SOCIAL WORK
AND
SOCIAL CHANGE

SOCIAL WORK
AND
SOCIAL CHANGE

A CASE STUDY IN
INDIAN VILLAGE DEVELOPMENT

Sugata Dasgupta

JOINT DIRECTOR OF THE GANDHIAN INSTITUTE OF STUDIES

EXTENDING HORIZONS BOOKS

PORTER SARGENT PUBLISHER   11 BEACON STREET, BOSTON, MASS.

EXTENDING HORIZONS BOOKS

Co-editors W. H. Truitt, Dept. of Philosophy, Suffolk University; A. Engelman, Dept. of Social Sciences, Franconia College

HN
683
5
D34

CONTENTS

25 3272

SV

To Leonard K. Elmhirst
a friend of rural India

ACKNOWLEDGMENTS

The present treatise is based on an earlier unpublished study entitled "A Survey of Social and Emotional Needs of a Group of Villages in Birbhum" conducted by the author. The data collection work for this earlier study and its preliminary report was made possible by a grant received from the U.G.C. through the courtesy of the Vishvabharati University. The present book is based in part on the former study. The author is grateful to the members of both villages whose kind cooperation made this book possible, and is indebted to the Vishvabharati University and the U.G.C. for their support.

Sugata Dasgupta

EDITOR'S PREFACE

Traditional sociologists have tended to view their categories of explanation as static, generally applicable from one community to the next, and as uniform and comprehensive. But new developments in the field of social research tend to stress equally the need to revise many of these categories. In the light of more recent investigations it has become abundantly clear that societies and communities generate their own, and very special, ways of appropriating reality, of social cognition, of causal perception, of social space and time. And in turn, the actual social processes themselves become an autonomous and determinate function of the needs and social perspectives in a given community. Although, in any culture, these perspectives, as they are manifest in the hopes, ideals and neuroses of the inhabitants, may be homogeneous, it is not the case that cross cultural generalities can or should be proposed in respect either to explanation or the implementation of control and planned change. The unique aspect of Dasgupta's work lies in his synthesis of the general theoretical presuppositions of *Wissensociologie* with *praxis*, or of social-perception and implementation.

This book is an empirical study of actual processes of change as they were induced and as they occurred in a number of Indian communities. These changes were the outcome of consciously designed programs of interference and re-socialization. The principal working technique employed by the Sriniketan was one familiar to American scholars, but one insufficiently used in our own "underdeveloped" communities. The technique employed here is the "social work" technique, but in a highly sophisticated and sensitized form. Great effort and care on the part of the investigators lay in ascertaining the social and emotional needs prevailing in the villages studied. Once these needs were thoroughly understood, and only then, was it possible to introduce new institutions that could be accepted by the inhabitants and thus integrated into the social fabric and mainstream of their lives. The investigators had to learn— relearn—to see with the eyes of the indigenous community. This was prerequisite to bringing about the desired changes.

vii

SOCIAL WORK AND SOCIAL CHANGE

This is a revealing investigation in a second respect. As a comparative study it shows with clarity the necessity of coming to grips with perceptual and cognitive categories of community members, before any attempt at change by an external agent can be initiated. It is obvious that in those communities where *non-social work techniques* were employed by the government the desired revisions in social structure failed. In short, there was no internalization process by which the community members could factualize and incorporate new and unfamiliar elements.

Underdeveloped communities can be characterized as "functional wholes." What then is the implication of this for introducing cultural change? One cannot hope to introduce new ideas, practices and institutions by simply thrusting them upon a community from without—superimposing education, building a school building. The importance of the application of social-work techniques is that they afford the sociologist an opportunity to invest the modification or new institution with a living vitality, making it a part of the life of the community as seen by the members of the group. Social development is dependent upon placing the controls of institutions in the hands of those people who are to be served by the institutions—making them social realities and a functional part of the community. And this, of course, is not possible until community members have internalized the meanings of the new institutions. Accordingly, Professor Dasgupta's study reasserts four significant aspects of community development which may be delineated as follows:

1. The importance of a method for working with people which is capable of providing self-education. This is the method of community organization prevalent in social work literature.

2. The importance of providing this method with a flexibility of approach that will make it effective in the context of the needs and aspirations of culturally diverse communities.

3. The importance of continuing sociological and axiological analyses of the social work process itself.

4. And lastly, the importance of utilizing a variety of research methods which focus on the perceptual processes of the subjects.

EDITOR'S PREFACE

This last aspect eventuates in the sacrifice of a degree of "quantitative" objectivity, but the benefits derived in terms of insight into more qualitative facets of the cultural studies more than justify this loss.

It is, in fact, the aloof objectivity surrounding many efforts at community development that has led to negative results. Failure in development programs has not been due so much to a lack of resources or technological aid, but to a lamentable failure on the part of the external agent to gain the confidence and cooperation of the people with whom they work. Few have recognized that the essential foundation for stimulating development lies not in the superimposition of technologies for the development of material culture; rather, the first step must be the discovery of an effective method for working with people.

Small rural communities may be sparked into a sense of dynamism, direction and purpose only when an effective, communicative and re-educational technique has been devised which is capable of transmitting motivational elements at a personal level. In the final analysis it is the peoples of such communities themselves who must serve as the mainsprings in the process of self-perpetuating development or recovery.

This book is a study of the social and economic development of two clusters of villages in East India, and as such it analyzes the practical contributions of an important program of social development, a particular method of working with the people, and the actual processes through which villagers learned and implemented rational and self-generating methods of democratic change.* Professor Dasgupta has described this theoretical technique very vividly and has introduced significant generalizations and observations in the last section of his book dealing with modifications to existing theories of community organization and methods of scientific social work.

Several conclusions force themselves upon the reader. The findings of this program place the social work techniques for future socialization and democratization at all levels and stages of society. The methods seem not merely relevant to "developing" nations but equally well suited to those blighted and depressed sectors of even the most

---

* Many of the methods adopted for use in this study were drawn from an integrated scheme of rural development first initiated by the Indian poet-philosopher Rabindranath Tagore.

SOCIAL WORK AND SOCIAL CHANGE

affluent societies. This modified theory of community organization is in a special sense, a unique theory of "social work"; it elevates "social work" to the position of a practical and theoretical frame of reference which holds promise for the disadvantaged in all countries. As a major contribution to the field of sociology of development, it is hoped that *Social Work and Social Change* will stimulate new thinking among development planners, professional sociologists and social workers in all phases of the community development enterprise.

WILLIS H. TRUITT
Editor

INTRODUCTION

I. SOCIAL WORK AND SOCIAL PROCESS

Social work as it has emerged from the dedicated effort and groping theory of past decades is something so new that we find it difficult to relate to our traditional understanding of man and society. It is still easiest to dismiss it as large-scale charity and miss its point altogether. For the significance of contemporary social work is precisely that it is not charity. Its ultimate aim is not primarily relief of individual mental or physical distress, but something far more basic—giving all men the ability and opportunity to be fully human.

The problem is not new. Human communities throughout history have had their hewers of wood and drawers of water, men whose lives were spent in a struggle for barest survival in the margins of society. One of the basic tasks and the ultimate criterion of the success of a community has always been its ability to incorporate its marginal members, to give them the opportunity to appropriate the life and values of the community and find personal fulfillment in them. Social work today is a conscious attempt to accelerate and guide the process of social integration.

The need to integrate marginal members is a perennial one, and when it is not met, the non-participating members of a society act as a brake on social development while the participating clique becomes stale and inbred. But the need to accelerate and guide the process through conscious social work is one of which we have only recently become aware. The reason for it may be in part rapid technological change, population explosion, or any of a range of factors. Whatever the reason, however, the striking fact of our time is that the rate of social change has far outstripped the capacity of spontaneous integrative processes. In order to survive, a modern society has to guide and accelerate the integrative process through conscious, purposive social work. The hallmark of a modern age has been precisely the transformation of spontaneous social processes into social work.

Social work as we know it is both a continuation and a transformation of the integrative processes. Because it is a continuation, some of its practitioners have been content with encasing traditional processes within an institutional shell. But it is also a transformation, and again some of its practitioners have tended to overlook the continuity and create solutions *de novo* and *ex nihilo*. Yet neither extreme does justice to the complex demands which the problem of social integration makes on society. To do that, we have to take into account both the continuity and the difference between social processes and social work.

II. THE CONTINUITY: SOCIAL *Ethos* AND SOCIAL *Eros*

Modern social work is continuous with traditional processes of social integration because the basic structure of human communities remains constant. The cohesion of a community parallels the cohesion of individual existence. In both cases we are dealing with an act which unites in the present moment past memories and future anticipations. Man, unlike a stone, cannot be defined in terms of an atemporal segment of his existence. Rather, like a melody, his existence is what it is at any given moment because of what he anticipates and what he remembers, and because of the way he perceives his memories and anticipations in the present moment. If we want to define an individual and distinguish between characteristic acts and acts we consider accidental, out of character, we have to refer to these three moments of man's existence.

These are also the three moments which define the identity and cohesion of a community. Society, like existence, is a human act, something men do and are. Its identity is again structured in terms of a past and a future and in terms of their fusion in the social perception of the present. To understand the principles of participation and exclusion in a community we need to understand these three moments.

The cohesion of a community is based in part on its past, or, more accurately, its facticity. This broad term includes a broad variety of a community's common givens. It does not matter whether the community is one of three men remembering an hour spent together in a stalled elevator or a nation remembering its past suffering or glory. In all cases it is the common facticity which makes a man part of a group, which makes him accept its authority as legitimate, and which leads him to support the acts which perpetuate its common heritage. To participate means to share common memories.

But to participate means also to share common hopes. An individual's identity is constituted not only by his past but also by his aims and goals. The same is true of communities: the cohesion of a community is based not only on a common *ethos* but also on a common *eros,* common striving, common aims, common ideals. Again, it does not matter whether we are dealing with a community of three men joined together by the common aim of starting a stalled Volkswagen or a nation united in a determination to realize an alleged manifest destiny. On all levels, to be a member of a community means to give allegiance to a common goal, to accept its demands as normative, and to support the acts of the community which tend to realize it. To participate means to share a common hope.

A community forms a cohesive whole to the extent to which its members share a common facticity and a common possibility, a common *ethos* and a common *eros.* To be sure, the two do not always coincide. Community *ethos* is essentially conservative, seeking to preserve a common facticity. Community *eros* is essentially progressive, seeking to reach a common goal. A given individual may share fully in the one and yet reject the other. Each can find concrete expression in a potentially infinite number of forms and symbols. Yet ultimately *ethos* and *eros* are the principles of cohesion and criteria of participation in the life of a community.

Memories and anticipations are the building blocks of identity of men and communities alike. But, as anyone who has worked with the mentally ill can attest, a theoretical awareness that there has been a past and that there will be a future is not enough. The individual becomes a man in appropriating the past and the future, in coming to *see* them as himself, as an expression and fulfillment of his existence.

The problem of social integration is closely analogous. The marginal members of a community need not only to become aware of the common *ethos* and *eros,* but to appropriate them. The difference is a difference of perception. The outcasts see the community's memories and hopes as alien, as belonging to others. They are outsiders because they do not *see* the community *ethos* and *eros* as extensions of their individual memories and anticipations, even if they acknowledge them abstractly. The third moment in a community's identity is precisely the element of appropriation. Anthropological research has made us clearly aware of the extent and the ways in which human communities through the ages not only articulated common *ethos* and *eros*, but also generated *techniques of appropriation*. This broad category would have to include the many and varied educational techniques which communicate the common stock of memories and hopes to the young and marginal members of a community, as well as the acts and the rituals which earn the individual the right of participation.

In all three moments which constitute the identity of a community and define participation in it, modern social work is clearly continuous with spontaneous social processes. It is different only because it is a *conscious* attempt to develop more efficient means of accomplishing the task.

III. THE DISCONTINUITY:
SOCIAL MANIPULATION AND SOCIAL PERCEPTION

We have stressed the continuity of social work with integrative social processes, and not without reason: creation *ex nihilo* is a privilege reserved to God and attempted by social workers only at their peril. But the discontinuity of social processes and purposive social work is equally significant. For when social change becomes a product of conscious activity, it no longer automatically follows the pressures and needs of a particular community. The goals and techniques of social work become a function of a conscious decision, and inevitably reflect the implicit philosophical orientation of their practitioners. Philosophical critique becomes immediately relevant to daily practice.

The earliest attempts at conscious social work clearly reflect the dominant philosophical orientation of their time. These include early Sunday schools, various Fabian schemes and modern phenomena like the attempt to bring about social change by massive infusion of Mao's thoughts. The philosophical basis here is idealism, and the technique of social work is appropriately enough one of moral exhortation.

A second group of phenomena reflects a materialist revolt against idealism. Here the technique is essentially materialistic, an attempt to change men through more or less forceable changes of physical environment. This includes phenomena such as agricultural collectivization, slum clearance *cum* public housing, and the attempt at social reform in Group B of the Indian villages described by Professor Dasgupta.

Each of these attempts had its apostles and its moments of glory. But both share a common weakness, basing social change on social manipulation rather than social perception. In our time their failure has become no less obvious than the inadequacy of the traditional options of idealism and materialism. A significant new departure in social work would require a new foundation, a foundation in social perception rather than in an attempt to manipulate the minds or the bodies of men.

Philosophically the most interesting development of our time has been the phenomenological attempt to avoid the dichotomy of idealism and materialism altogether. Phenomenology refused to identify reality either with the privacy of a subject's mind or with the objective entities of his world. Rather, it has sought to recognize that reality is experience, the unitary act of *being-in-the-world,* the cognitive, conative and affective act of actual existence. Man is here seen in the first place as an act of being-in-the-world, and the world as a world-for-man. Neither what has been traditionally called "mind" nor "body" can be considered primitive. The starting point, the basic datum, is the act, consciousness-in-the-world. Both man's "mind" and his world have to be understood as they appear from the standpoint of man's existence, his act of being.

In a sense, what phenomenology brings to the fore is no more than the lesson of ordinary experience consistently ignored by philosophy. But this lesson has far-reaching consequences whose exploration has occupied much of contemporary writing. And, to the extent to which social work has become conscious and so part of contemporary social consciousness, it has no less significant consequences for it. For the task of social work can no longer be conceived as manipulation of men by transforming either their beliefs or their physical environment. The task is rather one of transforming their basic experience of being-in-the-world, their basic social perception. Only in terms of this basic transformation does a change of beliefs and of physical environment become meaningful.

The significance of the Sriniketan experiment and of Professor Dasgupta's work is precisely that it translates this reorientation of social work into concrete terms. The process fostered in Group A villages and analyzed theoretically in Professor Dasgupta's concluding chapters is one which does not attempt to manipulate the villagers, to "reeducate" their minds or rebuild their villages. Rather, it starts with their basic experience of being-in-the-world, in terms as basic as a common contribution of labor. This is an act, an active being-in-the-world, but one which transforms both the consciousness of the participants and their physical environment. Through a systematic change in the social perception of the villagers, in their basic experience of the world, the Sriniketan experiment seeks to bring about the double change and so create a genuine community, a genuine "participatory democracy." In spite of the distance between Husserl's epistemological analyses and the daily realities of social work in an Indian village, Professor Dasgupta's work reflects a basically phenomenological and existential orientation to the tasks of social integration.

Sriniketan is not the millenium. Mistakes were made, difficulties encountered, problems raised. Even a universal adoption of the strategy and tactic of Sriniketan would not resolve the world's social problems. But on the frequently discouraging horizon of trying to offer all men the chance to be fully human it is both philosophically and socially one of the most interesting and encouraging signs I know.

ERAZIM V. KOHÁK
Boston University

CHAPTER I

IDEALS OF SRINIKETAN—AIMS OF SOCIAL WORK

An American specialist in community organization quotes the following interesting experience: A housing engineer visited a newly-constructed naval barracks where a group of young cadets undergoing naval training were residing. When, after visiting the area, the engineer called at the office of its Chief, he was asked to give his comments on inspection. "First thing," said the engineer "which we require in these barracks are bigger windows." "No," intervened the Chief, "the first thing we require here are to have the boys demand bigger windows." The suggestion of the Chief obviously was based on the idea that unless the boys had felt the need for bigger windows and demanded the same, it was no use offering them this amenity. The truth of the principle that unless a need is well-recognized by a community, a social worker would do well not to rush in with programs of social services, could be illustrated with a number of such live instances drawn from the experiences of social workers from all parts of the world.

The workers of the Department of Rural Reconstruction at *Sriniketan* faced the same situation when in the early forties they supplied mosquito curtains to the villagers of a nearby village and found, on later inquiry, that the curtains were being used as bedding, while the villagers lay under the hovering mosquitoes. The dejected social worker learned his lesson that the step was premature. The community had not yet realized the need for mosquito curtains; there might have been a number of socio-psychological factors standing in the way of the development of the required consciousness, which would put mosquito curtains to their proper use and rescue the villagers from the threats of malaria. The new concept of scientific social work stresses the necessity of enabling a community to recognize its needs and to mobilize its resources for their fulfilment. To Rabindranath Tagore, the founder of *Sriniketan*, the maximum emphasis of its method was similarly to be laid on enabling a community to attend to its own needs, by organizing its own welfare. Needs, and the growth of an awareness of new and growing needs, therefore play an important role in the planning and implementation of any program of social services and community development. It is for this reason that we hear today such jargon as "felt needs," "creation of needs," "basic human needs," "common human needs," and of concepts like "rock bottom planning," and "planning by and with the villagers," thrown about in abundance in the field of rural community development. It is for this reason that the workers of *Sriniketan* had concentrated, from its early days, on creating an intellectual and emotional awareness in the minds of the villagers of their day-to-day needs, and made an effort to develop such resources by their united action as could help them in meeting community requirements by their own effort. We might distinguish, however, between immediate needs and the larger, collective needs felt by the individuals belonging to a community. Each individual may well feel the brunt of such pressing immediate problems as those of food, shelter, and clothing, whereas the same individuals may be totally unaware of the need to combine together, conserve their diffuse energies and pool those divided resources without which even their primary problems, which are their chief concern, could not be solved. The whole emphasis in the method of working with people today lies, therefore, on the ability of the worker to create an environment in which a community could be motivated to perceive its own needs, and be prepared to organize its resources to achieve their fulfillment.

The present study is in a way a study of the perception of needs: the needs firstly as felt by the people in the villages in isolation, and later, when they start working with each other under the guidance of well trained social workers and dig into themselves and into the inner layers of consciousness of the community, the realization of the deeper needs which lie apparently dormant. Needs have been studied, or at least could be studied, from various points of view; they could be studied from the angle of an economist, from the point of view of an educator and that of a psychologist or sociologist. The present study is of needs from the point of view of social work; a concrete, nonabstract practice which in order to be effective must take into consideration the "total social phenomena," and at the same time utilize the combined points of view of a number

2

of other sister disciplines like those of economics, education, psychology and sociology. It will not be inexact to say that social work has a special field of its own, and that the "people in need" appear under a very different spotlight while studied from the viewpoint of a social worker. The concept of "need" referred to in social work is somewhat analogous to the term "demand" used by the economist as distinguished from the concept of "desire." To Tagore it appears in the following way: If we wish to meet each and every need of a community with outside efforts, that will hardly be desirable. What is required, on the other hand, is a determined effort to create, in the community itself, its power to resolve its own needs.[1]

The object of *Sriniketan* was, therefore, not merely to offer cereal, water, education and health services to the villagers, but to create that power of self-development in a community which would enable it to determine its own welfare. *Sriniketan* realized quite early in its career that this power of self-development would come through an organized effort made by the villagers themselves to solve their own problems by setting up their own institutions, run and administered in a democratic manner under the leadership of the village itself.

As compared to this, social work has been defined by the Sixth International Conference "as a process which makes it possible for the individual to achieve his maximum potential through existing institutions or to modify existing institutions to provide a healthier environment (physical, emotional, social and spiritual) in which the individuals may grow and function to the fullest of the individual capacities." [2] The conference further described the role of a social worker "as that of a catalyst of social change. His aim is to discover means or to break through the crust of inertia and to help realize the latent powers in the common man to be used for meeting his needs, physical, social and cultural." To Gordon Hamilton "Social work has to date clarified three distinctive methods of approach, called respectively 'social welfare planning' or 'community organization,' 'social group work' and 'social case work.' " He admits that in the context of professional social work there

[1] Free translation is ours.

[2] Report of the VIth Annual Conference of Social Work (Madras, 1952). Published by the International Conference of Social Work.

are mass needs and mass solutions, group needs and group solutions, individual needs, and individual solutions." [3]

It is interesting to study the objectives of *Sriniketan* in the light of the above statements and to find how those objectives and their *modus operandi* tally with those of professional social work. "The object of *Sriniketan* is to bring back life in its completeness into the villages, making them self-reliant and self-respectful, acquainted with the cultural traditions of their own country and competent to make an efficient use of modern resources for the improvement of their social, physical, intellectual and economic conditions and to so endeavor that a power within the villagers themselves may be working alongside of us albeit indiscernible by us. The ideas of *Sriniketan* were more appropriately described in the following words of Rabindranath Tagore:

1) to win the friendship and affection of the villagers by taking a real interest in all that concerns their life and welfare and by making a lively effort to assist them in solving their problems.

2) to understand the "villagers" daily routine and the varied pageant of his life.

3) to form a picture of the village of its outward form and its inner story in order to bring home to them the benefits of associate life, mutual aid and common endeavor.

To give the community through its individuals and groups of youth, adolescents and children, the wish, the impetus and the method of making use of their own aptitude and dormant potentialities for the solution of many of their problems was the fundamental aim of the program introduced by the Department of Rural Reconstruction at *Sriniketan*. For satisfaction of the needs of the villagers, through the action of the community itself and through organization of village agencies and development of village leadership, *Sriniketan* had ever toiled to introduce programs of social development. Theirs, however, was a slow and seemingly formless process of helping a community to awaken. This was indeed a way of acting as closest collaborators and consultants to the community, in helping them to evolve their own program. *Sriniketan's* village workers were thus directed to establish their acquaintance and asso-

[3] Page 14, Theory and Practice of Social Case Work.

ciation with this slow but gradually growing community, and help its pace of growth by their association.

To enable a community to realize its own needs, and to understand the difference between group action and pressure groups, was the primary purpose of the social work process initiated by *Sriniketan*. The social worker was warned not to act as a leader in the sense of a dictator, but to ensure that the people meet their needs by themselves and did not look only to external leaders for solution of their day-to-day needs and problems. The village worker was to be made aware that he was not there to establish his line of thinking or his way of working or to "organize" "establish" or "impose" anything. He was there to ensure that any action taken was the action of the community itself. Talking together and planning together was to develop silently into 'acting' together; and perpetuation of this togetherness into institutional shapes and forms would be, it was presumed, the greatest guarantee for meeting the needs of the community, by the efforts of its own members, on a permanent basis.

The ideals of social work were thus identical with the goals which were held before them by the workers of *Sriniketan*. These ideals manifested themselves through the actual tools of working with groups and communities in an effort to enable the community to develop its dormant potentialities and to solve its own problems through its own institutions and indigenous leadership. Among the manifold programs of work of *Sriniketan*, training of workers through continuous organization of training camps and short term courses occupied an important position. Workers were thus to be well-wedded not only to a vague ideal of the above description, but to the detailed methods of program planning, raising of funds, organizing recreation groups, framing plans for survey and study, acting as consultants to the organizations and village institutions, and of training village leaders. These techniques of working with people manifested in *Sriniketan* through the following programs of work:—

1. Organization of educational classes with adult groups.
2. Organization of recreational programs with children's groups developing into 'Braiti' Organization. (Scouts)

3. Organization of:
   (i) Recreation Clubs; (ii) Youth Clubs; (iii)
   Mahila Mandals; (iv) Health Cooperatives (on
   social insurance basis) ; (v) Craft societies; (vi)
   Village Welfare Councils; (vii) arbitration councils; (viii) Basic Schools.
4. Organization of extension education for the villagers through demonstration farms.
5. Organization of training courses for the village.
6. Organization of village study circles (thus helping to carry the problems of the village to the
   class room and laboratory and of the class to the
   village).
7. Organization of Training Camps for the training
   of paid staff as well as voluntary leaders.

A group of eighty-five villages spread over an area of
ten square miles had felt the brunt of this program and
the creative impact of its continuous process for some
thirty-eight years. The purpose of our study is to evaluate
the impact of programs following the above philosophy of
social work and techniques of social action on a selected
group of villages. This study asks, where do the people of
Sriniketan's work area stand today, vis-a-vis their own
needs through self-help?

Sriniketan's area of work is spread far and wide. A
group of four villages was selected from this field for the
purpose of our study, in order to discover the effects of
the "methods of working with people," which *Sriniketan*
had so long practised, on individuals, groups and communities of this area. As a result of its sustained work, social
groups, program leaders and institutions are to be found
in abundance in this group of villages (hereinafter termed
the A group). The B group comprises another four villages
which lie on the other side of the river and are normally
unapproachable to *Sriniketan's* village level workers. Programs and institutions, however, had sprung up here as
well; the B group had its own peculiar set of institutions
and leaders.

In the primary phase, the purpose of this study is to inquire into the needs, (which, interpreted from the social
work point of view, will mean dynamics and motivations)
of the many individuals—adults, youth and adolescents—
who man these institutions and to find out what role they

play in meeting their own needs. Do the institutions, which appear in these villages, meet these needs? What is the impact there of these institutions? Those programs of social group work and community organization, the relationship and processes of adjustment between programs and persons, groups and leaders—their interaction and *modus operandi*—do they express the awareness and consciousness of a growing community? Are the targets and physical achievements of the community products of the conscious efforts of the people? Are the processes of these achievements based on democratic awareness (everybody's consciousness and democratic or joint action) and efforts, as far as possible, of the people? Are these institutions the media of expression of the community's will and the agency for its action? Do these agencies, and the village activities initiated in these villages, meet the real needs of people? Have the communities in these two groups of villages grown into emotionally mature, socially conscious and physically capable groups, competent to meet their own needs through their own action? Have these institutions grown into vigorous and viable organizations of the respective communities?

The second but perhaps equally important phase of the study was to make a comparative analysis. This was to be done with the help of the data collected from the two groups of villages on the basis of the same set of schedules and questionnaires, to determine whether the state of events, the quality of the individual's and the communities' estimate of their own needs, and their methods of realization of these needs, are identical in two groups of villages—or, should they be at variance, whether the difference is ascribable to extraneous factor of social manipulation method of approach or techniques of working with people.

It must, however, be pointed out that the present study is not an evaluation report, but an attempt to test the validity of certain approaches and methods of working with people, and it may not be out of place here to bring out clearly in this context just what we feel the main objectives of our study to be, as compared to an evaluation report. Our aim is not to evaluate the work of an agency or of any of the members of its staff. The purpose of an evaluation report is to judge and to check errors in the methods of working of the thing evaluated. The purpose of an evaluation team is to assess whether the effort put forth has attained certain targets or fulfilled certain ideals which have been previously announced. The evaluation agency seeks to find out whether the results obtained tally with the announced aims and targets and it is within its bounds to even suggest corrections. The agency which seeks to be evaluated is necessarily expected in its turn to provide the evaluating authority with its charter of targets containing its aims and goals.

The purpose of this study is not to assess the physical achievement of targets, or to examine whether any of the professed goals have been arrived at. What it does aim to find out, on the other hand, is the present position of a group of villages where some work has been going on, in an acknowledgedly planned, well determined and well organized manner from some time in the past. The conditions prevalent in this group of villages, where work had been going on for the last three decades, have been studied with reference to a comparative analysis of work in another group of villages, where different types of development have taken place by a different process of initiation and under different stimuli or methods of work.

The purpose of the study is, therefore, to find out whether the growth achieved in these two areas is identical, or differential, in its quantity and quality. The aim, at the same time, is not merely to brand any of the results which have appeared in either group of villages as better or worse, but to explore the possibility of a relationship between the processes of work employed and the differences (if any) in the resultant social atmospheres of the two groups of villages under comparison.

CHAPTER II

THE PLAN AND METHOD OF STUDY

Two groups of villages were selected by the author in consultation with the Director of the Department of Rural Reconstruction. These groups of four villages each, will be designated A and B groups. They comprise an approximate population of 1390 and 1185 each.

The A group refers to four villages within the orbit of the work area of the Department of Rural Reconstruction, to be known hereinafter as the Department. These four villages, Benuria, Bahadurpur, Islampur and Lohagarh of the Ruppur Union, are located at a distance of five miles from the nearest railway station (Belpur-Santiniketan) and equidistant about 3 miles from the bus route and paved road. The road which connects these villages with the Department's headquarters is a muddy and fair-weather road over which, especially during the rainy season, no conveyance except the bullock cart could make its way. The road which connects Belpur with these villages branches off southwest of the fair weather road, making its way through the government-sponsored reforestation project.

These villages lie on both sides of the road. The first village on the right is Lohagarh—and then comes Islampur. Bahadurpur and Benuria are on the other side of the road. This part of West Bengal—and especially this part of Birbham is known to be the poorest in terms of agricultural or industrial prosperity, and the fact becomes evident from the very look of these villages. The soil of the area is sandy; in some parts, irrigation facilities (excepting the newly constructed Mayuraksi canal) are limited. Houses are made mostly of mud walls, thatch roof and tin sheds. People are generally of medium build, sun-tanned and emaciated; villages are multistreet, each street having a cluster of houses; and the land of the villagers is on the outskirts, sometimes located in distant villages as well.

SOCIAL WORK AND SOCIAL CHANGE

Some important basic data about the A group of villages are appended below:

A Group of Villages

1)	Total population	1390
2)	Number of families	278
3)	Average size of families	5
4)	Percentage of Adult male population	33 percent
5)	Percentage of Adult female population	35 percent
6)	Percentage of children (infants)	5 percent
7)	Percentage of children (school going)	27 percent
8)	Religious groups	(1) Hindu—70 percent (2) Muslim—25 percent (3) Santal—5 percent
9)	Caste Groups:[1] (main groups)	a) *Brahmin* b) *Vaidya;* c) *Sadgope;* d) *Tili;* e) *Benia;* f) *Kulu;* g) *Baisnab;* h) *Dome;* i) *Bagdi;* j) *Kaibarta;* k) *Namasundra;* l) *Bayen.*
10)	Main occupation groups	1. Agriculturist 2. Agricultural Laborer 3. Business 4. Service 5. Smithy (Blacksmith) 6. Fishing 7. Carpentry
11)	Average per capita income per month	14.24 rupees ($1.90)
12)	Percentage of literate Adults (male and female)	65 percent

---

[1] Four facts are important:

  (a) *Sadgope* are "dominant caste" economically as well as in number.

  (b) So called backward class (from d to i) of 9 are in majority.

  (c) Upper caste Hindus are in minority.

  (d) Landless laborers are in majority.

THE PLAN AND METHOD OF STUDY

13) Percentage of children
    actually attending school
    in relation to total num-
    bers of children of school
    age.   75.5 percent

The Department started its activities in these villages in the year 1922 and with intermittent breaks has carried on its programs into the current year. These villages thus fall within the Department's work area, which originally comprised 85 villages. For the convenience of operation, the total area of work of the Department was divided into three zones—the intensive area, the extensive area and the area of radiation. In the intensive area, all the services referred to earlier (see chapter one) are organized by the Department through a network of community organizations. In the extensive zone the Department is only able to take up isolated projects; the chief aim of the Department here is to get the people together for particular pieces of work. In the area of its radiation, which comprises the villages at the periphery of the extensive zone, the villagers organize themselves by hearing and learning about the Department's activities from their friends in the intensive and extensive area.

The A group of villages did not belong to the Department's intensive area until the year 1954, when activities were intensified in this zone and the area came to be included within the intensive circle. The activities which were organized since then and the programs which developed between 1954-56 have been mentioned earlier.

The program of the Department, however, took a very different turn in the year 1956, when a National Extension Service[2] block was set up for this area and most of the workers of the Department were transferred under the block with a multitude of responsibilities.

This represented a period of break and departure from the main current of activities, and the emphasis of the Department's work from that time onwards has remained exclusively in educational, social and cultural activities— the economic and the administrative activities being taken over by the N.E.S. block. Even in this limited sphere, however, sustained work had not always been possible due to incessant rains. The approach road to this group of villages was severely interfered with from time to time, and the

---

[2] Organized for community development work by the government.

11

main bulk of the Department's activities had to be given up at a certain stage.

The B group comprises four villages: Sattore, Khiroli, Bergram and Rahamatpur, belonging to the Sattore Union. They are located about 10 miles away from the nearest railway station (Belpur-Santiniketan) and roughly one mile each from the nearest bus route and hard road. The road which connects these villages with *Sriniketan* is paved in most parts, and partly muddy. The B group lies on both sides of the road itself—the road which connects Belpur with Sewri. The first village on the way is Bergram. Villages of the B group, in general description and structure, are very similar to the A group itself. Some important basic data about these four villages are appended below:

B Group of Villages

1)	Total population	1183
2)	Number of families	236
3)	Average size of family	5
4)	Percentage of adult male population	
5)	Percentage of adult female population	31 percent 32 percent
6)	Main caste groups:	(a) *Brahmin* (upper caste and in minority) (b) *Sadgope* (Economically dominant caste are in majority) (c) *Bagdi;* (d) *Bauri* (so called backward class)
7)	Main religious group	Hindu 75 percent Muslim 25 percent
8)	Main occupation groups	a) Agriculturist (dominant vocation) b) Agricultural laborer— (landless labor are in a majority) c) Business d) Service e) Carpentry
9)	Average per capita income per month	13.13 rupees ($1.70)
10)	Percentage of children (including infants)	6 percent
11)	Percentage of children (School age)	31 percent
12)	Percentage of children actually attending school in relation to total number of school-age children.	60 percent

12

13) Percentage of literate
    adults (male and female)   35 percent

Unlike the A group of villages, the B group did not belong either to the intensive or the extensive zone of the Department's area of operation, nor did it acknowledgedly belong even to the area of its radiation.

These two groups of villages were selected for the purpose of the study in view of their proximity to the headquarters, and due to the fact that the two zones, one touched by the Department's workers and the other untouched, lay so near to each other.

As the basic data reveals, these two groups of villages are almost identical in their socio-economic *cum* religiocultural background, although the A group stands much ahead of the B in terms of educational attainment and the number and types of community institutions existing in the area (see chart). The Department had initiated and carried on its activities in the A group of villages since 1922, and with vigor since 1953, whereas the B group of villages lay outside its orbit of influence. As a result of the work of the Department, a number of groups and institutions have emerged in the villages of the A group. One thus finds its leaders and its people making efforts to solve their own problems through a network of institutions. In the B group of villages, however, the activities of the *normal departments* of the government of West Bengal [3] had not been wanting, and as revealed by this study, an "outsider" group of constructive workers and political emissaries stood solidly behind the B group and initiated a number of educational and welfare activities with the help of a few enthusiastic village leaders. As the research team attached to this project entered the B group of villages for the purpose of the study, the eyes of a number of governmental development agencies also fell on this barren field. It was thus interesting to find that quite a few social welfare agencies quickly sprang up in this area within a few months, after the investigation work had started. Let us postpone for the time being any further analysis of the social situation of the two groups of villages (a subject to which we shall have occasion to return later), and instead have a close look

---

[3] This refers to "nation-building" departments, such as Education, Health, etc., which are distinct from the Department of Rural Reconstruction and the community development work of the Indian government.

at the methodology of work followed for the purpose of the study.

The study proposes to inquire into the position of the village organizations, of the social groups and of their indigenous leaders, and to review the state of affairs prevailing in both groups of villages. Primarily the aim of the project is confined to a study of the impact of the tools and methods of work initiated by the Department, in the A group of villages, but in order to achieve this, the B group of villages and the position of its organizations, groups and leaders, have also been studied. In order to arrive at its results, however, the present study did not follow only one particular method, or use a single tool for analysis. Rather, the package of tools used covered a wide range, and the results achieved are thus the products of a multiple approach adopted for this purpose.

TOOLS OF STUDY

A comprehensive questionnaire, which comprises a number of schedules prepared for this purpose, has been one of these tools. Others used are (i) case studies of leaders and of action situations, (ii) case histories of community institutions, (iii) attitude study, and (iv) opinion study of a selected sample each from either of the groups.

It is pertinent here to mention that in framing the questionnaires, schedules and attitude-scales mentioned above, the author found little information on any comparable schedules and questionnaires that might have been used earlier by other research agencies or workers, for any kind of similar study. The questionnaire and schedules which were thus framed were drawn solely from the limited experiences of the author. To evolve these had, itself proved to be a formidable task at the initial stages of the study.

A few questionnaires for opinion and attitude survey were available, however, as reference materials. These were subjected to strenuous scrutiny in a number of discussions, meetings and seminars, which were held with the teaching and field staff of the Social Education Organizers' Training Center, in order to suitably modify them to meet the specific purpose of this particular study.[4] Considerable thinking, re-thinking and hard labor was required to prepare the ground before the final questionnaire could take

---

[4] The Social Education Organizers' Training Center was headed by the author.

shape. The framing of these questionnaires and schedules was by itself a pioneering task and massive in content, inasmuch as elaborate and detailed analysis of character of the groups and of the local area of the inter-group processes, together with their dynamics, had to be undertaken before one could finally adopt them for the purpose of the present study. Immediately after this task was completed, a series of test interviews were conducted first by the author and then by two other trained social workers who were especially chosen for this work. The latter were not only trained workers, but persons of considerable experience in the field of rural welfare and community organization. Their reactions had naturally called for substantial amendments to the original set of schedules and questionnaires and in view of the new experiences, the questionnaires and schedules were further modified.[5]

In conducting actual field work for collection of data, the research workers were warned not to carry the bulky questionnaires to the field, but to get themselves thoroughly acquainted with them beforehand, carry on interviews on the basis of their study, and make scrap notes on the spot. Apart from these questionnaires and schedules a number of other tools were also used for collection of field data from a variety of other sources. Some of these are noted below:

The research workers who assisted me were from time to time asked to maintain comprehensive diaries which were checked and cross-checked in the periodic conferences which the author had with them for verification of the data collected by the investigators. Regular conferences were thus held on almost every questionnaire filled in by the field worker, and elaborate notes of these discussions were maintained. All this accounted for a large volume of important and interesting data which was incorporated into almost every aspect of this study.

The major portion of data was collected by trained social workers who were employed as research investigators. Three part-time village level workers were also employed, at a later stage, to assist the author for the same purpose.

---

[5] Data collected in the course of the study were tabulated in parts. These were used by Dr. Hashem Amir Ali in his book entitled *Then and Know* published by the Indian Statistical Institute with suitable acknowledgment. I have since then substantially revised his plan of study.

SOCIAL WORK AND SOCIAL CHANGE

These village level workers were all matriculates and employed in primary schools as teachers, but they, apart from their educational qualifications, had considerable experience in research work to their credit. Most of these questionnaires and schedules were administered by them, and the manner in which this was done is described later in detail. A pre-survey orientation training was arranged for them in 'methods' of collection of data. They were thus introduced to the various schedules and questionnaires in a systematic manner, and these training conferences particularly helped to orient them to the aims and objectives of the research study well before they were sent into the field. Special care was taken at this stage, when the village level workers came into the picture, to ensure that they maintained proper diaries, and regular conferences were held by the author on each of the questionnaires and schedules filled out by these auxiliary personnel.

But all this work—the administration of the questionnaires and the collection of data—thereby represented only one set of our tools. The organizers of the study had employed from time to time a number of other tools and methods for collection of data, of which the administration of specific questionnaires and schedules represented only one segment of the total plan. Case studies of selected leaders of community institutions and action situations, some of which were introduced in an experimental manner, formed the other facets of our study. A few members of the teaching staff of the Social Education Organizers' Training Center, and its senior trainees specially selected for this purpose, were from time to time requested to submit their own observation reports on these leaders, institutions and action situations, some of which were utilized in the materials for case studies, presented elsewhere in the book.

A number of tables prepared from the data collected by schedule A were directly useful for framing case studies of community institutions as well as for opinion and attitude studies.

The reports collected from selected staff of the S.E.O. training centers (senior students undergoing training and the village level investigators), regarding the organizational history of the different social and educational agencies of these villages, and case records of a number of specific action situations which took place in both the groups of villages during the period under study provided, along with

16

the main volume of data, materials for this study. For all these various levels and facets of study, the questionnaires (including schedules A and B) were used as guide indicators, and enhanced the collection of notes on village situations of varied dynamism. Guide points, as per A & B schedules, thus provided the broad outlines on the basis of which action situations were observed and records were compiled. Detailed notes, as mentioned before, were also maintained by the investigators after they had closely observed specific action situations, i.e., selected committee meetings, conflict situations, day observations, village seminars, guardians' meetings, recreational programs and leader-follower relations obtaining in the two groups of villages. The core of the data did not, therefore, consist only of the direct answers elicited as a result of replies to the questionnaire and schedules. In addition, elaborate notes collected by the workers on groups and group functioning in the two universes of study, with the schedules and questionnaires serving as guide indicators, also formed an important part of the total plan of work.

A number of case studies of selected action situations were thus conducted where observations were to be made regarding the points indicated by schedule B and the data collected from all these sources went to provide the large bulk of the material for research. Action situations were found in abundance in the A group of villages, and group activities were daily features of life here; whereas in the B group there was a total dearth of such situations as the leadership in these villages functioned in isolation. The research workers motivated the leaders in the latter to introduce a few action situations, with the idea that a social, anatomical analysis of them would provide suitable data for comparative study of their impact on the general democratic situation obtaining there, together with those of group A. These opinion studies, case studies, and histories of community institutions were supplemented by an attitude study conducted through interviews on the basis of a set of questionnaires and check lists.

The project, the result of a sum total of these varied approaches of study is thus by no means only an opinion and attitude study of certain selected members of the village communities under review. Rather, its overwhelming emphasis lies, if one may say so, on the study of action situations where social groups—and the interaction of groups and sub-groups of leaders and followers, and of persons and environments—could have been carefully studied and recorded for analysis.

THE METHOD OF SAMPLING

The three schedules known as *a*, *b*, and *c* aimed to study (1) organizations and institutions, (2) groups and group functions, and (3) social case-histories of selected leaders, respectively. The two groups of villages A and B, comprise a total population of 2,573. Out of the above, 10 percent (the children of the area), were eliminated from the universe of the study. The women of the villages have also likewise been excluded since there were no women investigators to assist the research team in its study. The total number of people covered by the research project was thus 1452. One of the main tasks of this project was to study institutions and to find how people, i.e. the clientele, of these institutions use them to meet their own needs. One could conceivably treat the entire population of the two groups of villages as beneficiaries of all the institutions located in these villages, irrespective of the fact that a large number of them might not have still become formal members of either or any of these organizations. To take an example in point; a Defense Party's or a Health Society's beneficiaries are not limited to its formal members or executives, as a vigilant defense part or the impact of the preventive health measures act as safety valves for the entire population of the area. However, for the purpose of this study the sample was confined to the active beneficiaries of these organizations, those on whom the impact of their programs was found to be more pronounced. The acknowledged leaders, members of executives, and non-members who took 'active' interest in the institutional activities and benefitted from them, therefore formed the specific focus of this study.

THE SCHEDULES

Schedule *a* consisted of questions relating to the organization and process of work of the social and educational institutions of the area. This also contains tools (i) for measuring the recreational and cultural facilities available in the villages and, (ii) for a study of social and political attitudes of the people of both groups. Schedule *b* consists of questions which help to analyze the dynamics of group actions and leader-follower relationships. Both the schedules were administered in an "institution-centered" manner, inasmuch as only such villagers were interviewed as had some connection with any of the various institutions functioning in either group of villages. All the leaders of all these institutions were thus interviewed as per schedule *a* which included committee members of institutions; others interviewed on the basis of this schedule were 10 percent of general members and 5 percent of non-members. As per the table given below the total number interviewed was three hundred and ninety six, which formed about 25 percent of the total universe of our work, and comprised nearly all the people who had been functioning in the institutional sectors of the two groups of villages.

Schedule a

"A" group of villages
(Benuria, Lohagarh, Bahadupur & Islampur)
Population: 1390

Category	Percentage of clientele	Approximate number of persons to be contacted (overlapping excluded)	
Leaders	100 percent	(35 in each schedule)	35
Committee members	100 percent	(100 in each schedule)	200
General members	10 percent	(50 in each schedule)	50
Non-members	10 percent	(25 in each schedule)	25
i.e., the people			200

"B" group of villages
(Bergram, Khiroli, Rahamatpur and Sattore)
Population: 1185

Leaders	100 percent	(26 in each schedule)	26
Committee members	100 percent	(70 in each schedule)	70
General members	10 percent	(50 in each schedule)	50
Non-members	5 percent	(50 in each schedule)	50
			196

Schedule *b* was to be administered to an equal number of people but it was found, after the work of collection of data progressed to some extent, that the opinions expressed by the villagers reflected grossly subjective and idealistic statements. The administration of this schedule was thus found difficult mainly for two reasons: first, the institutions in B group of villages were all *ad hoc* bodies and no useful purpose could have been served by interviewing the non-members (i.e. general public) and committee members of these institutions, since an examination of their dynamics did not provide any clue to the understanding of the relationship of these institutions with the greater community; and secondly, it was evident from the data collected as per Schedule *b* that all these contained subjective answers. The questions contained in Schedule *b* were thus accordingly modified, and these were then used as guide indicators to the investigators for case studies of selected action situations. This step, which changed the originally contemplated role of Schedule *b* was taken after much careful thinking, when the author came to the conclusion that it would be more worth while to collect data on group dynamics from direct observation of situations of group interaction and leader-follower relationships, than to acquire data from a mere opinion study.

As has been stated earlier, most of the institutions of the B group of villages were found to be in a moribund condition. Consequently, one could select for the purpose of this comparative study only three organizations from B group which yet remained in a more or less functioning order, and compare these with four institutions of group A. To have taken a great many institutions from A group and compare them with only a few of group B, would have been unnecessary and unscientific, inasmuch as the data from A group would then have been weighted heavily on one side. The present study, then, embodies only limited data collected from only a few institutions which the researchers found were in functioning order and were therefore directly relevant for the study.

The total number of questions in the two schedules was more than 150, and since about 396 persons were interviewed, a bulk of data was available at the disposal of the research team. About 700 tables were prepared in this connection, and after wading through all this data the author found, at the time of their interpretation, that most of the so-called organizations of group B were defunct bodies. In our final analysis and at the time of presenting the report we thus had to leave out of the orbit of our study a number of institutions, and focus our attention only on a few virile organizations—primarily for the reason that the data related to such organizations as were no longer functioning had to be taken out of consideration and eliminated. The idea of writing separate chapters on these organizations to prove their irrelevancy was abandoned, mainly for want of time. The number of people who have been included in the ultimate analysis, has not, however, been less than 25 percent of the total universe.

Schedule c contained questions and guide indicators for case study of selected leaders. At the initial stage a roster of names of village leaders was prepared by inviting panels of names, from the authorities of the N.E.S. block and the Department of Rural Reconstruction, as well as from the Union Boards of the locality. Names of about sixty leaders from the two groups of villages, thirty from each, was thus received; out of these, six leaders, three from either of the groups, were carefully studied; and when the time for interpretation of this data arrived, case studies of only four leaders were taken up for effective interpretation. It was discovered that only these four, out of the six interviewed, were really effective community leaders. The case study of selected community institutions and of carefully chosen action situations threw a new light on the prevailing leadership and brought out in the open the real position of this panel of sixty leaders. The data of action situations and case study revealed the leader-follower relationships in these two villages; this enabled the sponsors of the study to pick up six vital personalities who, instead of being leaders for name's sake, were the real effective manipulators of the destiny of these villages. A careful analysis further revealed that not four, but only two of these leaders were main pillars of the two groups of villages, and able to provide interesting and useful case materials for study. In the ultimate review of leadership of these two groups of villages, maximum focus has therefore, been laid on these two leaders.

In selecting age groups for this study we have confined ourselves to people of 16 years and above, i.e., people belonging to adolescent, youth and adult groups. A study of children, both as individuals and as groups involved in programs of action, was not undertaken in view of the fact that the study of the advanced age groups yielded more interesting and useful results. At the same time, it was recognized that the reactions of the present-day adults were to a great extent the product of their childhood experiences. The state of adjustments or frustration which the adult villagers revealed in their day-to-day work were, more often than not, the the results of their own early experience. A study of the children of the area, it was therefore considered, would have been incomplete unless one could have also studied the same group at a different point of time, when they would have reached adulthood and functioned in the larger institutions of their respective areas as full members.

The quantitative sampling for this study was made in a random manner, although it took into full consideration the factors and stratifications mentioned earlier. The specific universe of work was, in the ultimate analysis, limited to the male adolescent youth and adult population of the area.

PERIOD OF STUDY

The data of this study was collected in 1959-61. The actual field work was conducted in the summers and the winters of these two years, as no contact could have been established with the villages during the rainy seasons. It required about fourteen months to collect the field data with intermittent breaks due to rains and my own pre-occupations. It must be mentioned that the author's aquaintance with the villages of group A dates back to the year 1953. The data was tabulated in 1962, and the first draft was completed by December 1963.

LIMITATION OF OUR STUDY

The framer of the present study, more than anyone else, is very much aware of its manifold limitations. The project is a study of the needs of a regional community, maintained, nourished and changing under the impact of the methods and techniques of social work as introduced by a time honored institution of the country.

As stated earlier, "needs" have, from time to time, been studied from the points of view of various other disciplines, by a number of research workers. A study of needs, as perceived by the members of a specific community, from the point of view of social work, or with reference to any specific growth or change of its potentialities, aimed at meeting its own needs by dint of its own efforts was, however, an altogether new venture. The present study has had, therefore, no access to any comparative material which could authoritatively indicate to the framers of the research scheme the exact methods to be adopted, and/or the area to be covered. No other questionnaire or schedule, or for that matter no other systematic plan of study of a like nature, could thus offer any firm indication as to the validity of the method followed by the present study. But the pioneering nature of this research project, as well as being a source of great hesitancy, was also a source of great inspiration to its framer. For the very hazard of opening up an unexplored territory more than anything else, made the author not only extremely cautious in guiding his every step, but enabled him to realize at the same time the possibilities of the contribution that the study could make to the new field of methodology of social work research, and more generally to the sociology of development.

A NEW METHOD OF WORK

Another limitation of this study lay in the very method of work which the framers adopted for the purpose of this project. The study aims to compare two groups of villages at the same point of time. This method of comparison was itself a new approach, as one hardly had any precedence of a similar comparative study in the field of social science research in India to fall back upon. The author would have been much more definite on the results, or at least of having gone on a beaten track, if the same set of villages could have been studied at two different stages of their development after an interval of time, in place of this attempt to study two groups at the same point of time.

There were, however, a few studies which had some acquaintance with this type of methodology and which were somewhat similar to ours. The Tata Institute of Social Sciences carried on an opinion survey of the impact of All-India radio programs on radio listening groups, by interviewing the same group before and after radio broadcasts. The Program Evaluation Organization (P.E.O.), which periodically reviewed the impact of social education programs and published reports from time to time, did not, until 1956, take to the method adopted by this study. The procedure followed by the P.E.O. was to study and assess the efficiency of social education programs only in selected block areas, without making any comparative references to the state of affairs which existed in any non-block villages of a comparable socio-economic status. The Planning Research and Action Institute of Uttar Prädesh which studied social education programs in 1956, however, had adopted a somewhat similar line of approach as that of our study. They based their inquiry, made at a few selected Social Education Organization Centers (S.E.O.T.C.), on a comparative study of the students of a particular center with a number of "non-students." None of these studies were, however, of an exact or even of a very similar pattern. As has been indicated earlier, the framers of the present study were fully aware that this form of comparative inquiry as a means of judging the validity of certain approaches of work was altogether a new method. The entire plan of work, consisting of the total scheme with its various questionnaires, schedules and the contemplated methods of comparison was published in the form of a loose brochure and forwarded, before they were finalized for adoption, to a number of research bodies for their comments. The Institutes to whom these were referred, at least some of them, carefully analyzed these questionnaires and schedules and forwarded their comments on most of the features of the scheme. The two inspiring foreign critics who had favored the writer with their enlightened review were T. R. Batten of the University of London and F. L. Madge of the N.F.E.C.[6] Their suggestions were incorporated in the plan of work and had substantially influenced its character.

The Program Evaluation Organization however, took a special interest in this study and wrote to the author for a detailed description of the project and its scheme of work. The framer of this study was understandably encouraged when the P.E.O. brought out its 1958 report on social education, in which, to his pleasant surprise, they had discarded their earlier method of studying, for the purpose of evaluation, the impact of social education in a particular selected block in an absolute manner, and adopted a new method analogous to one followed by the present study. The P.E.O. attempted in this new report a comparative analysis of data collected regarding the impact of social education programs in some selected block areas, with similar data drawn from certain non-block villages where no social education work was initiated by the Community Development organization itself.

CHANGING PHENOMENA

A third limitation of this study came to the fore when it was discovered that the two phenomena which were being

---

[6] National Fundamental Education Center, New Delhi.

studied and compared did not remain constant but were fast changing their original shape and form. The differences between A and B groups were thus diminishing at a rapid pace inasmuch as the B group of villages was not situated far enough from the A to avoid its influence; it lay as if within the area of its radiation. If one could have thus selected a more distant group of villages the contrasts between the two could have possibly been more vivid.

The comparison would also have been all the more evident, if the A group had been longer in the inner circle of the Department's intensive area of operation. However, it was not possible, due to paucity of funds and other resources, to select a group of villages which might have lain in the inner circle of the Department for a longer period of time. The author thus had to select only a few, and if one may say so, rather backward villages for scrutiny which had till then experienced only in a limited manner the full impact of the program and methods of work of the Department.

As the work of this research study proceeded, and the investigators entered the B group of villages, they gave, in spite of their every effort not to do so, severe jolts to the dormant energies of the people of the area by the fact of their very presence. Even with the most objective administration of the questionnaires and schedules, the process of interview and of contacting various people of the B group seemed to have stimulated the villagers of the area, and the process of development, to a limited measure, was initiated. This is, however, by no means an unexpected or unnatural phenomenon; for since research is itself a method of work, all social studies of this nature are bound to suffer from this limitation. The contacts established by our research investigators thus created an urge in the minds of the people of the B group to initiate social action; they started contacting on their own the authorities of the local N.E.S. block and the Department, and insisted on initiating social work programs for their villages. "B," therefore, became less and less an untouched area, and due to the intermittent breaks in the Department's work at the A group of villages, owing to poor communication and heavy floods which frequently occurred during this period, A also tended to lose its "activized" and "contaminated" character.

SOCIAL WORK AND SOCIAL CHANGE

THE DIFFICULTY OF SAMPLING AND OBJECTIVITY OF APPROACH

After the study had progressed to some extent, the research workers came across severe difficulties in selecting proper methods of sampling and establishing a required standard of objectivity among the investigating personnel. It was, however, a matter of great surprise and satisfaction when one discovered that the untrained village-level investigators, with only a short orientation to this work, succeeded in maintaining in great measure a high standard of integrity and objectivity of approach and could bring in much data regarding the various opinion studies and action situations in an acceptable form.

The main reason for their success was probably that these investigators came from the work area of the Department, and had long been exposed to ideas and methods of work that emphasized objective approaches to all existing human problems. The success of village investigators who belonged to the work area of the Department, was, at a later stage looked upon as a useful finding in itself.

THE METHOD OF WORK

A number of methods were thus adopted for the purpose of this study. By the help of the statistical method, about 700 tables were prepared by editing the answers to Schedule A, which also required a number of variety of permutations and combinations. Case study methods for study of community leaders, institutions and action situations went hand in hand with the above. Specific action situations were also introduced in the B group of villages in order to test the effect of these actions on accredited leaders and their process of work. All these methods produced a vast amount of data—and the most important phase of the study was the interpretation of this data from the point of view of the intimate knowledge of the author as to the inner functioning of these villages, which he had acquired as a result of long acquaintance with the social structures of the two communities under review. Although many schedules have thus been filled in and many tables prepared, the emphasis of this study lay throughout on the understanding of the village situation, in the light of the research worker's own objective experience and knowledge of the specific area under study. The emphasis was thus, not so much on a mere counting of human heads as on understanding the behavior pattern and dynamics of social functioning of the human beings who formed the groups and communities selected for review. This is not to underestimate the contribution of the quantitative methods, but to realize that, by the very logic of the situation, a study like this cannot be completed by mere statistical analysis of mathematical data. Any effort to gain an insight into the behavior pattern of the communities and their process of interaction, however time-consuming that may be, is essential for this type of research. No other than that savant of a sociologist, C. C. Zimmerman could, however, describe the above proposition more adequately and in so few words, when he said the way of reasoning is not limited to one method, but to several: logic, statistical analysis, observation and even developed intuition. The development of this intuition could only be the result of long acquaintance with the communities under review, with whom the author had been able to establish a successful rapport. Throughout the course of this study the aim was to stabilize this relationship and to develop it further with the adult members of the surrounding villages. The fact that our study took a long time to be completed is therefore not altogether without significance.

The framer of this study, however, still cannot claim to have made a very accurate measurement of the social situations obtaining in the two groups of villages. Our generalizations might yet contain many probabilities, errors and shaky testimony, which are the inevitable concomitants of any pioneering study of this nature.

THE VALUE IN OUR WORK

The value of this research work, in our opinion, does not so much lie in what its achievements are; its use should be judged more from the point of view of the reaction it might create in the contemporary field of village studies, social work research and development.

This project, the author trusts, is thus but a first faltering step in an important direction. Its effort, to bring in methods of scientific social work under tests of validity and scientific scrutiny, would be of value only when the fallacies and points of errors of this study are pointed out by vigilant critics, and when further studies in the same direction are stimulated so that the applicability or otherwise of the methods and techniques of scientific social work become, in course of time, evident to rural social workers engaged in the task of social planning and development.

CHAPTER III

MOTIVATIONS OF SOCIAL ACTION & GROWTH
A CASE STUDY APPROACH

The A group of villages were not included in the intensive zone of the area of operation of the Department until July 1953. Concentrated efforts were made from then onwards to initiate development programs in the four villages of this group in a planned and determined manner and with special help of the staff and trainees of the Social Education Organizers' Training Center. The trainees were assigned to these villages for their field work training under the departmental leadership, and as apprentice workers of the agency. At the initial stages they were attached to the area organizer (analogous to a village level worker of *Sriniketan*), and at a later stage the worker was transferred to the center as a full-time officer under its field work department. The field worker in charge of the training center thus fulfilled a double role of a teacher-guide to the trainees as well as that of a welfare administrator of these groups of villages.

When the activities were initiated in 1953 in the A group of villages, it was found that a handful of leaders, elderly men mature in dealing with public affairs, dominated the scene. Each leader worked primarily in his own village, but cooperated with others of the nearby villages in matters of common concern. Some of these leaders were well meaning people who made many sacrifices for their communities, and received in turn recognition and social status. Some of them did, of course, by dint of their position, also secure personal and material gains. They were thus the undisputed and indispensable leaders, to whom men of all age groups and ranks from all over their respective villages paid their tribute. In all developmental matters the department, and even the governmental agencies, negotiated with the villages of this area only through these accredited leaders. The reason for routing all services to the villages through these leaders was simple: these village leaders,

29

when they accepted a program on behalf of some external agency, could enlist a good deal of popular support and implement even difficult projects with considerable ease. These leaders, two from Benuria, four from Lohagarh, two from Islampur and two from Bahadurpur, were of the upper-fifty age group.

As we have mentioned earlier, the A group of villages did not belong to the orbit of the Department's intensive area of work, although it lay just at the periphery. The Department's workers had, therefore, to depend on this network of leaders for reaching the groups and communities of these villages, and help willingly, or otherwise, the growth of this leadership. This led in turn to the establishment of a traditional hierarchy of leaders in this group which, composed of village elders functioning primarily in their own villages, developed collaborating links with each other for the organization of developmental work over the entire area through the assistance of their inter-village institutions. A number of organizations, detailed analytical treatment of which follows in the chapters to come, had also likewise sprung up in this area.

Each village had a school, and in the entire group of villages there were two night schools, three credit societies, four village development councils and a well-established cooperative health society. The area of work of the health society extended up to Nachansha—a village located at a distance of seven miles from Benuria, the center of the A group. The Union Board of the area, and all the developmental work routed through the normal nation-building departments of the State and the district, were under the control of these leaders. Decision-making on all important matters, external contact with outside agencies, and control over the destiny of village officials and village funds were their monopoly.

The background of the traditional leaders of the area makes interesting reading. Out of the ten leaders mentioned above, four were engaged in the national struggle for independence before 1947. Each of them had some land and was engaged in professional activities in some manner or other. Most of these leaders had, during the earlier days of the freedom struggle, worked with the Congress Party, but were now, except during the time of elections, the party's most vocal critics. They were undoubtedly men of honesty and integrity, but had at the same time joined hands with the communal leaders of the only Muslim village of the area and the Naib of a Zamindar, who was previously a police informer and now a contractor-cum-local representative of a most powerful party of the country. Of the majority caste, of their respective areas, they belonged to the middle income group in general.

The Department had always insisted that all forms and manner of work in this group of villages should be conducted in a democratic way; people's wishes should be ascertained, and democratically-constituted committees must function in charge of every institution of social and economic service. As a result, all these leaders had to win the vocal support of their own people. This support, earned partly by the developmental contribution of these leaders, and partly by their personal abilities and social background, had qualified them to speak on behalf of their villages in those bigger committees of the zone which conducted the affairs of the inter-village institutions. They were certainly, therefore, the leaders of their own communities, and sat in the village institutions as elected representatives of their respective people. Once elected, however, the leaders never bothered to consult their colleagues, those primary members who did not belong to the leadership hierarchy. Neither did they hesitate to commit their villages without consulting the *vox populi*. As a logical corollary they, the unchallenged leaders, steadily developed despotic tendencies and indulged in trivial acts of privilege, such as keeping the village radio in their own sitting rooms, and taking it for granted that all benefits of village improvement must start from their own street corners. Their special relationship with the Department was certainly responsible for their enjoying this situation of control over the destiny of their colleagues and maintaining their own position of power and petty privileges. As a result, the elections to the various bodies, although held at regular intervals, were reduced to mere formalities. The same set of leaders being elected again and again to the same committees reduced the village institutions to self-perpetuating agencies, instead of the democratic bodies of popular belief. Although the institutions in these villages drew their sustenance of finances and membership from their respective clientele, the latter had only a very loose manner of influence over them. There were no reciprocities of relationship between the clientele and the leaders, and no social mobility worthy of the name to allow old leaders to be replaced by new ones, or fresh elections to choose fresh leaders. A set formula of institutions and leaders had accordingly emerged in the area. The same set of leaders, with the same set of people collaborating with them in different villages, shared the powers and control of the established network of institutions—which neither waned nor grew in strength—and thus became responsible for maintaining a mere shadow of democracy in the area.

This created, it is interesting to note, a sense of stagnancy in the pace of social action and growth. The chief motivation of the leaders, and therefore of the ruling groups of the area, was their own sustenance, and no steps for the general furtherance of work which might have disturbed the status quo were taken up with much enthusiasm or care. Although ideologically the leaders were committed to democratic development, democracy in the area was in fact reduced to the rule of an oligarchy which, formally elected year after year under democratic constitutions, provided only an unalterable source of power in the area. The optimum of development and movement was accordingly limited by intention of these leaders to draw from outside help no more than they could comfortably assimilate into their own energy system. The system itself being of limited capacity, the democratic process had fast managed to slip its hold over the area! The established leaders obviously preferred the peace of equilibrium to rapid progress, and a slow pace of minimum growth to jerky uncertainties of quick development.

The democratic process of group formation and distribution of service by the Department, which originally produced this set of responsible leaders, was soon to take its toll, however, and create an inner dynamism to upset the equilibrium. A group of younger leaders came forward, in course of time, to accomplish this task. They rose above many barriers of caste, and regional and religious considerations, and impatient with the inertia and drudgery of the change-resisting situation, demanded greater paces of development. More efficient administration, greater speed in implementation of development projects, revitalization of old institutions and initiation of new ones, were what they were eagerly looking for.

The tools with which the Department started working in the local communities of the area, as soon as they came to belong to the intensive zone, accounted for this changeover in the total social climate of the place. These tools, the forms of relationship established in the area and the services provided, catalyzed the younger generation, made them a self-motivated group, and helped them to restore the pace of welfare work and democratic development where both were seemingly missing. It led to the rise of a new group, who practiced new programs and adopted a series of new schemes which they thought were more urgently needed to solve some of the more basic needs of the community. The old complex of the traditional leadership of the area was unable to bear this strain and therefore had almost melted away before the rising tide of this new enthusiasm. Two outstanding leaders from the old school, however, would remain as equally important in the next regime. These two men, of special characteristics and talents, had earlier acted as mere second-fiddles to the traditional leaders, and were picked up by the new ones as their inspirers and guides. The new developments which produced new leadership stabilized the process of welfare growth, and helped the seeds of democracy to take deep roots in the social system of the village communities of the A group. A new network of institutions was created, and a cadre of welfare workers. Given below is a case study of the social action programs which led to the new structure of development in the A group of villages, and provided the pace of growth with new meaning and motivation.

Since the villages had earlier belonged outside the intensive area of the department, its extension agents acted mostly on a surface level till the Department found in the batch of trainees of the Social Education Organizers' Training Center, a group of apprentice workers who could penetrate the community and act as catalytic agents. The trainees, of course, concentrated primarily on social education programs only, and were concerned with the children, youth and women of the area. Their main job was to offer adult education programs for the under-educated and under-privileged population, and to promote village organizations of children, youth and women. The enlightened and aged leadership which held a firm grip over the minds of the people of the area welcomed these trainees and patronized them in their sincere and hard labor.

As a result of the social education programs, the volume of welfare and educational services increased manyfold.

A youth club for each village and ten recreation centers for children were set up in the area. (Of these, three were for the children of Lohagarh, two for Islampur, three for Bahadurpur and two for Benuria.) Similarly, there came to exist eleven women's clubs and adult education centers, in place of the original two in the area: four for Lohagarh, two for Islampur, three for Bahadurpur and two for Benuria. A number of impressive cultural and recreational programs marked almost every day's activity in the villages of this area, and as a consequence the children of the place joined the clubs and organizations in large numbers. The women also started taking faltering steps towards their own centers, and the youth of these villages, belonging roughly to the age group between 14 to 28, enthusiastically rallied around their youth organizations.

The youth clubs of Benuria, Lohagarh, Islampur and Bahadurpur became very active during this period and took a leading part in organizing a series of cultural and recreational programs. A number of dramas were staged at regular intervals; cultural shows and study circles were held frequently; and *Kirtans, Sankirtans* and other folk songs refreshed the villagers in their selected evenings. The youth of the area, who hitherto looked only to the elderly leaders for their lead, and led an idle life, organized all these activities by themselves, and the whole territory during the years 1953-56 was thus dotted with a series of cultural, recreational, educational and organizational activities. This brought the youth of the villages nearer to each other psychologically as well as from the sociological point of view, secured their emotional integration, and developed a process of mutual give and take. The youth clubs had their own secretaries, presidents and committee members, and a senior trainee was attached to each of these clubs as consultant. They held fast to these organizations and sustained the flow of interest of the youth of the area through intermittent activities.

The S.E.O.[1] trainees and the youth clubs did not however directly take part in any developmental or economic activities. These were left to the elderly leaders who still continued to negotiate with the external agencies and accepted responsibilities for community programs directly from the Department. Whenever these leaders wanted the

---

[1] Social Education Organizer.

help of the youth they got quick response, the youth and the children of these villages coming out willingly in large numbers to aid them in the planned developmental activities which were still their exclusive concern. But the youth clubs as such were kept away from the developmental activities of the area and had to concentrate on the recreational and cultural aspects of the program; they had no say in the conduct of the political authority of the village. There was, perforce, at earlier stages, a broad division of work. The new youth organizations and cultural associations, although their workers contributed their small part in developmental activities, were kept away from the decision-making process, and were treated as wards of the established organizations' traditional leaders. The new entrants in the field of work were satisfied with their role of second fiddle, and accordingly were neither looked upon as rivals to the established organizations nor with suspicion by senior leaders. The latter, on the other hand, patronized the former and enjoyed a good deal of comfort, finding their young wards getting a lot of fun out of their activities, which they considered of a juvenile character. Little did they realize that the conduct of the recreational activities and the consequent process of socialization were the early-day rehersals of a more important drama, whose dimensions were bound to become political as well.

Determinedly and without interruption, the flow of events fast developed in which the younger generation of these villages were brought nearer to each other. They no longer wasted away their leisure in idle gossiping but spent all their time in activizing the youth clubs. Youth clubs raised their own subscriptions, maintained their own records and gradually developed a good deal of leadership potential from among themselves. As they started coming into their own, the S.E.O. trainees were directed to recede to the background and act as aids and helpers. The two leaders, however, Mr. X and Mr. Y, who were respected by the elderly leaders of the area as well, did not adopt a patronizing attitude as their other elderly colleagues did. They joined the trainees as aides and guides of their youth clubs.

The youth of these villages gradually started feeling responsible. In their organizational work it was insisted that punctuality in attendance should be observed, procedures maintained and records kept properly. Disorderly behavior in their meetings was condemned by all concerned, and thus dragged through the fire of activity and discipline, a wholesome leadership, under a network of wholesome organizations, gradually started coming into being. The elderly leaders enjoyed from a distance these "mock-shows" of their younger colleagues.

The youth of the area had from then onwards increasing opportunities of working together with the elderly leaders of the village, as these leaders increasingly sought and readily secured their cooperation in all developmental activities.

Definite lack of much sense of punctuality, the disorderly behavior of the elders on occasions when the two groups worked together, their dictatorial temper and patronizing attitude, however, pained the younger generation a good deal. The latter had, it must be remembered here, already started becoming self-conscious and had developed the requisite skills for conducting meetings, running organizations and establishing contacts with the outside world. They were also getting trained in raising funds for their own organizations. Gradually, the youth clubs came nearer to each other and developed an inter-village youth organization which staged inter-village cultural programs and sometimes took upon themselves, under the guidance of S.E.O. trainees, specific constructive programs of work. These include cleaning of the school surroundings, road making and construction of community center buildings. This was the time, therefore, when the social contents of the action programs, having already created democratic structures of organizations and leadership, took a new turn, and the youth of the area aspired to move towards concrete programs of economic development. That would have given them, they conceived, higher status in the authority structure of the village, so that their leadership could no longer be ignored or dismissed as juvenile. As their sense of responsibility and their awareness of the strength which they could now draw from their unity became evident, they started getting disillusioned with the frailties of their seniors. A "we can do it better" feeling came to dominate the scene and gradually got the better of them. The feeling was heightened by a sense of frustration which came to the youth, as they found that the elderly leaders only used them as instruments for 'their' developmental work and did not think that they merited any more attention. The fact that they were looked upon by the elders as mere organizers of cultural programs and no better, and that the Department continued to negotiate with the elderly leaders for all important developmental schemes, gradually aggravated the feeling further.

The boys felt that they lacked recognition from the elders and to some extent from the Department as well; there gradually developed along with the prevailing sense of frustration a feeling of aggression against an undefined opponent, and led to the growth of a firm determination. Since the youth of the village were still not sure, on a conscious level, that what they were reacting to so violently was the policy of disregard of the elders, or the Department, or both, the emotional suffering continued to grow and further brought the youth closer to each other. The feeling of discontent began to assume serious proportions. During this period, a sudden development took place which added insult to injury. A sense of vacuum was immediately created in the youth group, owing to the collapse of their pet projects, the youth clubs, which they had so fondly nurtured over the last few months. This happened when the Social Education Organizers' Training Center had suddenly to discontinue their regular visits to the A group and to gradually shift their field work area elsewhere, to a different set of villages. This withdrawal of the trainees, and the lack of effective support from the elderly leaders, disorganized the youth clubs and in course of a year or so, the clubs as such became defunct.

It must however be recognized that a growing neighborly feeling and sense of togetherness had already developed among the village youth by this time; and although the formal structure of the club organizations had collapsed, an integrated relationship among the youth leaders of the area was already a settled fact. This awareness of strength, which originally came from a formal union, was intensified by a sense of aggression. The deepening frustration—a result of the vacuum created by the collapse of the formal structures of their organization and the withdrawal of their trainee advisers—made the youth of the area increasingly intolerant of their elderly leadership.

The age group combination now broke barriers of religious, caste and kinship solidarities. The youth of these four villages joined hands and decided to contest their elders when the next general election for the offices of the cooperative health society came up. The elders were defeated, and in one clean sweep the group of young leaders filled in all the posts of the health society. Later the youth group further consolidated their position and within a few days' time successfully contacted the State government to set up a cooperative oil pressing society. This cooperative was a scheme which the elders had been trying to secure for the village for the last two years, and now the formation of the cooperative mobilized the entire oil presser's (union) group behind the youth. The youth group included the sons and nephews of the leaders of the older generation and they were drawn from a variety of castes and from both the major religious groups of the area, the Hindus and the Muslims. The tribal population was kept out of the show.

The elders were greatly upset. But they consoled themselves with the idea that theirs was only a temporary setback. They now openly asserted that the youth of the area had become impertinent and would not be able to hold these institutions for long, and would bring the latter to inevitable ruin within a short period of time. This widened the rift further, as the conflict which existed till recently on a sub-conscious level became a matter of a real test of strength, and helped both the groups to get emotionally stirred and physically prepared for a social clash. A headlong clash came in the next year, when the youth decided to contest the Gram Panchayat elections; they set up candidates, and went on to successfully defeat all the elders. This created a terrible feeling of animosity between the two groups, the new masters of the village and the rejected old guard. They vied against each other for the time being, and the departmental workers offered informal counsel to both the groups. They requested the elderly leaders to bless the youth and to cooperate with them by acting as their advisers, and called upon the youth to give the retiring leaders a position of honor. The youth, dazed with the first flash of victory, rejected these advices and went ahead with their plans—completely eliminating the elders from the plans and programs of work.

The new group that came to dominate the scene were people who had come through the fire of activities. They managed the health society extremely well; the membership of the society increased considerably, and the deficit budget was converted into a surplus. The new leaders, who had been critical of the anti-democratic behavior of their elders, were now careful to safeguard democratic procedures and traditions. They realized that they were the products of the groups with whom they worked, and that the groups of people for whom the services were meant could easily have thrown them out of office if they did not conduct themselves properly. The village community in general seemed to be happy with their new leaders and went on rejecting the whole group of traditional leaders in election after election.

The elderly leaders had obviously had closer and more intimate relationship with the Government, and other respectable and powerful persons of the outside world, than with the people. The people of the A group of villages had accordingly known that the actual quantity of services would, for some time to come, show a retarded growth in their area due to the rejection of the elderly and influential leaders. The experiences showed that this had actually happened at the initial stages, and the new leaders of the A group were viewed with suspicion by many outsiders; yet the people of A group showed an awareness of their own strength and preferred to depend on their young leaders, who were selected according to their own preference. Correspondingly, the community was required to, and did, make increasing sacrifices to give its new leaders support. It contributed more money and increased the number of members of the health society, integrated the three cooperative credit societies of the three villages into one, and floated a new cooperative venture. The needs, dynamics and motivations of the groups of individuals of the area—adults and adolescents—were evident. They obviously were eager to emphasize their ability to choose their own leaders, rather than standing by a few domineering leaders who might have promised more efficient services.

The villagers of this area had admittedly secured a good deal of return in the past from the traditional leadership; but the new leaders were dearer to them, not because they made no mistakes, but because they were of the people's own choice. They had come to know these leaders intimately, at first through the cultural and recreational activities and then through actual work. They had seen them in action and were impressed with their sense of punctuality, their feeling of responsibility and their zeal to do something new. This acquaintance, which rapidly grew intimate, made them confident that their needs and interests would be more secure in the hands of the new group. This confidence ultimately did it. It motivated the people to venture into great social risks and to take the big step of rejecting *en bloc* all their traditional leaders and installing a new framework of leadership and institutions in the area.

THE B GROUP—ANALYSIS OF THE BACKGROUND OF WORK

The nerve-center of the B group of villages lay in Bergram, the next important segment of this group being the village of Sattore. Two leaders, Mr. P and Mr. Q—and mostly Mr. P—had wielded great influence over the destiny of these village communities. Both these leaders were susceptible to outside influences, and held leadership mainly due to external support and control: Bergram was guided by a set of constructive workers and Sattore by politicals of the nearby town. The leaders and activities of the B group had thus taken shape over the last decade mainly due to the interest of a band of external leaders, although a handful in number, they were well-meaning and influential, and took these villages under their protective umbrella. They depended on the village leaders, mainly two in number, to sell their ideas and programs to the village communities. Being men of very heavy preoccupations, the external leaders who provided the main source of stimuli for social growth of the area had no time to look into the process and methods of work of their accredited agents. Unlike the Department they did not even verbalize the the need, (possibly taking it for granted), for a democratic framework. The village leaders of B group would not, therefore, look to their own communities for support. They won financial and material aid from outside the village and could thus on their own build a number of institutions in the area. Most of these were schools—primary, post-primary and secondary ones—with big buildings, polished libraries, and well-decorated class rooms. Detailed study of some of these institutions, embodied elsewhere, would reveal that most of these schools did not even have enough students, and that the books in the libraries still gave off the odor of newness. An interesting commentary on the whole situation was that the village leaders of the area did not even bother to win the cooperation of the parents of the area, or to look for new students for the school. They considered that the setting up of the school itself was a favor done to the clientele of the area. The social institutions of the area were likewise, even by constitution, self-perpetuating and undemocratic.

A study of the pace of social growth of the B group would reveal that here too, as in A, many conflicts had taken place between the established leaders of the area and a new bunch of impatient aspirants. But since the old leaders felt no manner of obligation to the area, and depended on the latter neither for finances nor for any other support, the conflicts, which always raged outside the institutions, only resulted in greater isolation of the established leadership. Yet, this did not create any hardship for them, since all these conflicts and confusions put together could not isolate them even from the fringe of their main support, whose chief source lay outside the area.

Given below is a short review of the leaders' organization and methods, as well as their relationship with the catalyst agencies, which existed in the B group of villages over the last few years.

As described earlier, social work activities were initiated in the A group of villages by the Department of Rural Reconstruction. It had a unified agency of administration and an accredited philosophy of work. A scientific program of social education and welfare was thus introduced by the Department in the A group of villages in its attempt to awaken the village communities and bring out their latent strength. In this task, the Department helped the villagers of the area by supplying them the necessary aids of technical advice for planning of programs and construction of social services, so that they could face on their own some of their basic problems. Workers of *Sriniketan* also visited the area year in and year out. They held regular meetings to discuss and critically evaluate their ways of work. Staff meetings and other training schemes were periodically launched and village leaders, young and old, women and children, from the A group of villages were directly involved in social action through a series of village level programs.

No such systematic attempts were made by any central agency in the B group of villages to touch the rural community at its base and to awaken its dormant potentialities. Two interested and conscious workers of the B group had, on the other hand, contacted a few influential outside leaders and organizations from time to time, in order to bring certain services and amenities to the villages of the area.

SOCIAL WORK AND SOCIAL CHANGE

The avowed objectives of these benefactors were either to extend services to the villagers for their own altruistic motives, or to win them over for political ends. The two leaders from B group who are subjects of our study in the next chapter were connected with two such organizations, one political in its character and the other associated with constructive work activities of a few reputed leaders of the State. In both cases the organizations or individuals who stood behind these two leaders and helped them to float a number of social service institutions and welfare projects (such as buildings, roads, land reclamation projects, sub-canals, etc.), always depended on the village leaders for completion of these works. All the schemes of development which were secured for the village by outside support certainly needed some amount of local or popular participation. These village leaders, aided as they were by outside agencies, secured these matching grants by employing whatever methods they considered fit for the purpose. There was no time for the well-wishing patrons of the village whose influence helped these leaders to secure their schemes, to contact the people directly or to organize them in a manner that would have motivated the entire community to participate, as in the case of A. Similarly, due to political influences pushing him forward, Mr. P became the President of the local Panchayat; but the doubtful methods by which he won the decisive vote, a grossly negative step from the point of view of scientific community organization was not taken too seriously by those who wanted him to win the election and retain his leadership.

The *Palli Seva Niketan* of B group ran all the schools of the area and had, as an institution of service, done work of great merit. A mighty structure of concrete was constructed for this agency. A school building standing in this interior area has been maintained with a high standard of efficiency. Surroundings of the building are clean and the internal set up is tidy. This efficiency is impressive and the "outsiders" who helped from behind could not and did not have time to see, in their sojourns to the area, beyond this layer of efficiency. They were more interested in the product, which they could see in terms of big buildings and well laid out roads, etc., than in the process which secured these products. As a result, the institutions which have cropped up in B have had little or no contribution from the people for their support. Even whatever contribution the villagers of the neighboring areas had once provided for the road project and school buildings of *Palli Seva Niketan* were later regretted by them. The leaders of the Palli Sevaniketan too, as a result, had turned their back to these critics. There is however no doubt about the fact that the leaders of the B group of villages were well meaning stalwarts, although they were far from democratic in their outlook. Neither did they have the requisite acquaintance with the objectives of social development. Their catalysts or inspirers, as the Department was in the case of the A group, had no time or motivation to orient them to those objectives. The objectives of rural reconstruction, as viewed by both the outside leaders and local enthusiasts, were thus merely to raise certain structures for services rather than to work *with* the community.

In the A group of villages, leaders had to look for support to their people because that was the aim of the sponsoring agency—the Department of Rural Reconstruction. They could not exist except by enlisting popular support behind them, and by avoiding isolation from their clientele. They had therefore to educate their groups in their ideals and objectives, and win their sympathies; in other words, leaders in A group of villages needed the people whereas the leaders of B group could progress in spite of the nonsupport of the *vox populi*.

In the B group of villages, leaders therefore had to stand alone, isolated from their clientele. As a result they created antagonisms among many, and some hostile groups planned to retard their progress. This did not however have any socializing effect on the leadership, but instead led them to ignore the hostiles with great feelings of anguish that their own laudable objectives were misinterpreted by the misguided. They hoped that the day would come when the critical community would become mature enough to understand them! Mr. P's reaction to his recalcitrant neighbors is amply expressed in his admission to the researchers that he was not ready to retire, as he did not think that he could yet see anybody good enough to be his successor from among his community (see chapter IV). The institutions in the A group of villages, on the other hand, had democratic constitutions, and were such that the leadership there could not have guaranteed themselves a permanent foot-hold in times to come. Not infrequently, leaders in the A group had to consult their committees and the people of the area. More than that, instances were not wanting when in the A group the general body of the villagers were to reject the committees and their leaders *en bloc* and replace them with new hands. Here in A people were probably more aware of their rights and knew how to practice them for their own benefit, too.

Most of the institutions in B group were schools; these were set up with one hundred percent government support, and did not need much contribution either in cash or in kind from the people. Social service agencies in A, on the other hand—at least many of them—were self-financing bodies and had to look for interested participants who knew democratic procedures of work and liked to observe them. Aware of the importance of maintaining decorum at meetings they were therefore keen to train their members and to make up their deficiency with effort and earnestness. The leaders in A had thus set up paraphernalia, procedures and methods by which they could formally ascertain the needs of the community and plan their own program by operating on the basis of a consensus. The leaders of the B group however had no such dependence upon or concern for the people. The committees here were *ad hoc* bodies, and the leaders were chosen by the granters rather than by the beneficiaries. The initiation of a democratic process of growth was therefore by no means incumbent on the leaders. Meetings of committees in B were held with a handful of members, and no positive attempts were made to associate the general public with its decisions. No cultural shows, literacy drives or open dialogues between leaders and people were featured in the B group. Institutions with settled finances and self-perpetuating leaders faced no hazards in the area at all, and being run on a bureaucratic model by a handful of village leaders who acted as self-appointed umpires and executives, life in B flowed on with steady efficiency. Never imperiled by any probable upsurges of emotions and aspirations, the prevailing status therefore became the order of the day in B.

Yet the B group of villages viewed in many respects certainly stood at par with the villages of A group. In terms of their knowledge and academic understanding of everyday problems, they are not much behind their brethren of the A group, whereas in terms of physical structures of agencies, their achievement is even greater. The interests of the people of B group were however not taken into serious consideration by the elite who functioned as self-imposed and self-perpetuating leaders in their own institutions. The agencies that functioned in B group were thus more or less defunct bodies since, seen from a democratic perspective, they were "leader-centric," and run without the help of the people looking for no continuous association of groups or any democratic inspiration for guiding their own destiny, organizations in B were more 'management' than 'client-oriented.' They therefore look more to the outside world for support than to their own kinsmen and friends of the community. The people in the B group not very frequently consulted by their village leaders to whom they looked up for grants and benefits, and they had learned to adjust to this fate and treatment with cool unconcern! Even when the leaders of the B group seek to consult the people, meetings are called in such a hurry that most of the people do not turn up and even those who come to attend submit unconditionally to the dictates of their leaders. Most of the beneficiaries of the B group would thus be unable to say how and why the impressive Community Development projects in the area (e.g., of roads and buildings) were constructed and who ran them with what finances. They know however this much for certain, that the institutions in B have not been built by their co-operative effort and neither did they require local support for survival. The people here made their contributions if and when they were called upon by the leaders to do so and sometimes even under the illusion of being made partners in the policy-making bodies. The leaders here, it seems, were not a product of the group, but the group functioned as an unconscious appendage of the elite.

It is not the purpose of the present study to affirm, even for a moment, that the leaders of the B group of villages were of doubtful motivation, although some of their disgruntled colleagues had harbored such doubts. The leaders of the B group, on the other hand, were sturdy individuals and men of sterling character; they could thus certainly be classed as leaders—although their sparks of action had been limited within the four walls of their small communities. They had won for themselves honored positions in the minds of many intelligent outsiders who are respectable leaders of the present day society, and yet these very leaders of the B group of villages had failed to touch the hearts of their own people.

SOCIAL WORK AND SOCIAL CHANGE

The reason for such an anomalous situation is not hard to find. The needs, objectives, dynamics and motivations of the local leaders of the group were a result of the fact that they, as initiators of welfare programs, had very different ideals in view, and had to employ different methods and techniques of work than those which were employed by the Department in A. More interested in constructing buildings than in building communities, the leaders in B had forgotten to create the necessary awareness in the minds of the people and to leave it to them to determine their own plans of work. Not mere initiators and stimulators, they were workers and doers *par excellence*. They therefore wanted to go the whole way of development all by themselves, and to do it by their own superhuman strength. "Many a seemingly successful leader seems to delight in trying to do the whole job himself; but his success is only superficial for as he leaves or is displaced the group is not stronger than it was before he assumed leadership. This is one of the paradoxes of the best leaders. The less he is indispensible the greater he is leader."[2] Leaders who did the whole job by themselves were found in abundance in the B group, and therefore the leadership and the people of the area lay apart from each other by self-imposed, artificial cleavages of mutual separation.

The methods used by the Department in their area of operation, on the other hand, were different from those used in the B group of villages by its outside well-wishers. As a consequence, the quantity and nature of results achieved in the two groups of villages were not identical. The programs and processes which have led to this differential growth has to some extent been mentioned in this chapter and in the previous ones. But the impact is visible on leadership, organizations and events of the two groups of villages; this is treated in the ensuing chapters, which will go a long way to demonstrate the differential characteristics of the two sets of processes, programs and approaches. This chapter merely provides an introduction; the more detailed and multidimensional study is to follow.

---

[2] Sanderson, Dwight and Polson, R. A., *Rural Community Organization* (New York: John Wesley & Sons, 1939), p. 365.

CHAPTER IV

GREAT LEADERS OF SMALL COMMUNITIES —
(A Case Study of Village Leaders)

It is said that a country gets a government that it deserves. It may equally be true that a village community gets a leader which it deserves. The barometer of growth of a community could easily be found in a measure of the quality of its existing leadership and its future potential. The present state of leadership, the opportunities which are provided in a community to facilitate growth of new leaders by replacement of the old ones instead of allowing prolonged and monopolized domination of a few are some of the ranges on the barometer which may provide clues for studying the structure of leadership in a particular community as well as for assessing the stage of democratic development at which the community is resting at the moment.

It is, however, certainly difficult, if not impossible, to state categorically what are the qualities of a good leader and to point out that here is one who is the best of all the leaders. The endeavor in this chapter is not to look out for any particular leader and to say that he is the superior one among all the rest. But the findings of our research studies here are an attempt to discover whether the qualities manifested in the leaders studied from the A group of villages, i.e., the area of operation of *Sriniketan*, are in consonance with those which *Sriniketan*, as a result of its activities, desired to develop among the indigenous leaders of the area. The other purpose was to find whether the qualities observed among the leaders of A group are precisely the same as we found in the leaders of the B group.

A leader of a village, as visualized by *Sriniketan* should have an understanding of the problems of those whom he seeks to lead. Leadership should have its base rooted in the confidence of the people. The leader must handle situations by winning over the majority of the group as well as by enabling the majority to accept impartial solutions

47

which would help all the members of the group, including the minority, to realize their needs and thereby seek fulfillment of the needs of the community in general. The leader leads not merely because of the fact that he represents any domineering sect or group, but because he has a superior, amiable behavior, and is able to plan and execute decisions of the group with adequate integrity and a high degree of honesty of purpose. As a leader one should, in short, be a product of the group he leads. It is not expected that he shall be the dictator of the group, rather only its effective mouthpiece.

Nor should the motivations of the leader be personal gain. A leader, being a normal human being, certainly looks to fulfill many of his own needs such as seeking recognition, sharing gains with the rest of the community and so on; but the true leader must have his immediate personal gains superseded by the gains of the community of which he is a part and whose spokesman he is. All his motivations should be tinged with the spirit of the sacrifice of immediate personal gain in favor of realizing common human needs which the community under his leadership is still struggling to fulfill. He should consult his colleagues and not impose, but offer, leadership when situations require it.

Our Present Study

Case studies of six leaders, three from each of the two groups of villages, were accordingly made, in order to find out how much of the qualities of leadership listed elsewhere are found among the cases studied. The three leaders of the B group of villages are known for the purpose of our study as P, Q and R and the other three belonging to A group as X, Y and Z.

A preliminary scrutiny of the six case records, however, clearly shows that a special study of the leaders X and P provides the most important clue to the understanding of the state of leadership prevalent in the two groups of villages. It is also true that both Mr. X and Mr. P have played the most dynamic and vital role in giving shape to the community services holding sway in their respective areas, and have distinguished themselves as important personalities, each in his own field. They have been the centers of gravitation around whom all activities in their respective villages have been built up. Both Mr. X and Mr. P, as their case studies reveal, are leaders whose background, ways of work and motivation are out of the normal run of average men. It is interesting to find how their leadership careers provided them with important sources for satisfying their own ungratified needs.

Leaders Y and Q are the two next important personalities and a subsequent reference has been made to them by providing comparative data on the structure of their leadership. Leaders Z and R have been left out for the purpose of our study as they did not seem to have either the influence, or the potentiality of growing into influential leaders in the immediate present.

AWARENESS OF THE CONCEPT OF MOTIVATIONS

Most of the leaders interviewed for the purpose of our case study seemed to have been aware that a leader should reflect a number of popular qualities, some of which have been mentioned earlier. Being men of exceptional intelligence, which has qualified them to climb up, they could forestall our leading questions and in answering most of them gave socially desirable responses. All of them seemed to express what one could legitimately deem as the right answers for our questions. The study that follows, does not, however, indicate that all these leaders have identical structures and motivations of leadership and of ways of work; on the other hand, it was discovered while interpreting the data thus collected that, although these leaders were aware of the popular notions of socially desirable qualities of a leader, not all seemed to agree with them. These four leaders, therefore, particularly supplied us not only with stereotyped replies to our questions, but also went on freely to express their own objectives. It is remarkable to note that almost all of them expressed themselves freely and boldly. The real positions of these leaders were further revealed during the course of discussion of a number of other connected issues, recorded elsewhere in the book. Their reactions on these allied matters, more than the direct questions, provided substantial data for our study. This work is thus a product of not only the case materials collected through interviews and discussions with these leaders, but also of what was gathered by observation of the leaders under direct action situations in which they were involved from time to time during the period of our study.

The task analysis of the two leaders, Mr. X and Mr. P, provides interesting material. Mr. X is a member of a number of committees of various institutions in his area. His tasks mainly are to help those who keep records by advising them on the *modus operandi*. The meetings he attends are usually presided over by the accredited chairmen of these institutions. While most of the speaking in these situations is generally done by the members of these committees, Mr. X is usually found to sit quiet and step in at the right moment to explain the inner meanings of records and issues, pointing out possible alternatives to the various policies and suggestions which the meeting might have ignored. If this is his role in committees and meetings, whenever he goes on occasional visits, his tasks are to observe the reactions of the various people of these institutions and policies and to bring them to the notice of their *de jure* leaders. He would then sit with the committeemen and devise ways and means to improve the quality and methods of work of the respective bodies, so that the reactions he had obtained were set at rest.

He is also occasionally found settling conflicts between the members of the organizations outside the committee rooms, and playing the role of mediator and harmonizer. His main job is, therefore, to give advice, formulate policies and put them up for the consideration of the formally recognized leaders of these associations.

Mr. P on the other hand, is primarily a 'doer.' He presides over the meetings and somebody else keeps the records.

It is not his business to go out and meet people; nor does he entertain many at home. His external contact mainly consists of long bicycle journeys when he goes out of the village to meet his consultants and guides for support and advice. Mr. P is a hard worker, who supervises the affairs of his organization, whereas Mr. X would collect data on supervision and place it before the real supervisors for consideration. The relationship of Mr. X with his committee is that of a consultant and advisor-leader, and of Mr. P is that of a father-figure to his immediate followers and "dominator" to the community at large.

THE TWO LEADERS MR. X AND MR. P

Both the leaders were of Hindu caste and whereas leader "X" refused to mention his sub-caste, Mr. P revealed his caste sub-group without any hesitation. Both belong to joint families, although Mr. X lives away from his home.

Mr. X came several years ago to the village of his present habitat, from outside, in order to take up a job. He fast became a member and a part of the community itself. Mr. X can thus no longer be treated as an outsider to this village.

Both the leaders have had formal education and read up to intermediate standard. Mr. X had completed his Inter Science (B.S.) and had taken a further course in medicine. Both Mr. X and Mr. P seemed to devote their whole time and energy to village development work, although Mr. X remains by occupation a service holder. Being the doctor of the village, Mr. X has to devote a good deal of his time to attending to patients, in which manner he earns his living. Even then, it will not be wrong to affirm that he is a full-time leader in the truest sense of the term; for even when he is on his professional work, his behavior, his opportunities of contact, not only with the patient but with the patient's families in the villages he visits, all these are looked upon by him as opportunities for studying the problems of villagers and of helping them in their day-to-day difficulties. He is, by virtue of his superior education and long contact with the village, the ideal of the youth and is consulted by them in almost every action they take. As a leader, however, Mr. X does not act in isolation. He frequently consults his colleagues of the younger generation and seems to have contributed a good deal to the building up of their organizations. Accordingly, he moves among them with perfect ease. Whenever he represents a point of view or suggests a program, one may be sure that he has consulted the group on whose behalf he makes the commitment. He emphasizes the need for making mass contacts on the part of his followers and feels most at home in large meetings and group discussions.

He is in his early fifties and had once suffered from a disease of the lungs. By his own admission he was much cared for by his parents. Being the first male child, after three successive daughters, and since his maternal relations were many, he got overwhelming affection and was in fact overprotected by his parents. He had, he feels even now, a happy and well-adjusted home. He lives in the rural community represented by villages of the A group and has become one of its integral parts; yet he harbors, he says, a feeling of acute loneliness and although he works and lives along with the rest of the villagers of the area and does not look outside the village for any companionship, he has, a sense of real isolation and he feels so even when he is among his own neighbors. This feeling of loneliness and isolation, he admits, has been with him from the very beginning and is still there. This then is by and large a subjective feeling, which would be evident if one studied objectively his ways of day-to-day living. He has won in abundant measure the love and respect of his fellow villagers and has become a member of the community in every sense of the term. When his old mother died recently the villagers of even a higher caste, considering him to be of "almost their own caste" (although he comes from a different caste which is immediately lower down in the scale), carried his mother to the cremation ground and raised contributions so that he could perform the religious rites in connection with the *Sardha* Ceremony of his departed mother in a princely manner. In view of the fact that he was overprotected in his childhood and hardly had opportunities of taking part in games and sports he did not however seem to acquire specific experiences of socialization by functioning as a member of groups composed of persons of equal status.

He comes originally from East Bengal and was uprooted from his home as a refugee, and had thereafter come to this village to make a home and a vocation on a very meager salary (he had not completed his doctoral degree in medicine). He has since then attained a good deal of social and moral stature with many in the village, although there are still quite a few who would attempt to deny him all that. He is an employee of one of the village organizations and yet has become a leader of that very institution, as well as of many others, if not of all other institutions which function in the A group of villages. He holds this position of leadership not by being a formal officeholder of any of these institutions, but because he is a very efficient worker on his own merit. He acts as the informal and yet the undisputed leader. He is held in the affection of a good many young men and for the rest, who might not give him that affection, he is looked upon as a very necessary executive leader without whose sustained interest some of the institutions would collapse. By his own admission, and with all these achievements to his credit, he has yet been unable to find himself in the company of the villagers and feels rather lonely in the village.

GREAT LEADERS

The villagers, the young and the old, with whom he works are today unevenly divided in their loyalties to two sets of leaders. The elderly leaders had once held all important positions in the village until a new youth group gradually grew up and replaced them (see chapter III). Mr. X was looked upon by the elderly statesmen of the village, in their heyday of power, as a very efficient aide and was respected and well thought of by them. The younger generations in the earlier stages of their movement worked well with Mr. X. Now that the leadership of the youth has been well established, he is today held in high esteem and respected as a very useful consultant. All have thus paid their tribute to him, the young and old. The elderly leaders are now somewhat disillusioned with him as he did not withdraw his support from the youth when the latter, grown and nurtured under X's leadership, ultimately decided to hit back at them. Yet Mr. X continues to be respected by both and serves, to a very great extent, as the meeting ground of the two groups—the retiring and frustrated traditional leaders and the new. He has been responsible for sponsoring a number of institutions in the village which grew up under his leadership with fairly rapid strides. He however still feels unhappy and unadjusted with their pace of growth. Essentially in constant and acute subjective distress, he is unable to achieve for the community, as he says, greater bargains of welfare measures due to lack of financial resources. He is in the habit of purchasing lottery tickets in the hope of obviously securing a sudden windfall. The utopia he dreams of is still a distant mirage, and his successes fail to combat his frustration and unhappiness. As a result, he frequently tends to become aggressive; but being unable to turn his aggression towards the community without whose willing allegiance he cannot function effectively, he directs it to the outside agents, who approach him either on behalf of welfare agencies or other sources offering help. To the village he appears as a lovable leader who continuously devotes all his time for social work activities; but to the outsiders he often appears as a hard, anguished and bitter individual who seeks to accuse the rest of the world for his miseries. But once this outer crust of cold disregard melts, he offers unstinted and ungrudging help to any external agent who is prepared to recognize him and decides not to disturb his position in the village.

Mr. X provides good example of a noteworthy social

climb. Entering the village as an employee of one of the organizations of the area, he rose, by dint of his astute and mature functioning, to become leader of the two most powerful factions. Trained and skillful in managerial work, painstaking and apparently self-effacing, he was long recognized by the elderly group of leaders as their consultant. At a time when they were in power he was consulted on a wide range of matters and his advice, technical support and help were sought. Mr. X did not misuse the position which he had acquired in the reflected glory of the traditional leaders of the village community; neither did he at a later stage, when the traditional leaders were swept off their feet and yielded to the hegemony of the youth. Mr. X was again successful in keeping up his image of an impartial counselor to both the groups. He was however drawn nearer to the aspiring youth who had become the chief custodian of all developmental power, and he became their adviser. The defeated faction had, at first, hit at him with sarcasm and vigor. But as the social climate cooled off and Mr. X was found to be the only possible link between the new and the old, the rejected leaders of the elderly faction also veered toward him.

The key to Mr. X's rise to power was not only his skill, but also the sustained interest he manifested in the day-to-day developmental activities of the local community. A friend of the young and the old alike, Mr. X, a migrant from East Pakistan, had come to the area in search of a vocation with three distinctly visible feelings: he was anti-authority, suffered from acute emotional isolation and needed to sublimate his feelings of earlier frustration by submerging himself in hard community work. This, he found later, had also earned for him recognition from the community of his adoption. He was, as the case history reveals, an overprotected child with a satisfying past. The sudden reaction following the partition of the country which threw him, like many others, overboard, created an intense sense of frustration which gradually grew into a recognizable form of aggression generally expressed towards an "outsider-leader" of the government. He also often identified the Department as the symbol of authority which had conspired to drive him out of his own homeland. Yet Mr. X showed great power of adjustment and this more than anything else helped him to sublimate his immediate need for expression of hostility, and to look for support in the multifarious activities which were going on in the community. This too intensified the frustrations and acting as a lever stirred him to action. Increased opportunities shaping his destiny and providing him with substitute satisfaction also helped him at this stage to stabilize his role in the new community.

Mr. P, an agriculturist and owner of lands, is of medium height and fair build. He is forty and a resident of the village. He too was well cared for by his parents, being the second eldest child of the family. He, too, was no great mixer in his boyhood days. He used to be, in fact, uncontrollable in the company of his relations or neighbors of equal age and status and did not take much effective part in childhood recreation. Mr. P is a full-time leader and a formal leader as well. He is the Secretary of the mammoth educational institution located in his village and thereby also the Secretary of the only agency of that village which is carrying on important social service work. His economic conditions are better than those of many others of the same village and he is therefore in a position to devote substantial interest for rural development work.

He was born in the house of a farmer in one of the villages of the area, but the birth actually took place in the house of Mr. P's maternal uncle at a village located seven miles away from his parental homestead. The hereditary avocation—paternal and maternal—has been one of farming.

The childhood days of Mr. P were days of inadequacies and wants, which used to afflict the respondent. His father was learned, though not educated according to university standards, and had nothing of what is called paper qualifications. Mr. P had his first schooling at home, under the care and guidance of his father, and as he grow up he came to study in a middle English School. It was then that the young boy first experienced a bereavement in the death of his grandmother. But this incident passed without leaving much mark on the family or in the life of Mr. P, who was at that time only ten or twelve years of age.

The next period of his life saw the fruition of his secondary education, when he was matriculated and was placed in the 1st division (high academic ranking). He says, he had all along been a serious student of the rural type (by rural type he means that he was both a bookworm and interested in outdoor activities), and was given to reading books more than being involved in any other extra-curricular activities, e.g., games, socials, cultural activities and the like. After his matriculation he got himself admitted to *Santiniketan*, into the I.A.,[1] class under the syllabus of the University of Calcutta. He suffered an early emotional setback, along with the other members of his family, when he was still a teen-ager and his brother died, leaving him to become the eldest surviving son of the family. His father was so much overwhelmed with this grief that he retired and Mr. P could not complete his studies in intermediate arts. His educational career had thus come to an abrupt end.

This event of death, Mr. P reports, created a serious emotional disturbance in him and pitched him into acute economic distress. Thus ended, he says, one chapter of his life; he then moved to the next chapter which enabled him, he says, to cast his lot for the betterment of the people of his village. From his childhood he had wanted to be a teacher, but obviously his educational career did not enable him to go very far that way, beyond helping him to join a primary school, which he himself had started in his village. In course of time and by the strength of his contacts with a number of important persons of the State and (by his own admission) being an instrument in their hands, he had succeeded in building up a multipurpose Senior Basic School under the agency of a village welfare council, of which he became the Secretary.

It may be noted here that somehow or other the career of a teacher had an intense appeal to this person from his childhood days, chiefly for the following two reasons:

First, he became a believer of "school-centric" education for the villages where poor boys and girls do not normally get even the minimum opportunity for schooling. Secondly, the career of a teacher, he acknowledges, brings on the one hand some income to the person and on the other (no less important), it opens up the avenue for the performance of social work. Even though Mr. P had early frustration because he was unable to become a full-fledged "bookworm," by now, he feels, he has been able to draw substitute satisfaction by developing sufficient interest in other aspects of village life. To him, his life has seemed one more of "being" than of "becoming."

---

[1] Intermediate Arts (four years from matriculation).

He settled down, in the next phase, in his own home-stead and had started working on his own farm, marrying at about the age of twenty-two. During this decade of his life (when he was about 27-28) [2] a middle school was sprout-ing at Digha about a couple of miles off from his village; he went there to serve as a teacher and remained for three years. This period as a beginning school master could offer him nothing more to his credit except helping him to ac-quire an aptitude for the vocation of a teacher.

His domestic life suffered and he had to come back to his own village in 1951, when he took to farming and started a primary school at Bergram. Now he was thirty-one or thirty-two, and in this adventure of village service he had the help and support of one Shri AKR, another village worker of his own village. For about eight months both AKR and Mr. P were working without any remuneration; thereafter they started collecting a small pittance from the income of the school and gradually they built two big educational institutions in the village.

He is not a teacher in either of these schools but as sec-retary of both he is the employer of all other teachers. He works hard over days and nights, and emphatically admits that he does not think of retiring from his position of leadership even for a brief respite. He is a person of strong will and does hard work for his community. He is revered by all outsiders, loved by a few of the community and feared by many. Mr. P's chief source of strength in the village had not been popular support. By strength of his character, determination and devotion, he earned the blessings of a few constructive workers of the outside world who have country-wide fame; they gave him support in his educational and constructive ventures. By his own ad-mission, Mr. P does not wish to be led by popular opinions but takes pride in doing things which he considers right. A handful of persons in the village forms his group of workers, and he has taken up big projects at hand with their assistance and loyalty. Outside leaders trust him im-mensely and he does not have to depend on support of the villagers for winning outside help.

Mr. P says that he has cast his lot with the villagers and lives in the village, but it is interesting to find that while he spends his whole day in administering the school and

[2] Exact age is not always identifiable in rural areas.

in supervising other projects, every evening he (along with two others) invariably goes out of the village to a location eight miles away to spend his leisure in the company of the irrigation personnel who have camped there for the maintenance and supervision of canal work. Apparently, in spite of the best wishes of these leaders to emotionally identify with the villages of the area, they have been unable to relate to the people of the locality. Mr. P in particular does not enjoy the company of the villagers and prefers to move out to spend his leisure. There seems to be little doubt that the villagers in their turn have not also been very charitable towards him in spite of the hard work he does and the flow of money he has brought into the village for the benefit of the villagers—he himself living a life of simplicity. While the people of Bergram (with a very meager population) possibly accepted him—to some extent, the people of Khiruli, Rahamatpur and other neighboring villages questioned his motives and complained that, although they had contributed much of their toils and labor in putting up the institutions of which Mr. P was the leader, he had totally ignored them. They were thus bitter about his activities and gradually grew jealous of him and his success.

As a result of this, Mr. P also became cold towards the people of the area. The villagers, one presumes, do not influence his decisions; he admits that and goes on to comment that whatever the people of the village might have to say, he would advance the cause of "his" institutions in spite of them. Consequently he drew up a bylaw, as a part of the constitution of his welfare organizations, that no villager would be allowed to become a member of the association by his own right. All members would have to be appointed by a council in which Mr. P, his father, and those who agree with his ideals, have high influence. The constitution further provided that membership of other villagers to this council would have to be renewed from year to year.

Mr. P by force of circumstances and by his inner calling has become an indispensable executive of all these institutions, if not of the communities which these institutions serve. He says he is sometimes fed up with his own leadership; but he can never think of giving it up, for he then has to ask himself the question "what else to do?" The thought of giving up the leadership leaves him cold, since it seems to him that if these institutions go out of his control, he will have to function in a vacuum. He thus certainly considers himself as very indispensable, and never allows others to dominate him in his work. He cannot think of retirement as, he says again, he does not find any one good enough in his own community, to take charge of the affairs which he is now managing. He agrees that he imposes his decisions on his colleagues, since he does not feel that any of the members of his community are enlightened enough to question his deeds. None of his colleagues, he reports, even think of complaining to him that he does not consult them. He thinks that he himself understands the problems of the whole group, and of the individual members as well. He thinks that solution of any problem should be made to look impartial and good to the members although they may not be necessarily good for all. He feels he can always handle group meetings, organize programs and guide members of the groups all by himself. He is completely satisfied with his own performance as a leader and with the achievements of his own leadership.

Mr. P owes his leadership to a committee which may have "popular" support but is not certainly the committee of the people of the village. The committee is composed of very respectable and esteemed citizens of the State, but none of them belong to the village. The committee and the leader thus act in isolation without taking the greater community into their confidence. The leader acts to bring social services to the community by mobilizing outside help for them, but does not care to think of working with the community. Thus, although one finds that the physical structures in the community keep on growing, by adding new bricks and buildings to their fold, the community seems to lie unaware of its own destiny and its role of handmaiden to its powerful headmen.

Mr. X on the other hand has not been able to work out such a stringent organization for himself. Neither does he say that he thinks it necessary to have an absolutist leadership for himself. He says he never imposes his decisions, and he himself thinks that he ought to retire at an early date. He does not think that he is at all indispensable for most of the institutions which he has helped to build up. He says he recognizes the fact that each individual and each group has its own needs, but he also feels that he is able to understand the needs of those with whom he works, at least to some extent. He says he acts for the satisfaction of common needs of the village as a whole and makes sacrifices for the groups with whom he deals. He emphasizes that he never uses the institutions to which he is attached for his selfish ends or gains. He, however, admits that while aiding the villagers he also realizes some of his own personal gains as well as recognition from the community. He is aware of his limitations and of the reality-situations in which he functions. He realizes that although he serves to fulfill the needs of the villages, he serves to work out his own needs as well. He has thus, it seems, attained a high level of mental maturity, a state where one is aware not only of his strength but of his weakness as well. He feels that he functions as a leader only because situations require his lead. He thinks that villagers admit him to a position of leadership since he is able to plan and execute village programs competently. Yet, he admits, he continues to handle situations only by appeasement and persuasion. He is far from being completely satisfied with his own performance as a leader; he feels he has yet to develop enough confidence in himself to become a more perfect, capable, and competent leader.

By virtue of his educational qualifications which are much higher than those of Mr. P, and in view of his experiences and maturity, also of a higher order than Mr. P's, Mr. X functions as a very efficient leader. By testimony of all important persons who have come in contact with both, as well as by the findings of the present study, Mr. X does not seem to be of any less efficiency in the setting of his own community, as compared to Mr. P in his own group of institutions. Mr. X has acquired an important influence over the youth group, and has been able to help some of them to make out their careers in different fields. He has always acted as their guide and adviser. Yet Mr. X is not a dictator in any of these institutions. He works in several institutions where he finds himself a member of the respective executive committees. He is thus associated with the health cooperative society, basic school, oil pressing cooperative society, and a number of youth clubs of the area. But he is only a member of each of these committees and nowhere does he function as a formal leader in the sense of being either the Secretary or the President of any of these institutions. These positions in these institutions are filled by election among its other members.

Mr. X has thus been a leader in these committees without assuming any definite official position anywhere. The executive and general members of these committees have always been appreciative of his services, but he has not been allowed, nor has he made any serious attempt, to attain the position of a dictator of any of these institutions. He thus works with the members of these various committees, and not for them, acting through persuasion and appeasement and not by distribution of favors and rulings. He depends more on the villagers of his locality for his position than does Mr. P whose chief source of strength lies outside the village with the influential men of the State. There are a number of important institutions and some impressive buildings in these villages of A group as well, but these buildings are nothing in comparison to the structures built by Mr. P in the B group of villages for his educational institutions. The Committees in the A group debate every scheme before it is accepted, and even the most efficient of the workers among them, Mr. X, is not provided with the opportunity to control or organize, as one supreme head, all or any of these programs. The health society has its own President and Secretary; the oil pressing cooperative has its own Secretary. The basic School has its own organizer. These Secretaries are certainly not half as capable as Mr. X is. The fact that Mr. X has not been allowed to assume a supreme controlling role, and that the divergence of control vested in different hands continues to retard smooth functioning of these institutions and considerably minimizes the rate of their progress, remain as hard realities. While all activities in the B group of villagers (i.e. of the particular ones with which Mr. P is concerned) have been able to receive the benefit of efficient and united direction from Mr. P, Mr. X has not been allowed to assume that position of direct control.

Mr. X is more of an informal adviser to these various Secretaries. As these youngsters are themselves still fresh and immature, this group of villages has not been able to secure that impressive physical development which the B group has won for itself under the continued command of one all-powerful leader. Committees in A group are composed of villagers. The leader depends on the members of the group with whom he works for his leadership and not to any outsider for the same. He has to wait until others approve of his programs. A bunch of young leaders have grown up under the shade of Mr. X, who now acts as their mouthpiece and not as their dictator. He is head and shoulders above them in intellectual eminence and that is why he feels lonely and isolated intellectually. Mr. X feels that an effective leader needs a strong personality of dash and diligence, and must be very rich to influence men and matters. Although he has all along been a co-worker with his men, yet it seems that there still lurks an unfulfilled desire in his mind to have a strong enough personality and plenty of riches and wealth so that he could be more than what he is. He aspires possibly to be something more than a co-worker, perhaps an absolute leader, whose way is obstructed neither by democratic control nor by dearth of resources.

This desire is in time with his basic inspiration for leadership; but the visibly conscious and dynamically active community composed of the younger leaders and other participating members has refused to create situations for the growth of such an absolutist leader for him or for that matter for anyone else. What is of greater importance is the fact that Mr. X, at least on an intellectual level, realizes and expresses the value of growth of the community and of the groups with which he works. He has developed respect for his new and younger colleagues, and a tendency to share power with them. He frequently admits that he is not an indispensable member of the group, and that he could retire at any moment. He admits that he is not leading but is only guiding a well-equipped community that enjoys well-developed alternate leaders. He admits that with all his qualities he can influence the members of his group only on occasion, and can initiate the group into action only to a limited extent, although he continues to guide them whenever they need such guidance. He admits that he gives in to group pressures and sometimes to personal considerations as well.

Mr. P does not admit that any of these difficulties ever surround him. He always manages group meetings and programs according to his likes. He always is capable of initiating the groups to his ways, and never yields to group pressure or to any other consideration. Mr. X, in short, is not what Mr. P is. It seems from a study of their biographical data that both had started their career with the same basic motivation and with somewhat identical talents; but Mr. X is what his community and his clientele have allowed him to be and so is Mr. P, in the context of a non-participating community which has never retarded his way.

The two groups of villages, A and B, thus seem to stand on different levels of development, and to have established different patterns of relationship with its leaders. One uses the leader as its consultant and guide, and works with the leaders to meet its own needs. Here not only the community looks to the leader but the leader also looks to the community for his support and guidance. The action of the community here is not that of the leader alone but is a combined effort of both. In the B group of villages the leader uses "his" community as he likes. The community looks to the leader and the leader looks to outside influences for bringing benefits to the community and thus in fact use the community for perpetuating his unchallenged leadership. Here it is the leader which establishes institutions, imposes decisions and interprets the community's needs. He builds the services accordingly, and does not need to wait for even a primary apparatus to develop which might provide the community with an agency to express its views and aspirations, if not a mechanism to control its leader.

THE TWO OTHERS: MR. Q AND MR. Y

The two others belonging to the two group of villages are leaders of softer metals; they are common men who do not enjoy any talents and have been unable to move their respective communities as much as Mr. X and Mr. P have been able to do. Yet they have been recognized as established leaders, able to win the affection and confidence of at least a limited number of people. Mr. Q from the B group of villages works independently of Mr. P in a limited field, while Mr. Y has established a close organic relationship with Mr. X's way of work.

MR. Q

Mr. Q hailing from the B group of villages is 40 years of age and had completed his studies up to the B.A. standard;[3] although he owns some land, he is not very rich. The primary reason for his rise to leadership seems to be partly religious, and partly political. Mr. Q is of Brahmin caste and he had attained this position of leadership from this high caste status; at least that is what Mr. Q believes to

---

[3] Bachelor of Arts, First degree of an Indian university.

be the reason of his success as a leader. A closer association with Mr. Q however, will reveal that although his source of influence in the village may be due to his superior caste status, his primary support comes from outside. He is a member of the leading political party of the locality and he can offer a good deal of benefits to the members of his community. Acting as an agent of this party, he is one of those who casts the vote-getting net of the political leadership during times of general election, and becomes their chosen man for lesser elections and positions of power in which the higher-ups themselves are not interested. All his power, influence and prestige comes from this source of strength.

Mr. Q feels that he is a real leader and that he is in a perfect position to understand the needs of all the members of the groups whom he leads. He liked to state emphatically to the investigator that he believed in imposing his decisions on others. He could certainly not think of retiring as he thought that he was very indispensable. Mr. Q flourished in the village by forming a group of vocal people who had effectively united under his inspiration, and whom he helped in turn by granting a variety of benefits acquired through his political connections. Here again the leader does not look to the group for his support but the group depends on the leader for grants and favors to be procured from outside sources. Mr. Q, therefore, says that he does not wait for winning the majority opinion but pushes along his own way of influencing a small minority. However, he feels that he is able to influence the minority only because he offers impartial solutions to all problems referred to him. An interesting clue to Mr. Q's leadership vis-a-vis his awareness of his social position could be found in an incident which took place during the last elections, when Mr. Q had contested for Presidency of the local Panchayat. Quite a few persons belonging to the so-called lower castes were elected to the committee which was in its turn to elect the President. The vote which would have decided the fate of Mr. Q was that of a Harijan woman who was particularly opposed to his election. Mr. Q tried to persuade this lady but having failed to do so, as the final hour for voting drew near, he suddenly placed the sacred thread of the Brahmin, dangling around his own neck, on the feet of this Harijan woman, threatening her with dire spiritual consequences should she still refuse to cast her

vote for him. The bewildered Harijan member got fright-
fully exasperated and cast her vote in his favor.

In sharp contrast to Mr. Q, Mr. Y comes from an average *Sadgope caste*. He has been educated only up to the
primary stage, and has been connected with the basic
school, the health society, and the cooperative of his village. He is 64 years of age and has lived long enough in
the community to know and estimate its problems. Mr. Y
does not think that his caste or religious status has anything to do with his position of leadership. He, on the contrary, feels that he owes his influence over the people only
to his own ability to interpret their needs and those of the
community. He thinks that he works to offer opportunities
to all members of the group to freely express themselves,
and that the organizations which he serves have never
been used for his personal gain. Mr. Y is a fairly rich
man, has a happy and well-adjusted home and does not
depend for his leadership on outside support. Now that
he has grown old, he thinks that it is his duty to give the
youth a chance to take over. Mr. Y's recent role in an election contest which had sharply divided the A group of villages casts an interesting light on his personality make-up.
The youth and the enlightened young men of the A group of
villages had set up a united common front against the
established and traditional leaders of these villages. The
latter, who were the elderly leaders of these communities,
were life long colleagues of Mr. Y. The youth group set
up their own candidates against all of them during the
recent elections to the health society and the village
Panchayat. These leaders who had long held power in their
hands, felt unhappy at this threat from their young wards.
They veered toward Mr. Y for his support, but contrary to
all expectations Mr. Y extended his blessings to the rising
generation. He himself stood out of the election contest
and advised his elderly colleagues to stand out. One of the
elderly leaders of the area, who belonged to Mr. Y's caste,
was his life-long rival. Other leaders and Mr. Y's rival
finding their own position threatened, came forward to
yield to Mr. Y, the place which his rival had been so long
monopolizing, finding it prudent to hand over charge to a
leader of their own generation than to a representative of
the new! This would have provided Mr. Y with a position
which was long denied to him; many thought that he
would yield. But Mr. Y remained steadfast in his support

of the younger generation and preferred to remain in the background. Mr. Y has also more often than not acted as the arbitrator of village disputes, especially of the *domes*[4] and tribals of the area. He has always been there to guide and lead people, although he has not accepted any position of leadership in a formal sense. Whenever situations have required, however, he has undertaken from time to time to work in different capacities in the various institutions of the village.

It could be gathered from the above that both Mr. X and Mr. Y have unequivocally expressed that they were there to function only as responsible democratic leaders. They did not wish to, nor could they, impose their views and dictates on their own people. It must, however, be recognized here that a mere oral assertion by a set of leaders, even if these are reiterated from time to time, do not necessarily indicate that these leaders are really as democratic as they confess to be. One has, however, to conclude from the above that the situations in A group of villages are different from those obtaining in the B group. The programs and the process of work in the A group has created, to say the least, a climate where the leaders have at least to admit that they are democrats and mere consultants of the community and not a bunch of bullies. The climate in the B group is, on the contrary, conducive enough for any leader to parade his independence from the rest of the group and express his utter disregard for the capacity of the members of the group to function as an effective check. The B group of villages thus permit a few to play a dominant role. Caste leaders still linger there and dominate the scene. The A group of villages, on the other hand, have not been led by considerations of religion or caste, at least in the matter of choice of its leaders. Another important factor which seems to be common to both the leaders of the B group of villages is the weight of outside influence which tends to control them both and lend them all their strength. They are influenced, it seems, in both cases by powerful forces which are not a part of their respective village communities. In the case of Mr. P the committee that rules him is composed entirely of outside members, while in the case of Mr. Q, it is the political party, whose agent he is in the village, that seeks to foster and guide him, in his leadership tasks.

---

[4] One of the lowest untouchable castes.

GREAT LEADERS

The leaders of the A group of villages do not look to outside support for their leadership. This is so in spite of the fact that outside ideas and professional leaders of a powerful social service agency have been in the area over the last thirty-eight years. Both Mr. X and Mr. Y, although they have been surrounded by the programs and processes initiated by the welfare agents of *Sriniketan,* have looked for support and sustenance, to the members of their own community. This the leaders have expressed time without number in answers to the various questions put to them by the researchers engaged in different phases of this study. The inability of the leaders to assume the position of absolute importance in controlling the affairs of their own community, which will be evident from the data supplied in chapters to follow, goes to show to some extent the truth of their expressed objectives. Welfare activities and services are thus organized in the A group of villages with the help of the leaders and in collaboration with the people. The leaders here are a direct product of the groups they serve. The personal aspirations and ambitions of the leaders might well have been the basic motivation for which the leaders of the A group had sublimated their immediate needs and started their career of hard and patient work; yet the fact remains that they have had ultimately to bow to the wishes of the people and act as catalysts and consultants of the community in order to help the latter to find and stick to its own needs. The data required to prove the validity of the above contention has been partly presented in this chapter. Other portions of similar data will however, be found in the chapters dealing with village organizations and groups, and in those chapters which are concerned with the role of these leaders in relation to their committees and to other members of the various institutions with whom they work.

LEADERS OF A AND B GROUPS OF VILLAGES AND THE PROCESS OF SOCIAL WORK: A SUMMARY ANALYSIS

As one makes a brief review of the various characteristics of the leaders of the two groups of villages, it seems evident that the leaders of A have their own different ways and methods of work in contrast to those followed by the leaders of B. It has been noted earlier that a number of new leaders had grown under the inspiration of Mr. X, while Mr. Y directly aided the coming into power of the younger generation. Mr. P, on the other hand, has had no relation with other members of the village. He strongly gave vent to this feeling when he admitted that he could find no possible successors to his own leadership from among the members of his own group.

The leaders in the A group of villages (especially Mr. X) have, among their other achievements helped the creation of new leaders. This, Messrs. Sanderson and Polson, the authors of *Rural Community Organization*, hail as the characteristics of the most successful democratic leaders, and more so from the point of view of the objectives of rural community organization. "Lastly" says Sanderson "a measure of the best leadership is the amount of leadership which it develops in others." [5] The success of Mr. X lay in the fact that he had groups to fall back upon, and it was as their spokesman that he was privileged to act. When the two groups of the old and the young vied with each other, it was to him once again that many had turned for a harmonizing influence. Mr. X primarily thrived as a member of the village, and as an equal co-sharer of the interests of the villagers' groups which he chose to guide. He depended for support of his leadership on the village groups, and his chief success lay in enlisting their cooperation with the programs suggested by him.

Mr. P on the other hand had to do without people and popular support. He endeavored to and succeeded in building an organization where people had little or no role to play. His was not an attempt to enlist popular support, but one of acting alone in isolation in the village. Mr. Ralph A. Felton, another distinguished sociologist, seems to have come across a similar type of leadership phenomenon elsewhere too. He says "that people don't rally around a leader unless the leader needs them." [6] Mr. P in the B group of villages did not need any people and, as others complained, and he admitted, he wanted to develop "his" institutions, in spite of all the opposition of his own and neighboring social groups. The institutions he thus founded were not open to all but could take in only a few selective members as its councilmen. He preferred indeed to stand alone, and not to fend for the whole community.

As one is confronted with the peculiar type of leadership presented by Mr. P, he feels particularly doubtful about the usefulness of P's role as a leader from the point of view of

---

[5] Sanderson, Dwight and Polson, R.A., *Op. cit.*, p. 365.
[6] *Ibid.*, p. 365.

the democratic growth of groups and their needs. The fears get confirmed when we find that the social scientists of the modern age still continue to affirm "that maximum membership and participation in the various organized groups furnishes the seedbed in which leadership may germinate." [7] Let us not, however, forget that although Mr. P has functioned without a *social* group built with the cadres drawn from his surrounding communities, and has cared little to look to the support of his people, he has been a successful leader from the point of view of some forms of community organization. "It is possible to get community projects done and to achieve certain sorts of community development work in which a few men put over a program.[8] " But this can be done, says Pigou, "by a dominator" as well. In leadership, says Pigou, "power is created through the integration of diverse purposes and the intelligent use of individual differences; in domination, on the other hand, power is monopolised." [9] Mr. P. from Group B by his own admission, and as revealed by his way of work (look at the constitution he drafted and according to which he works), has made of himself par excellence a monopolist and a dominator.

Mr. X, on the other hand, cannot and does not act independently of the people whose favor he seeks to win. He acts as the spokesman of the group and labors to gather them around himself. Although he still feels subjectively and psychologically a sense of near-isolation, from his neighbors, he has to fall back upon his community again and again for support and sustenance. "Any person who is more than ordinarily efficient," says Tead and Bernard "in carrying psycho-social stimuli to others and is thus effective in conditioning collective response may be called a leader." [10] It is here where the leaders of group A (especially Mr. X) have succeeded, and it is here where the leaders of group B (and especially Mr. P) have failed. Whatever might have been the original desires and primary motivations for their leadership, Mr. P has been able to function independently of his community. He therefore mastered the art of mobilizing outside support and con-

[7] *Ibid.*, p. 360.
[8] *Ibid.*, p. 360.
[9] *Ibid.*, p. 361.
[10] Tead and Bernard, as quoted by Sanderson and Polson.

tributed relentless labor to building up "his" projects all by his own individual efforts.

The community where Mr. X functioned could not be so ignored. Mr. X had instead recognized the need of winning the support of his community and spent long years to build up new groups and younger generations of leaders. In order to give shape to "his" ideas he had first to get the community to accept them, and to share the glory and responsibilities of his leadership with others, even with the representatives of the younger generation. That was also the advice which Mr. Y gave to his erring elderly colleagues and this, it will bear repetition, is the most important criterion of a successful leader in a democratically growing community. There could be many definitions of a leader, but from the point of view of social work and community organization, he is one who sees the need of the community and enlists others in its programs of self-help and inward development.

CHAPTER V

ACTION ANALYSIS OF RURAL COMMUNITY ORGANIZATION

VILLAGE ORGANIZATIONS AND PEOPLE

In a democratic arrangement, where the village organizations not unlike their leaders, appear as a result of integration of people's interests and aspirations, they find it natural to function as stimulators of new activities directed towards meeting the expanding needs of the community. A people may thus set up their institutions as a result of the understanding of their own needs, in order to ensure that these needs and interests are fulfilled through community action initiated under the community's chosen leadership. In any given community there are always certain common needs whose solution requires a willingness on the part of the individuals to sacrifice their subjective interests. Community institutions may then be formed as a result of this consciousness, and bind the villagers together for a common cause, enabling them to use the institutions as instruments of social change and goal-fulfillment.

Yet more often than not, under a sham democracy, the organizations instead of being instruments in the hands of the people appear as instruments of its leaders. The leaders under such circumstances control them in the name of the people, but use them for the satisfaction of their own individual needs: social, economic, political or emotional. Judged from the point of view of instrumental-expensive continuum (concepts inherent in the works of Wirth, Golshamer, Rose, Lundberg and Komarovsky), voluntary organizations of any area may be divided into instrumental and expressive types. The "instrumentals" are social influence organizations formed to achieve a condition of change in some segments of society, while "expressive" groups are formed to satisfy personal interests "held by their members." [1] "Expressive Associations," say Jacoby and Bob-

---

[1] Arnold M. Rose, *Theory and Method in the Social Sciences* (Minneapolis: University of Minnesota Press, 1954).

chuk, "provide the framework for immediate and continuing gratifications," [2] whereas the "instrumentals" seek to realize goals which are not the personal goals of its members. Although from the point of view of "motivations" in social work, the efforts of every leader have elements of self-satisfaction and there is nothing called "sacrifice" in the dictionary of social work, it would be at any time an interesting study to find out which village institutions weigh more heavily on which side of the instrumental-expressive continuum.

As a partial fulfillment of the objectives of this research scheme, it was thus considered useful to make a study of the institutions and organizations which exist in the two groups of villages in order to discover how these institutions function. What are their methods of operation? Do they act as handmaidens of their leaders, who use them to gratify their own personal needs, or do they help the growth of the people's initiative and resources in order to meet their own needs and their general social objectives? If the latter is the case, the study aims in the next phase to find out how the growth of people's initiative and resources, which is required to solve their needs, help to realize this end.

A list of institutions was prepared at the outset for both groups of villages. The histories of these institutions were then collected and, together with it, their constitutions and methods of work were compiled from the data gathered by interviewing the general members and executives of these institutions as well as a small section of non-members. In order, however, to gain a deeper insight into the working of these institutions, it was necessary to observe their members in action and to find how the institutions actually functioned. How are the meetings conducted, and how does the leadership function in making of day-to-day programs, and in what manner were the remotest and the most ineffective members of the organizations linked to the decision-making apparatus which enabled them to express and meet their specific needs? Our study of action situations in which institutions of both groups of villages were involved reveals interesting data, and this forms the mainstay of our work.

A number of dynamic and living institutions, which sym-

---

[2] Jacoby, Arthur P. and Bobchuk, Nicholas, "Instrumental and Expressive Voluntary Associations," *Sociology and Social Research*, Vol. 48, No. 1, Sept., 1963.

bolize the joint working of people of five villages, are associated with the A group. It was difficult to find such institutions in the B group. Since the developmental activities in the B group of villages had been achieved mostly through the initiative of a few leaders and not of any organized section of the population, it was difficult to find any institution of cooperative or democratic nature functioning there. In view of this, an effort was made to broad-base the study, and whatever informal groups[3] were found to be working in either of the village-groups were included for analysis.

A number of developmental activities were taking shape in both these groups of villages, and the quantitative structure of the services of the B group were of no less significance than that of the A. But the research workers, for the purpose of this study, were not so much concerned with the tangible products as with the intangibles, meaning the entire process of growth itself. The research scheme aimed at finding out how people themselves contributed and undertook responsibilities for organizing developmental activities. For it is only when people take part in such organizations that development becomes a social product; on the other hand, when the people stand aloof and schemes are pumped into a community through the medium of individual leaders or autocratic institutions, these fail to root themselves into the social structure of the community and remain as isolated symptoms of external growth.

In the A group of villages, even a casual look at the names, nature and number of institutions will reveal that activities here were a product of institutions—institutions built by the people of the area. In the B group of villages no such institutions existed in a formal manner. This comparative data is itself a revealing experience in a study which aims to discover how people are striving to meet their needs. But the research workers did not leave it at that. In order to make a thorough attempt to understand the procedure and methods of work in the B group of institutions, a step forward was taken in including in the orbit of the present study the list of informal groups of institutions as well. Here also, as in the case of formal institutions, the number existing in the B group was very small. Given below is the list of institutions, group-wise

---

[3] By informal group we have referred to traditional organizations such as *Bhajan* groups, etc.

and village-wise, together with their aims and objectives of work.

Institutions mentioned herein are of three different types and could be grouped under three heads: (1) informal institutions (such as traditional, and mainly religious and recreational, organizations) ; (2) schools, which are almost one hundred percent endowed by the West Bengal government; and (3) agencies such as the District School Board and others, run and organized by the people themselves. The informal institutions are mostly hereditary professional organizations of a specialized type, such as Manasa Mangal groups and Harinam Sankirtan parties, which are religious groups composed of people who sing "kirtan" or other traditional folk music and have no democratic constitution or rules to govern them.

The schools are obviously secular institutions set up under rules of government in order to meet the educational needs of the people of the area. These schools in West Bengal have attendance committees, elected by those members of the community who send their children to the school. These committees offer to a limited extent opportunities to the villagers to reflect their points of views on the affairs of the school. Formally, however, schools in this State are run by the headmasters appointed by the School Board and the villagers' responsibility seems to end after they have donated land for their schools and elected the attendance committee. They have beyond that very little or no role to play in determining policies and ways of work of these institutions. For an effective study of the role that the people play in a manner of self-determination to meet their own needs, a study of the third category of organizations, the service institutions, were found to be of utmost importance. Three institutions from the A group of villages have, therefore, been singled out in this Chapter for a comparative study with three others drawn from Group B. These are the cooperative *Ghani* (oil pressing) Society, the Cooperative Health Scheme and the three cooperative credit societies now integrated with each other, all of Group A; and *Palli Seva Niketan, Palli Mangal Samiti* and the Khiroli Defense Party of Group B. In subsequent chapters, a comparative study has also been made of a number of facts including a few actual situations in which institutions of both the groups were, at times, involved. A survey of educational and recreational conditions and resources of the two groups of villages has also been appended. These are followed by a study of general consciousness obtaining in both groups of villages, and a comparative review of the attitude of the two groups towards developmental work in general.

It was revealed upon strenuous scrutiny that the *Palli Seva Niketan* was the most viable and dynamic organization in Group B and that Ghani and Health Societies of Group A, run on cooperative lines, were the two most effective organizations there, seeking to cater to the economic and welfare needs of almost all the people of the A group of villages. The health society in particular was fast developing into a living symbol of health and welfare work which could easily be a model not only for other villages of the area but to some extent for the rest of the country. The cooperative Ghani was a modern replica of the health society, organized to serve the same group of clientele. This new institution was managed solely by the new leaders of the community. The most important phase of our study, therefore, concerns itself with a comparative analysis of the ways of working of these two institutions, and especially of the cooperative Ghani drawn from the A group of villages with the *Palli Seva Niketan* and the Defense Party of the B group.

One hundred and ninety six clients from B group of villages, out of which sixty people were associated with the Defense Party, thirty five with the *Palli Mangal Samiti* at Sattore, and one hundred people who were the beneficiaries of the *Palli Seva Niketan,* formed the specific universe of the study. In case of *Palli Seva Niketan,* the number of committee members were only a few, hence we classed them as leaders, and the guardians of the schools as members (both executive as well as general). Non-members in this case were those who did not send their children to school. The clientele mentioned here in this study were thus generally divided into leaders, members of the executive (and the general body) and non-members.

Appended below are brief histories of the formal institutions belonging to the two groups of villages:

PALLI SEVA NIKETAN SOCIETY

Palli Seva Niketan Society was founded in 1954 as a registered society with the object of promoting "educational, social and cultural activities for the generation of Indian life and society in harmony with principles outlined by Mahatma Gandhi." Its probable activities were listed as establishment of a center of education for production of research publications and educational equipment, and also for setting up health, education and recreation centers, rural housing and agricultural projects. The main activity of the society at present is, however, confined to running of a senior basic and multi-purpose high school; the total number of students enrolled in both schools will be about 200. The promoters of the institution mostly reside outside the villages. A detailed study of the methods of work and a review of the activities of these institutions will follow.

Mr. P and Mr. A.K.R. are two of the chief promoters who reside within the village and belong to it as well. The institution was established by one Mr. B.C. The executive committee of the institution consists of the following members:

1. Shri Nimal Kumar Bose, Professor, 37, Bosepara Lane, Calcutta (He lives 100 miles away from the village and does not come from the area)   President

2. Shri Bomkesh Chatterjee, Agriculturist, P.O. Raipur, Birbhum (He lives 10 miles away from the zone and does not come from the village)   Vice President

3. Shri Sakti Pada Ghose, Agriculturist, Bergram, P.O. Kasba, Birbhum.   Joint Secretary

4. Shri Hanseswar Roy, Teacher, P.O. Bolpur, Birbhum (He lives in the nearest town 6 miles from the zone— a former M.L.A., does not come from the village)   Joint Secretary

5. Shri Anil Kumar Roy, Teacher, Bergram, P.O. Kasba, Birbhum.   Member

6. Shri Nanda Kumar Ghose, Teacher, Bergram, P.O. Kasba, Birbhum.   Member

7. Shri Purna Chandra Dutta, Agriculturist, Bergram, P.O. Kasba, Birbhum.   Member

8. Shri Sudhir Chandra Laha, Auditor, 27/38, Hari Ghose Street, Calcutta-6. (He lives 100 miles away, does not come from the village)   Auditor

9. Shri Madan Mohan Ghose, Teacher, Bergram, P.O. Kasba, Birbhum.   Member

ACTION ANALYSIS

Out of these members only five belong to the zone and all of them are from the same village, although the schools they run are supposed to serve the whole area. Out of these five members, three were interviewed on the basis of a set of questionnaires contained in schedule *a,* in an attempt to find out their opinion regarding the working of the institution and the role that they thought it played in the village. The other two were not available for interview, as they said that *their opinions tallied with those who were already interviewed!*

The members of the committee interviewed described themselves as office bearers, founders and active participants in the work of the institution and on being questioned about the reason of their joining the institution, they observed that they joined it partly due to persuasion of the higher authorities and partly for their faith in the organization. Other reasons for affiliation as listed by them were desire for service, personal benefit, and pressure from friends. They felt that the purpose of the institution was chiefly to promote public works such as construction of roads, the spread of general education, and the offering of facilities for their own practical training. All of them felt convinced that the organization was extremely well-managed and that it was of great use to the community as well as to them. Next, the members were questioned about what they thought was the contribution of this institution to the development of democratic opportunities in the village. Two of them were of the opinion that they had to a great extent created an understanding of the need for this organization, as well as an awareness for meeting the felt needs of the villagers. It has, they emphasized, made them understand to a great extent the importance of group action among the villagers for solution of village problems; it has made them realize the need for accepting group interest over individual interests and for planning programs beforehand. The institution has also contributed, according to these two, to the training of leaders, and has familiarized its members with the maintenance of records and accounts. The organization, they felt, has made them realize the importance of self-help to a great extent and has infused in them a sense of service for the community. The third member doubted very much whether all these had been realized to any extent. Similarly, the two referred to earlier again agreed that success of the organization, in terms of its purpose (as understood by them) and in terms of the basic needs of the people, has been achieved to a great extent; while the other disagreed and thought that these were achieved only to some extent. All three, however, felt that they got help from "everybody in the village" in all their activities and that what they needed now was only some equipment and a good approach road for the school.

The management of the organization is conducted in the following manner:

A few original signatories of the Memorandum of Association continued to be the original members of the society for life; other persons above 19 years of age, who accept the ideals and objectives of the society in the form and manner to be settled from time to time by the council of the society, shall be eligible to become members of the society for one year provided they are accepted in a meeting of the council by a majority of three-fourths of the members present in person.

Those who will be deemed by the council to be in active sympathy with the ideals and objects of the society shall, while they continue to contribute 12 rupees per year or at least 200 rupees—at a time for life, or to do some work allotted to them, be reckoned as associates of the society. A separate list of such associates, with their address, shall be kept by the Secretary.

At an annual general meeting of the members of the society the members present in person shall consider the annual report and audited accounts, appoint an auditor and fix its remuneration, and elect the council such as that which shall manage all affairs of the society. The council will consist of not less than seven and not more than fifteen members including its President, Vice-President, Secretary, Assistant Secretary and other members and also a Treasurer if desired. Members of the council must previously be members of the society and should include a fair number of ladies if available.

Out of the members and non-members interviewed, their answers on the following scores seemed to be worth noting: *Eighty-five percent felt that the society had not created any democratic awareness although it had been of valuable service to the villages around. They felt that they were not consulted in the making of policies, and as such their answers could not include detailed reactions to the process of policy-making. Another 13 percent felt that the society was rendering useful service although they were not associated with its day-to-day work or formulation of policies. Two percent of the forms were rejected.*

The *Palli Seva Niketan* and its ardent promoters did a great deal of impressive constructive work in terms of building roads and preparing fields for cultivation for school children. The present researcher, once accompanied by a high official of the Government of India (resident at Delhi) visiting the village, found that after some time the officer was approached by the Secretary of the *Palli Seva Niketan* to enroll himself as a member of the organization and the officer having agreed to do so, was immediately admitted to its Executive Committee. The officer, however, has in the last three years never again visited the village. The method of recruitment of its members thus follows the constitutional pattern indicated above. In view of the peculiar constitution of the 'Samity,' which debars ordinary members from coming into its fold, the bulk of the data collected from the leaders and presented earlier merit the most serious consideration.

The organization maintains no paid staff from its own funds; teachers of the two schools are the employees of the organization, but they are paid solely out of funds disbursed from the board.

PALLI MANGAL SAMITI, SATTORE

This society was established some time in the past and it was not possible to trace its history in detail. However, it seems obvious that the society is now existing only in a moribund condition. It was not possible to find any constitution or any functioning working committee of the society. Out of the villagers interviewed in this connection who knew about the organization and styled themselves as members of the executive and general body, only six percent of the organization had been paying their fees. The rest styled themselves as 'participants.' Seventy percent out of the total interviewed said that they became members of the organization in order to secure personal benefit. A lone member expressed that he became a member because he had faith in the ideal of the organization. Another, a member, did not reveal the reason for his affiliation. Only 1 percent of the above total had even a vague idea about the purpose of the organization and could mention only road construction as one of the main activities of the organization. Eleven percent of the members interviewed were of the opinion that the organization is poor and ill-managed, whereas the rest of the 14 percent emphatically stated that the organization exists in name's sake only.

Most of the clients had doubts about the usefulness of the organization to the larger community; they felt that the organization provided services more to the committee members than to the community at large. In an attempt to find out the contribution of this organization towards the development of democratic practice in the village, it was found that the clients interviewed were of doubtful opinion. *Out of the total number interviewed only 60 percent stated that they had some vague understanding of the purpose of the institution, while another 21 percent maintained that they did not understand anything about its purpose.* The rest, 19 percent, avoided straight answers to this question. All of them emphasized that the institution could claim no concrete work to its credit, and that they were not satisfied with its way of working, if there was indeed a way at all.

The organization had no budget, no rules or regulations, and no paid staff on its roll.

KHIROLI DEFENSE PARTY

The Khiroli Defense Party was established sometime back in the past and it was not possible to trace its history in details. The party had no constitution or list of executives. The society exists today in a moribund condition. Out of the total members contacted only 70 percent of the villagers could be interviewed, others did not give proper answers to our questions and the forms had to be rejected. Out of the 70 percent, 50 percent were actively associated with the organization and the other 20 percent stated that they had been less active than the others. When asked about the reason for their joining the institution, 8 percent of the (valid forms) members stated that they joined the organization because of personal benefit and 12 percent of people refused to give any reason; 60 percent felt that they had associated with the organization partly for personal benefit, partly to offer services to the community, and partly as a result of pressure from friends and higher authorities. Fifty percent of the villagers out of the 70 percent interviewed in this connection felt that the management of the institution was of average standard. Others stated that the organization was poor. Out of the total interviewed, 49 percent of villagers were emphatically of the opinion that the party existed only for name's sake, while 20 percent of the total thought that the organization was of good use; 1 percent however felt that the organization was of more use to them personally than to the community in general.

Ten percent of members expressed doubts about the utility of the organization while another 20 percent preferred not to comment on this subject. Questioned about the impact of the organization on the growth of democratic opportunities, democratic training, and the success of the organization in terms of its purposes and programs, 40 percent of the clients were emphatically of the opinion that it had achieved nothing in these matters; 60 percent maintained that results have been achieved to some extent, and from time to time. All of them felt, excepting one, who refused to comment, that the organization could be more effective if the local police, who had originally recognized the organization and thus had helped to form it, could take more initiative to visit and check up on their activities at regular intervals.[4] They wanted more funds from the police to buy batteries and flashlights.

They also maintained that the police officers who now confine their tasks to merely offering "recognition" to the parties, and providing certain facilities such as grant of equipments and uniforms etc., should take direct responsibility for organizing the party. It could, they felt, then yield more substantial results. The organization maintained no paid staff.

Islampur CREDIT SOCIETY

The society was established in 1923 under the inspiration of Shri Kali Mohan Ghose, a worker of revered memory who worked at the Department of Rural Reconstruction at *Sriniketan*, Shri Radha Binode Pal and late Shri Sudarson Pal of village Islampur had been this society's Chief Patrons. A few elected members of the society who usually formed the executive committee and Shri Radha Binode Pal, who has been acting as the Secretary, were respon-

---

[4] The system in West Bengal was that defense parties formed by villagers were recognized by the Police of the area. The Police gave them legal sanctions to operate, and some material aid, but on the condition that the party should be strictly a village institution.

sible for the smooth running of the organization. After a good start the activities of the society were suspended for a long time and credit operations were discontinued. As the villagers gradually realized the gravity of the situation and experienced great difficulties, since easy credit was no longer readily available, the members met again and the society was restored. Most of its members say that they then realized the value of the society and when on occasions individual members became defaulters, others, their colleagues, took steps to persuade them to pay up. Frequently the neighbors pooled their own resources to pay back the loans of the defaulters in order that the stability of the society would be ensured. In order to further strengthen the society, the two credit societies located at Benuria and Bahadurpur are being integrated with this existing institution at Islampur. Nine members form the present executive committee and Shri Sanat Pal is its present Secretary. All these nine members of the committee were interviewed by our investigator; out of them, three are office bearers. A registered institution, the society maintained a balance sheet, its accounts were duly audited, and elections were held at regular intervals. As has been described in chapter III, a new group took over the management of this institution in view of its earlier malfunctioning.

Ninety percent of members interviewed in connection with the cooperative society stated that they became members for their own benefit as well as for the benefit of the community. All of them knew about the activities of the society. All, excepting 10 percent of the total, thought that the organization was of average efficiency, while all of them felt that the institution had been of great service to the community at large. Out of this total, 23 percent felt that the society was of some personal help to them, but of great deal of use to the community itself. Seventy-seven percent of the members felt that it was hardly of any use to the greater community of non-members. Questioned about the impact of the organization on the growth of democratic process in the village and the success it could gain in terms of the purpose, programs and basic needs of the people, 60 percent of the villagers felt that this had been achieved to some extent while 2 percent among these felt that achievement in this direction was of great significance. Forty percent of the members suggested that the society could be of greater use if sufficient loans would be forthcoming in time, and if the borrowers paid them back regularly. The institution maintained no paid employee from its funds.

BENURIA HEALTH CO-OPERATIVE SOCIETY

The society was established about thirty-six years ago, at a time when malaria and other diseases were taking heavy toll of life of the villagers, and no medical facility was available in the locality. The nearest place where medical facilities were available was at the town of Bolpur, located at a distance of seven miles. The workers of the Department of Rural Reconstruction used to visit these villages at that time, and they were deeply concerned with this situation. The chief among these workers was Shri Kali Mohan Ghose who, along with Dr. Timbers, a malaria specialist (then acting as a consultant to the Department) surveyed the needs of these villages. As a result, Shri Kali Mohan Ghose convened a meeting of the people of Benuria and Bahadurpur, Lohagarh and Islampur at Bemiria, in order to discuss with the villagers what might be the possible solution to this problem. There they discussed and came to the conclusion that a health society was required to combat the situation. A house was accordingly raised in an open space at the west end of Benuria, with contribution made by the people of all the four villages, Bahadurpur, Benuria, Lohagarh and Islampur. The health society was to be run by the subscription drawn from its members. The society thus started its operations in its own house, raised its own finances, employed a doctor and a compounder from its funds and set up a small dispensary in order to carry on both preventive and curative activities in these villages. The experiment was one of the first of its kind and saw excellent mobilization of the entire community under its own leadership. The society was run by a committee which was annually elected in its general meeting. The general body of members also elected a President and a Secretary for the society, who carried on the day-to-day work. Mr. X, referred to earlier, was an employee of this institution.

The Department of Rural Reconstruction at *Sriniketan* offers "organizational" help to the society and some of its workers serve on the committee as 'coopted' non-voting members. The Department arranged to secure medicine for the society at wholesale rates, and to make available to the clients of the society the free services of its chief Medical Officer who acts as a consultant to the society. The villagers were helped at the initial stages to run the organization, in the solving of the disputes and difficulties which obstructed their unison; they were also offered the necessary guidance required to set up an administrative machinery, to keep accounts, and to maintain records all by themselves. The workers of the Department who came to the village as extension agents thus acted as helpers at the initial stages. But now the villagers do all these things by themselves and the role of the Department is increasingly becoming a passive one.

The house built for the society caught fire after some time and a new house was readily acquired as a donation from its members. A piece of land was also made available to the society which yielded income to be credited to its accounts. The membership of the society is open to any villager of the neighboring villages; the size of the clientele is determined by the general body of members, who mainly keep in view the capacity of its existing service personnel and the economic needs of the society, to determine this size. Its membership fee is fixed at varying rates linked to the economic condition of the individual subscriber or of his family. A recent clause of the society threw its services open to the tribal villages of the area as well, and since the inhabitants of these villages were too poor to become individual members, the 'whole community' of each area were permitted to become community members on payment of subscriptions in kind. As a return for his membership, a villager or his family is entitled to buy medicines at nominal rates, and secure ready medical attendance on payment of a small fee for each call. The society also organized (in fact this was its main function) preventive health services for the entire community and for non-members as well. Among such services offered by the society were maternity aid and child welfare. Gradually the villagers of this area started realizing the value of the services rendered by the society, and not four but thirteen villages made use of the institution, and a sub-station was opened at a distance of four miles at Nachan-Saha.

The society today serves an area of four square miles and a population of 5,000 people and 1,000 families. Two hundred and twenty-one families are members of the society. To study the activities of the society in greater detail would form a treatise by itself.

Out of the total clients interviewed, two percent were officeholders, while all others were just members of the committee; two percent were non-members. Sixty percent out of these members stated that they joined the society because it brought them personal benefit. Forty percent of them stated that they became members chiefly to help the community to maintain its health services. Ninety percent of clients were well acquainted with the details of the working of the society, but eighty percent out of them said that the organization was running only "averagely satisfactory"; while the rest of the twenty percent thought that the organization could be improved. All of them were, however, of one mind that the organization was of a "great deal" of use to the entire community. Questioned about the impact of the organization on growth of democratic opportunities and the success it has achieved in terms of its programs and in meeting basic needs of the community, all of them thought that the organization had succeeded to a great extent. All members felt, at the same time, that if the society could draw in its fold all the villagers of the area, or in other words if all the families of the area would become members of the society, then and then alone would the society be placed on a firm footing.

The society stands as a paramount example of self-help. The whole organization is run by the villagers on their own resources without securing a bit of help from the Government. The association functions as an unregistered co-operative, but submits itself to regular audit. The N.E.S. Block of the area could have replaced this society by opening a Union Health Center in its place which would have been run purely on government grants and by the government staff. The villagers of the area would have been entitled to free medical services. It is significant to note that no sections of the villagers, neither the elite nor the weaker sections, ever agreed to take advantage of this union health scheme proposal which was presented before them in due course. They preferred to run their own lingering society and what they wanted instead from the authorities of the State was some government aid for their health society so that it could obtain the required financial stability. It was, however, strange to find that the Government which was committed through its N.E.S. Block program to develop-

SOCIAL WORK AND SOCIAL CHANGE

ing a self-helpful social order for each block area, could not see its way clear, in spite of the best sympathies of its officials toward this scheme, to offer it some grant. This inability on the part of the Government, which was very much regretted, was due to the fact that the scheme did not fit in with the normal plans of Community Development and National Extension Service. The society maintained a paid doctor, a compounder and a part time cleaner from its own funds.

COOPERATIVE GHANI

The village of Benuria had in the past a number of oil-pressing *Ghanis* run on indigenous lines. These had degenerated over the years due to competition from its oil mills. From the time when some work was initiated in this village by the workers of the Department, a consciousness slowly started gaining ground that the villagers must make efforts to restore the village to its old position; as this idea developed, the villagers started contemplating and planning for an opportunity to re-introduce the oil *Ghanis,* which the elders recalled had once provided the village with a great source of strength. After some time an opportunity came to them when the *Telis* (i.e. the oil producing community) and new aspirants drawn from other castes (of Benuria and of a number of other surrounding villages) approached the Government of West Bengal to offer them a village industry loan in order to set up a cooperative *Ghani.* The promoters of this organization hoped that the *Ghani* cooperative society, if formed, would help not only the oil pressing community of the area, but would pump enough liquid assets into the village to give them the necessary capital to start other industries as well. Twenty families became at first members of this society and raised a subscribed capital of 1650 rupees against which the West Bengal Government promised to remit a loan of 40,000 rupees refundable in three annual installments. The Directorate of Industries gave technical assistance to build the storage room and office accommodations for the cooperative, and supplied the cattle required for this purpose. The central oil pressing cooperative society granted 7,500 rupees for non-recurring expenses, of which 50 percent was given as grant and the rest as loan.

The administration of the society is vested in a Secretary, and the shareholders in general, who elect annually a representative committee. Members are responsible for organizing production and the sale of oil, and the society has undertaken to repay the loan out of the profits of the sale proceeds. Members take active part in organizing sales. In view of the fact that mustard, which is the raw material for *Ghani*, has to be imported from a long distance, the price of *Ghani* oil is higher by 15 percent than mill oil. Despite this enhanced value, the organizers succeeded in pushing the sale of oil in every shop of the village and almost in every home, of *Sriniketan* and *Santiniketan*, the villages' two immediate neighbors. We shall have opportunity to make a more detailed study of the contribution of its members in the administration of the society at a later stage. The society maintained its own paid staff, a storekeeper and a supervisor.

In studying the details of the workings of the society, it was found that 16 percent of the villagers interviewed were committee members, 82 percent were general members, and two percent were non-members. The non-members interviewed called themselves sympathizers of the society. All members say that they entered the society for their personal benefit as well as for the benefit of the community. All of them are acquainted with the activities of the society. Sixty percent of the total felt that the society was well-managed, while 20 percent felt that it was but run on average efficiency and 10 percent of the members opined that it was very poorly managed. The other 10 percent reserved their comments. All the members, however, agreed that the society was of great use to the community as well as to its members. Members were questioned regarding the impact of this institution on the growth of democratic opportunities, and its success—both in terms of its purpose and programs, and from the point of view of the basic needs of the community. Fifty percent of the total persons interviewed thought that all the above had been achieved to a great extent. Thirty percent thought that the achievements in this score had been only partial. Still others (20 percent) felt that the society provided potentialities for the development of the above qualities among the members of the participating communities. All of them, however, had plenty of suggestions to offer for increasing the effectiveness of the society—most of which were positive and constructive.

SOCIAL WORK AND SOCIAL CHANGE

THE INFORMAL ORGANIZATIONS

The informal organizations of these areas are mostly socio-religious and recreational organizations of the traditional pattern. These could be grouped under following heads according to the type of recreational programs served by them: *Harinam Samkirttan* Group (in the A group of villages) of Bahadurpur, Islampur and Benuria, and Rahamatpur of B group; *Bhadu Gan* Groups (in the A villages of Benuria and Lohagarh); *Raibeshee* (in Lohagarh); and the *Manasa Mangal* party in the village of Rahamatpur (B group).

The *Raibeshee* party organizes folk dance programs, *Bhadu Gan* and *Samkirttan* parties offer folk songs, and the *Manasa Mangal* sings religious ballad songs. The parties who sing these songs are composed of a permanent and self-perpetuating group of people, all of whom have great talent for these arts and have been trained in them. The leadership of these groups usually belong to the more technically accomplished members of the groups. These parties generally move from village to village and stage their programs on receipt of small payment in cash or kind. While the formal organizations referred to earlier draw their membership from a variety of caste groups, these informal organizations are generally composed of people of the same castes grouping into parties, although by tradition they are supposed to be multicaste, inter-religious cultural organizations. It is interesting to note that whereas the formal organizations described earlier which had modern developmental objectives as their aim were multicaste and secular organzations, the informal organizations which, under the influence of *vaishnavism*[5] were supposed to be secular, had developed caste characters. These organizations seldom came under the influence of developmental work. Although the personnel of these organizations stick to no communal or caste considerations in joining developmental organizations, in the traditional sector they show different preferences. The process of secularization of religious organizations is described later in some detail. The organizations, of course, have a sprinkling of members from other castes who have been drawn to the fold in view of their technical competence.

The *Kirtan* groups generally have one chief singer, two

---

[5] A secularised sect among the Hindus.

instrument players and a number of cooperating singers. *Bhadu Gan* groups similarly have a chief singer and a number of aides. Some of these groups are seventy to eighty years old. They are self-perpetuating organizations which gradually draw the younger recruits as trainees to their fold, and later, as the young ones acquire seniorities and proficiency, they grow into leadership. Among the caste groups which are organizing these parties, the Islampur *Bhadu Gan* party is composed mostly of *Domes*. The *Samkirttan* party of the same village consists mainly of *Sadgopes*. The Lohagarh party is composed of both *Domes* and Muslims. The *Bahadurpur Samkirttan*, however, has a Brahmin member[6] in its overwhelmingly Sadgope organization. The workings of these informal organizations are not taken into consideration for comparative study of their functioning vis-a-vis the growth of democratic consciousness in these villages, in view of the fact that these organizations are but self-perpetuating professional groups which do not permit or require democratic leadership.

Since they are traditional and undemocratic in character, the question of the general community's control over their affairs (from the point of view of the process of the satisfaction of needs), likewise did not arise. The organizations, as this study revealed, operated only in very limited areas in fulfilling recreational needs of the villagers, and as such a study of their impact was not warranted from the point of view of the particular project at hand. There were however a number of youth clubs (quite a few today), which also staged traditional cultural programs, offering recreational services to the community which were long the monopoly of these informal organizations. New secular and democratically-governed groups were thus taking to religious programs for meeting their secular and recreational needs, but the traditionals had still maintained their vigor. To the new youth groups however, staging of dramas and modern literary programs are of greater interest today than the traditional and religious programs, and although these groups of secular youth very much appreciate and take interest in those folk programs staged by

---

[6] This alienation of a few members of the other caste and religious groups is a concept peculiar to this sect. They sometimes have some members, who do not belong to their caste rank, but are taken in, mostly after due process of alienation from their own groups has taken place. Also see p. 28 for a further note on castes.

the professionally-trained self-perpetuating groups, when it comes to their own management they prefer to organize their modern varieties of recreational programs.

The number of informal organizations is high in the A group of villages, while there are only a few in the B group. These organizations meet to a great extent the recreational needs of the society, and strengthen social integration of their multi-caste, inter-religious audiences. These organizations are not democratically formed, but they act to lessen tensions in the community by adding to its virility and vitality, and by recreating the energies of its members. The fact that the organizations are numerous in the A group is not altogether without meaning. The key role which the informal agencies played in A was not a matter of mere coincidence; it was a result of planning. The policy of the department was to make the best use of existing recreational resources and to endow the informal voluntary bodies, which administered these programs, with a developmental function. The department was well aware of the fact that recreation and development were closely linked with each other and the indigenous assets of a community could provide the starting point of social planning.

The policy of the catalyst leaders, who played the role of the department in the B group of villages, was different and, in fact, one of studied indifference. They saw little strength in the existing structures. Considering them as outmoded and useless, they forged ahead to introduce new organizational innovations and imposed these on their clientele. The few traditional organizations still there were only those which had survived this indifference and apathy. Consequently these played a limited role in organizing social services for the area or for that matter in performing any developmental function; the latter remained an exclusive concern of the new agencies specially set up for the purpose. Thus, the informal organizations somehow lingered on in B and maintained a moribund state of existence. In A the situation was just the reverse.

The informal voluntary organizations in A were carefully studied and nurtured. Accordingly, they grew developmental perspectives and became a part of the community's total apparatus for social development. Interestingly enough the informal voluntary organizations were also, in their turn, substantially influenced by the developmental process and became secularized in the bargain. They developed a close link with new societal trends initiated by the process of rural reconstruction. The following case of a *Samkirtan* party will make this evident.

The *Samkirtan* party of Islampur consisted of *Domes* and could have been regarded as the only kinship organization of the caste. The members of the party were all *Domes* and the group, although a recreational agency, performed a political function. Yet when, some time back, marital discord led to a divorce suit involving two influential families of the community, the matter was, strangely enough, referred to a third party, a team of arbitrators. The latter, composed of a few acknowledged leaders of the area, included the secretary of the health society, its Doctor and its President, all drawn from a neighboring group of villages. Neither one of them belonged to the caste of the litigants. The trio appointed, with the consent of both, sat on judgment over the disputing families who belonged not only to a caste but also to a well-knit kinship group.

Two conclusions, it seems, emerge from the case materials presented above. The first is that the people of the area, irrespective of their religious affiliations, had become "secularized," well enough to accept the local elected leaders as their guides even in such sensitive areas which would have previously required the umpireship of a caste leader, and that the 'modern' welfare institution, set up in the area, had been able to establish their role firm in the web of social relations of the indigenous community. The former had in fact become a part of the rural social structure.[7]

The institutions in A, therefore, provide an excellent example of secularization and modernization. The new dynamics of social development were also gradually demolishing the artificial barrier that separated the formal agencies from the informal. Social service organizations set up by the people of the area had thus assumed here or were increasingly assuming the status of informal social institutions,[8] whereas the latter were gradually taking on tasks of social development. This ascendency of the formal institution to a new type of role had relegated the informal traditional organizations to a comparatively unimportant

---

[7] As defined by M. N. Srinivas vide his article entitled "Social Structure and Social Change" in *Sociological Bulletin*, Vol. 13 (Bombay: Indian Sociological Society, March, 1964), pp. 12-21.

[8] In the sense used by me in this chapter.

position and converted them to an agency of development. In the measurement of the instrumental-expressive continuum, the institutions in A were, accordingly, developing an instrumental bias although it was still difficult to separate, at a perceptual level, the impact of the two roles, which ordinarily seemed to be at variance.

CHAPTER VI

CRITERIA OF COMMUNITY ORGANIZATIONS
—AN ANALYSIS OF INSTITUTIONAL FUNCTIONS

The data presented earlier regarding the four formal organizations of group A and the three of B have been gathered from records available and maintained in these institutions, as well as from the office of the Department of Rural Reconstruction and the *Belpur-Sriniketan* N.E.S. Block. The history and short review of both the formal and informal institutions have been acquired in part by interviewing people connected with these institutions. The data on the formal institutions under study[1] has been further supplemented with facts collected by the help of schedule *a*.

Our purpose in studying these institutions was to determine the contribution that these institutions make in meeting the needs of its members. Is the realization of these needs by the members of the organizations based on democratic awareness? Are these institutions the media of expression for the communities' will, and agencies for their action? Do the people play any effective role in these institutions, or are they mere instruments in the hands of a few beloved tyrants or self-seeking careerists trying to impose their programs on the participating community? In order to seek answers to the above, it was found necessary to make a case analysis of these institutions and assess the progression of their inner dynamism. To understand the working of these institutions and the individual group framework, histories of each of these institutions were collected and an attempt was made to read in them the dynamics and motivation of these institutions, and the genesis of their growth. Simultaneously with this, the beneficiaries and the organizers of these institutions were interviewed

---

[1] i.e. the cooperative Health society, Ghani society of Benuria, Cooperative Credit society of Islampur, the Defense party of Khiroli, *Palli Seva Niketan* of Bergram and *Palli Mangal Samiti* of Sattore.

93

in order to determine their perception of the image of these institutions, and their own assessment of their respective roles. (The answers which we have thus received from the members were incorporated in the preceding chapter in the short reports made on each of the institutions of the two groups of villages). It was found, however, that the opinions of individual villagers regarding the working of the various institutions have not been very revealing inasmuch as the variations in the opinion scale were not great or even noteworthy in many respects.

This was primarily so in view of the fact that opinions are often relative statements and do not offer an absolute measure of any event or situation. Even the most satisfactory working of an institution, to take an example to the point, could be descirbed as unsatisfactory by a group of people who expect much more from it, whereas even a slight upward curve in the stereotyped performance of an institution which has been traditionally ineffective may be reckoned under certain situations as an excellent achievement. Opinions and attitudes of a group of clientele in social work situations are thus greatly conditioned by the expectations and aspirations of the group, which in turn is a product of the potentialities evident in a work milieu. This conditioning of aspirations makes a comparative study difficult, if not impossible, excepting in case of respondents who have been exposed to both stimuli in different or same points of time.

Unfortunately, no common beneficiaries of these various institutions were found to be residing in both the groups of villages so that we could gather a comparative estimate of the services offered by these agencies to the same group of clients. The opinions acquired in the course of our study can thus be described as valid, if not valuable, only when they have been emphatic about facts and events. To take a few examples: the expression that the *Palli Seva Niketan* was working "satisfactorily" coming from almost all the members interviewed does help to throw some light and enable us to believe that *Palli Seva Niketan* has been functioning as an effective institution. Similarly, the oft repeated statement that the *Palli Mangal Samiti* and the Defense Party of B group have become almost defunct was the unanimous opinion of a number of villagers of the B group.

COMMUNITY ORGANIZATIONS

In comparison to these opinions, the trend of the interviews in A group clearly revealed that all the institutions there had definite existence and specific roles to play. They were consequently of great relevance to their members. The credit society of Islampur has been reorganized after its merger with the credit societies of Bahadurpur and Benuria. The health society at Benuria has not impressed all its members by the efficiency of its organization, although none of its members doubted that it had rendered in the past, and continues to do so, a great service to the community at large. In setting up the *Ghani* society, where a loan of 40,000 rupees is to be repaid in three years, the undertakers and cooperators have undoubtedly taken upon themselves a great responsibility, and its follow-up is bound to be interesting. The fact that 50 percent of its members out of the total interviewed thought that the cooperative was running well may have some value in concluding that the organization was working on sound lines.

The data acquired from the sources mentioned above is, however, by no means complete or comprehensive. It only provides a preliminary view and casual acquaintance with the working of these institutions; thus, some of these could be selected for a more detailed study and closer scrutiny. This study would of course be the most important phase of our work and finds its place in the next chapter. It involves an attempt to analyze the functions of these institutions and of their various members in the wake of action and in the thick of reciprocal relationship. A few case records on action-situations compiled to this end are therefore the mainstay of the ensuing discussion. But before we proceed to discuss these case records, a few general comments on the characteristics of the community institutions of these two groups of villages may well be worth its while. For they provide, in the author's view, a summing-up view of the basic characteristics of a few of our community organizations. The discussion would also outline in this context, and for the first time on the basis of empirical analysis, a systematic understanding of some of the cardinal features of the technique of rural community organization. These will be of special interest to the students of social work literature inasmuch as they are the peculiar products of the needs and processes of social development taking place in the Indian rural community.

SOCIAL WORK AND SOCIAL CHANGE

GENERAL CHARACTERISTICS OF RURAL INSTITUTIONS

Out of the three institutions of B group selected for study, two of them—the Defense Party of Khiroli and the *Palli Mangal Samiti* of Sattore— serve only the respective villages in which they are located. They do not have any opportunity to develop broader inter-village programs or activities. By perspective and scope they are thus limited in their area of operation within the four walls of their sponsoring communities. As compared to them, all the three institutions of group A had long ceased to think in terms of their own villages and had broadened their fields of work. Both the *Ghani* Society and the health scheme seek to serve not only the villages where they are located but a number of neighbors as well. The Credit Societies of Islampur, Bahadurpur and Benuria have demolished their walls of isolation and have reorganized themselves by closer inter-village integration.

Little communities which can thus look beyond their narrow frontiers and realize that the needs of their members could best be met by integration of their interests with the interests of members of other neighboring communities provide excellent examples of a well developed community organization process. "Frequently the community is too small a unit to make possible the independent support of desired facilities. To obtain them, it is necessary to cooperate with neighboring communities."[2] Here in the A group we thus have for our study a *regional community* in the making which realizes that the interests of its component parts and therefore of all of its members have to be integrated, and that organizations have to be established in order to fulfill not only the needs of a particular village but of the larger community of the whole region. The A group of villages has thus it seems reached a high degree of organization from the point of view of what the social scientists would describe as the professed aims of inter-community integration.

The *Palli Seva Niketan* of the B group states in its objectives that it seeks to provide, not only for the village of Bergram where it is located, but for the whole area—and indeed for the country at large—an institution of education, welfare and research. But in actual practice even its constructive work activities have been limited to the local

[2] Sanderson and Polson, *op. cit.*, p. 364.

community. The senior basic school of the institution which is meant to draw people from all over the area, has been drawing only a few students from the villages next door, and its contacts with the distant areas have been few and far between. In its avowed aim the *Palli Seva Niketan* has, of course, decided to work for the whole country, but its benefits have in actual practice been limited to the small hamlet where it is located. The leaders of *Palli Seva Niketan* in fact go out every evening during their leisure hours to the officers of the local canal authority to seek companionship; they have thus not been able even to integrate themselves with the members of the local community, for whom they work.

All the three cooperatives of group A, however, cater to the needs of a number of villages, and the youth clubs of the area have also worked out an inter-village platform. In judging the degree of community organization which has been achieved by the villagers of these two groups, the above data is certainly not of mean significance. There is a growing tendency in India today to accelerate the pace of regional planning and sectional development. This acceleration is based on the assumption that small communities do not provide optimum resources for planning a growth-oriented program. The experiences of villages and institutions of A group seem to corroborate this theory and mark the early beginnings of the regional planning and community organization movement in an indigenous setting and atmosphere.

It is, however, not sufficient for a well-organized community institution that it simply draw to its fold beneficiaries from a wide range of area; what must also be ensured is that its participant beneficiaries achieve real integration by the growth of democratic awareness. They must then develop sufficient social consciousness to sublimate their own feelings and immediate interests in order to build such institutions and services which may offer greater common benefit, and limited individual return. *An institution, organized on sound principles of community organization, must thus be constitutionally governed and run by the people themselves.* It must have a democratic apparatus for expression of the community's will, as well as built-in devices to ensure that the communtiy maintains its grip on the institution. All its members likewise should possess adequate control over the community apparatus, and be able to exercise this control through accepted democratic procedures. *The two most important criteria of a good community organization, then, are that the common core of the organization be a product of integration of community interests, and that it be run democratically by the clientele of the need area.* Both the characteristics mentioned here are however of special significance from the point of view of the needs of the developing society as a whole. For, if the former helps the pace of resourceful planning, the latter sows the seeds of democratic behavior at the grassroots. If one sponsors growth, the other lends it a proper perspective and stabilizes its treatment in the cultural subsoil of the total milieu.

A third criteria which is likewise of utmost importance today has been passingly mentioned by Murray Ross.[3] It is essential in the context of an undeveloped economy and society that the community institutions and services must as far as possible be self-financing. Integration of community interests should enable a community to raise its own funds in order to maintain the services it needs. An institution administered outright by government grant or hundred percent endowment—be that charity or aid—cannot be considered to be a people's institution, viewed from the perspectives of the problems of the underdeveloped society. This particular twist in the emerging theories of community organization has special significance from the point of view of participation and resource-mobilization programs of the client community. Until the total resources of a community are mobilized, it is unimaginable today to conceive of a total program of social development and large-scale recovery.

Even a casual acquaintance with the titles and structures of the institutions of these two groups of villages will reveal that those of the A group are mostly self-financing, and that their members have methods (and apparatuses) to sustain a democratic yet firm grip over their institutions. The institutions of the B group, an equally casual survey would reveal, are proverbially poor in these very properties. Most of the institutions in A group, although they have received of government subsidies and loan, have also raised a good deal of finances on their own. The institutions in the B group of villages on the other hand are run

[3] Ross Murray, *Community Organization—Theory and Practice* (New York: Harper, 1955).

mostly on endowments from the government. There is not a single cooperative in this group; for cooperatives require cooperative contribution and joint working, and a cooperative must at least theoretically be run on democratic lines.

The Defense Party of Khiroli, like all defense parties in this region, was established when a group of people, combined together to form such a party, had approached the Government for recognition. The latter recognized them as the defense party of the area, and granted the organization its usual quota of flashlights, batteries and uniforms. That the defense party of Khiroli had thus come into being due to joint resolution of a number of people to work together for the common defense is evident. It is however interesting to note in this context that its organization collapsed within a short time, and when inquiries were made to find the reasons of this setback, its members unanimously revealed that the organization became defunct due to the apathy of the police; for, they complained that the latter had not been giving them enough funds to buy fresh batteries and new flashlights. Questioned further as to how the organization could be improved, the members of the party stated that if the local police officers continued to visit or check up their activities at regular intervals the organization could probably be restored. The Defense Party, our interviews revealed, came into existence only when the people of Khiroli became aware of a common danger to their life and property, and subsequently recognized the need for protection of these by mobilization of community effort. But the fact that even for such a serious matter as common defense the clientele of the party could not raise its resources to buy flashlights and batteries (obviously they had lost the flashlights the police gave them at the first instance), and that the feeling of the members was that the organization could only be sustained if the police came in and checked up their activities frequently, proved that the people of the area were more dependent on the help of the police than on the community's own resources. Obviously the community could make no big sacrifices, and only a very limited contribution, in keeping up the tone of the organization. Neither could it buy equipment from the community's own funds and arrange its supervision under its own chosen leaders. This case of the defense party, provides interesting material from the point of view of social work analysis. Here was an established organization whose initial grounding was the product of people's awareness and felt needs. But the failure of the community to follow up its determination with necessary sacrifices and sublimation accounted for its subsequent collapse.

In the *Palli Seva Niketan* similarly, the basic regulations in terms of its objectives had reflected the feelings of its sponsors, who had certainly desired to provide a very broad-based organization for the bigger community of the whole area. But neither the community nor its leaders had apparently been able to make such sacrifices for the institution as were required to win the cooperation of the members of the greater community in order to fulfill the aspirations of its founders. Even its memorandum of association very definitely precluded the general members of the community from having any say in its organization and vested all its effective control in the hands of a selected few, endowing them with full powers to run it as they liked.

The organizations in the B group of villages were thus of doubtful lineage. They hardly belonged to the family of community organizations. They were not based on any real emotional integration of the needs and interests of the members of the community; nor were they susceptible to any democratic control by its general members—the great many clientele who were not their sponsors. Most of its funds acquired from outside were gifts or endowments to this organization. These—the institutions in B—were thus planted in the soil of the community by a few well-meaning leaders who were determined "to be good" to the community and to shower free benefits in abundance! Yet by their own admission members of two of the three institutions in B group had felt that most of them were near-defunct bodies and just maintained somehow a moribund existence.

Palli Seva Niketan, the massive welfare institute of the B group, had in fact, for the reasons mentioned earlier, presented some difficulty to us. When the plan of study of the internal functioning of such institutions was taken up, in order to find the degree and manner of relationship which existed between the various elements in an organization— such as the elector and the elected, the representatives and those whom they represent and so on—the difficulty became particularly evident in view of the fact that the institute maintained no democratic paraphernalia. A study of the *Palli Seva Niketan* under this particular branch of analysis was therefore given up after efforts were made to separate its various elements and to define their functions. Case studies of action-situations had therefore to be confined to the beneficiaries of the other two institutions, which were not by their professions and announcement undemocratic in nature.

The institutions in the A group of villages, on the other hand, were either youth clubs or cooperatives run essentially under democratic constitutions. Any villager of the area could thus become a member of any of these organizations by payment of certain subscriptions, and could have a hand in electing its committees. The committees in A likewise held their offices for particular terms and reigned only so long they enjoyed the support of the general members. By their structure, profession and objectives all these organizations of A group provided its commonest members with an apparatus for controlling its highest executives—a means of change which *Palli Seva Niketan,* the only surviving and developing organization of the B group of villages, denied to all those whom it sought to serve.

The cooperative health society of A group has been similarily upholding a democratic constitution for the last thirty-six years, depending purely on its own funds, without endowment from the Government. The Benuria health society is thus possibly one of the few unique institutions in the whole country which has been able to so manage its affairs for such a long span of life. The youth clubs which were once virile and are today dormant, had also built themselves up on the strength of their own funds. The Cooperative *Ghani* society had loans from the government, but little of endowment or grant. The Cooperative Credit Society similarly had loan funds (as per the rules of the Government), formed on the basis of the share capital they could raise.

None of these institutions of A group however had any outright grant from the Government for maintaining their establishments. They were people's institutions, built by people's hard-earned money and labor, and had therefore to keep their gates open to everyone and anyone who might be ready to come in. The organizers of these institutions had thus shown, willingly or otherwise, a readiness to adjust with the dissidents' points of view and to accommodate the oppositionists within their folds.

It is not the contention of this chapter that all the institutions of A group presented a paragon of democratic virtues. What is evident however, and needs to be emphasized, is the essential difference between the two village groups, and especially the position of the group of institutions functioning in A. The latter, to sum up, had verbalized allegiance to principles of democratic development, sponsored democratic constitutions, and looked for community self-sufficiency. They had also successfully encouraged self-engineered decision-making. None of these were the characteristics of the organizations functioning in B group.

The institutions in the Department's area of operation had fulfilled, at least as it appeared from the data served here, the two cardinal principles of community organization. Furthermore, all of their inter-village institutions were organized as far as practicable with the funds available in the community itself. They thus represented the particularistic characteristics of rural community organization which are of relevance to Indian cultural conditions.

In the B group of villages neither of the above aims could be fulfilled as the institutions were not based on people's contributions, but looked to government for continuous endowment, and to outside leaders for all key decisions. In the case of one of these institutions, even its constitution stood in the way of the realization of democratic ideals in institutional administration. The members of the community, in this case, were even debarred from freely entering its portals.

The *Palli Mangal Samiti* of Sattore seems to be the only organization in B group which made efforts to run itself without looking for external aid or government grants, and sought to organize its members on the basis of a democratic constitution. But the institution, like the Defense Party, has been defunct for a long time and could not have been taken up for a detailed study under the impact of action-situations.

A great many of our readers who have had experiences with institutions run on the basis of so-called "democratic" constitutions cannot and should not, however, be satisfied with the arguments and data we have been presenting in our effort to conclude that the institutions of the A group of villages were democratically run and functioned in harmony with reciprocal relationship. For have they not seen many institutions in various places which have democratic constitutions in name, but permit of autocratic control by a few of its members? Of course, at the same time, situations are not unheard of where although a constitution may not be avowedly democratic, yet the leadership is dynamic enough to offer some scope of adjustment to the views of the general members of the community.

In other words, there is every possibility that there may be much more in a given situation than what meets the naked eye. The institutions in A group of villages could thus be, by character, constitution and nature, such that they vest the formal organization, direction, and administration in the hands of the many, but in effect are ruled by a few who may not be so susceptible to the needs, interests and likes of its clientele as may appear. In order to examine this new position, i.e. whether these institutions were actually so run on a democratic basis as per their professions and/or whether the needs and interests of the people were adequately reflected in the working of the institutions, more data is required. This is presented in the chapters to follow. Case studies of selected action-situations, and case analysis of the functions of community organizations of the two groups of villages are the subjects of our study and discussion there.

CHAPTER VII

PEOPLE AND THEIR INSTITUTIONS
— A STUDY IN ACTION

Review of certain selected case studies of action-situations form the subject matter of this chapter. These will enhance, it is hoped, the reader's acquaintance with the institutions mentioned earlier, and go a long way in indicating the role that the individuals and groups play in the inner workings of these bodies. In the preceding discussions we had attempted to compare the ways of both the A and B groups of villages, and we raised a few fundamental questions regarding the character and content of their social functions. The case studies which follow possibly provide greater clarity to our estimate of the intra-institutional process and its various dimensions, and answer some of the queries raised earlier and recapitulated below in brief. Do the people who are members of these institutions act democratically and jointly for fulfilling their common needs or is the democratic process blurred by personality cults, or individual domination, or leaders with vested interests? The methods of programming in a group, the manner in which meetings are conducted and programs selected, and the role which the ordinary members and leaders play in a group are of vital significance from the point of view of this study. Is the process of program-planning by itself a democratic and educative process? Or are these mere handmaidens of the dominant leaders? Do the groups which run the different institutions function as the representatives of the general members who elect or select them? How are the decisions arrived at? Are the decisions made by throttling expression, by coercion, or by majority voting, or is it possible that the decisions are arrived at by mutual discussion and healthy compromise, based on rational understanding of the need for sacrificing each others' conflicting points of view for the sake of common benefit? The way the community fulfills its needs is as important from the point of view of our study as the quantum of actual services available at its disposal. The process of social work is as important as the products social work might turn out. In the comparative study of a few action-situations noted below, an attempt has been made to provide a bird's eye view of this process, which took place and shaped the course of events in the two groups of villages.

CASE STUDIES FROM GROUPS A AND B

Six selected case studies and a descriptive account of certain developments in group A and B form the contents of this chapter. These are the case studies of three action-situations from group B and minutes of two meetings of the Board of Directors of the cooperative *Ghani* society. A record of the proceedings of an economic conference held at a village in A, is also appended. There were, it may be mentioned at the very outset, certain special handicaps from which the researchers suffered in adopting the line of investigation whose results are embodied in this chapter. This was due to the unequal pace of organizational development which had marked the two groups of villages. While the institutions in A were many in number and full of action potentialities, it was difficult to come across such action situations or democratic institutions in the B group. The actions inside and around the institutions of group B were unilateral, usually containing a streamlined process of decision-making in which the leader played the key role. Consequently, the process did not offer much scope for analytical study and did not present, as in A, a myriad experience of intra-group and inter-group action.

The *Palli Seva Niketan* of Bergram, the most important institution of the three studied in B group, had a working committee of nine, of which four lived outside the village (e.g. Belpur, Raipur, Calcutta), and only five lived in the locality. These five which, although not in a formal way, composed the working group for this institution, included a teacher of the school (an employee-member) and a father and his son. The son, whom we have studied earlier in the chapter on leadership, was the prime mover, being solely responsible for bringing most of the outside support, both financial and otherwise, for the growth of the institution. It was his sincerity and hard work that had endeared him to many leaders of the State and brought him resources for the setting up of the institution in which he was so vitally interested. He was the real leader in the committee and others followed him closely, almost in a manner of subsidiary alliance.

Since most of the members lived outside the village and considerable agreement and harmony prevailed among the five members of the working group, no meetings were usually held for transacting day-to-day business of *Palli Seva Niketan*. The research workers had therefore to initiate a few experimental action-situations in group B, and then study them for the purpose of this report. Consequently, the organizers of the two schools of *Seva Niketan* were requested to convene a meeting of the guardians of the school in order that the research team could study the process and *modus operandi* of the meeting, as well as the role which the leadership played in dealing with their clientele. A similar action-situation was also introduced in the village of Sattore. This time it was a recreational program. The purpose of the meeting, as the local leaders saw it, was to motivate the villagers—common people—towards developmental work. The third, not a case study in fact, relates a real conflict situation which coincidentally took place during our period of study in one of the villages of group B. This involved the members of the Defense party (of Khiroli) at work and was readily taken up for study. All of these action-situations, although they were in most parts stimulated for the purpose of this study, in sharp contrast to those which took place in regular course and in a natural manner in the A group, provided adequate insight into the nature of inter-group process concomitant to the B group of institutions and their behavioral results. Viewed in a comparative manner together with the institutions of A, the case studies also throw a special light on the relationship structure of the two groups of elites; this includes the relation of leaders and followers, of committees and their members, and between the members of the committees themselves. Described below are these situations of interaction:

ACTION SITUATIONS IN B GROUP—
A SITUATION OF CONFLICT (KHIROLI)

One of the villagers, Mr. Abdul Gaffur, who is a leader of the Defense Party, was interviewed. Cases of conflicts usually occurred, he observed, over damages done to crops by a neighbor's cattle, boundary disputes, and alleged deliberate non-cooperation of a few deviant individuals with village work undertaken by the entire community for common purposes. He quotes an instance:

The villagers were constructing a public road in the village of Khiroli, and almost every able-bodied person came forward to help in building the road. One particular person, persuasion notwithstanding, declined to cooperate. The defaulter, as a result of this, fell from the favor of his co-villagers. Later, another incident occurred, this time centering around the construction of the village primary school. A building had to be put up, and the leaders of the village called upon the residents of the area to contribute their labor for this purpose. As a result, the villagers came forward in large numbers to build their own school house; people came with cash and/or kind (materials); men made themselves available where they could give neither money nor materials. But the defaulter, referred to in the above case of road construction, once again refused to cooperate or participate in the program. He remained stubborn and turned his back to the project. He not only refused to join the community project, but carried on his usual duties as if nothing of consequence was going on in the village. All requests of the neighbors and mandates of leaders proved of no avail.

COMMUNITY MODE OF CONTROL

This repeated act of non-cooperation was construed as an attitude of challenge to community life, scornfully offered by a lone individual; and villagers were of a mind this time to enforce authority on the capricious individual. The villagers met at the venue of the school ground and at the suggestion of one of them, unanimously decided to impose a fine of 20 rupees, which the defaulting villager naturally refused to pay. As an act of reprisal, the villagers snatched away one of the cows from the custody of the defaulter. This was to be his penalty for non-cooperation.

It was now difficult for an individual to maintain a one-man show of defiance to the common will; he came to his co-villagers for compromise; and having agreed to pay a reduced amount, possibly 10 rupees as a fine, and this being agreed upon by both sides, he took back his cow.

It has been, according to Mr. Gaffur, the leader of the Defense party, a measure of control on the part of an organized group against an isolated individual; "but it was necessary, nevertheless," as observed by another group of people who were present at the time of this interview, "as a deterrent." The leader concluded that, in spite of the period of unhappy events which the villagers and the loner had to go through, their relation, after the end of the dispute, "has been as cordial as before and no discernible mark of ill-will was there at work basing the incidents discussed herein."

The conflict situation referred to above can occur and does occur almost every day and everywhere. The phenomenon of the deviant individual is not a rare incident, but is faced all over the world by social workers or indigenous leaders engaged in securing community contribution for community work. One of the most fundamental problems which a social worker has to deal with in the field of community organization is that of persuading the hostile, nonchalant, or unwilling members to come forward and offer their cooperation and contribution to the common cause! In all such cases, the worker-organizer must, from the psychological point of view, help the client to realize that there are certain common wants which have to be attended to even at the cost of one's own immediate needs. This is inevitably a long term process of socializing an individual and winning him over to the point of view of the community. Sociologically, the process involves generation of enlightenment in the community to enable a dissident along with the others not only to perceive the vital needs of the community, but to prepare him to sacrifice his own individual needs and interests and join others to work together for fulfilling the common need of an area or people. There are many ways of bringing in this process of change, either in a deviant individual or in a group. In olden times this was done by social boycott. The modern person of democratic orientation would probably try to understand the dissident's problem and remove the difficulties which keep him apart from the rest, or just persuade and even use subtle pressure on him. The exact mode that a community or leader would adopt will obviously depend on the state of sophistication of the parties concerned and their faith in democracy or the process of personal and social change. But to browbeat, coax, or force an individual member of the community (who does not agree with the point of view of the rest), to fall in line is a rather archaic way of handling a situation and has traditionally been used by communal organizations and institutions. Although such methods yield, as in the situation mentioned, some temporary results, these are not the ways of building a community based on harmony and relationship. Such coercion and control is unacceptable to any conscious community leader, and must be rejected by any one whose task is to stimulate a community. Neither does the above situation reveal that the leaders of the defense party had enough sympathy, maturity and patience to realize the difficulties of their dissident compatriot and wait till he could have been persuaded, rather than forced, to realize that his interests were of a piece with those of his neighbors. The fact that a leader of the defense party, even after employing the traditional coercive method on a revolting individual, feels that there was "no discernible mark of ill-will" in the individual, certainly does not go to show that the leader in question had a sympathetic awareness of the problems of the dissident. This instance, as a typical example of the old communal and tribal organizations' way of work, may be taken as an indicator of the level of social development, degree of social organization and the type of individual-group interaction that prevails among those people of Khiroli who run the defense party— a major institution of the B group of villages.

A Meeting of the Guardians of Senior and Junior Basic Schools and its Aftermath: Bergram

The meeting was held within the school compound as a part of the program of statewide observance of Basic Education Week. The last day of this week was fixed for the guardians' meeting, whereas the rest of the features of the observances were mostly concerned with manual work and other school-centric projects. The guardian's meeting was the only program of this type. The teacher, together with the students, did extensive spadework during all the previous six days to make the meeting well-attended and a success. They were not unaware that the meeting was going to be studied by trained research workers.

The meeting was scheduled to take place at three P.M. The research worker, accompanied by another investigator, was on the spot half an hour before and found only a few school teachers, some strolling and some relaxing on the green grass near about the main gate of the compound of the *Bergram Palli Seva Niketan*. There was the usual exchange of courtesies and the worker was taken around and introduced to the various wings of the institution. The tour was completed, and by now it was four o'clock, i.e. an hour had elapsed from the scheduled time when the meeting was to have started, but no sign of guests and visitors was visible even now.

As one visits Bergram he comes across inspiring developmental activities going on in the village centering around what is called *Bergram Palli Seva Niketan,* a registered organization. The list of activities of the organization will be evident from the Memorandum of Association and rules and regulations appended elsewhere in this book. Its developmental work includes provision for schools, roads, tanks, and ponds—their creation and reclamation—grain farming and other agricultural activities. All these projects, directly supervised by Mr. X and his aides, are being worked out with finances received from the local N.E.S. Block and the Education Department of the Government of West Bengal. It does not take much time for a visitor to be impressed by the quantum of the activity; the heat is apparently there. But the light that should accompany, to arouse and enthuse the people to common participation in a program, was not to be found.

The proposed guardians' meeting was almost in its abandoned stage when, late in the day, with the arrival of some ten to twelve persons, the discussion was finally arranged within the compound of the Senior Basic School. The discussion went on for about an hour. People one by one were asked to speak at the instance of the Head Teacher on the utility of Basic Education and on the means of enlisting the people's cooperation in making the institution at Bergram thrive and develop. The discussion was mostly influenced by the Head Teacher and his brother, who was prepared for a talk; and both of them in turn were visibly influenced by Mr. X. They all spoke about the many difficulties through which the institution called *Seva Niketan* was then still passing. They urged the people to appreciate them more and to bring in more and more students, so that the purpose and the benefit of the institution could be carried to every house within the area of operation of the organization. The discussion of the meeting was evidently based on the need for securing more wards for the school and not on any other aspect of the parent-teacher or parent-ward relationship. After a few speakers dilated on the same theme, with frequent punctuations by the president, the meeting terminated with a vote of thanks.

PEOPLE AND THEIR INSTITUTIONS

The discussions recorded above reveal in unmistakable terms that the developmental aspects—the conscious participation of the people and their willing cooperation in working out the programs sponsored by the *Seva Niketan* —are not in keeping with each other. Some instances collected from the post-meeting discussions by the field investigator in charge of Bergram group of villages also tend to disclose some tremor of discontent that exists in intervillage relationship of the neighboring villages (Khiroli, Rahamatpur and others) of the B group. These are noted below:

The field investigators quotes one SM of Khiroli apropos an adult school. SM, according to the interviewer, said "the number of illiterate persons in our village is much more than that of Bergram, where *Palli Seva Niketan* is located (when one refers to Bergram and its activities, *Palli Seva Niketan* and its programs are in fact referred to), but a particular leader of Bergram *Palli Seva Niketan* insists that the adult school now functioning in Khiroli should be shifted from our village and located in his. He is a man of influence, and he is connected with the adult school in question, which is being actually run by G.M. of Khiroli. Strange, he never cares to visit us nor possibly dares to do so for reasons best known to him."

SM next commented on the execution of a road construction program in Bergram, under the Test Relief Scheme, sanctioned for this village by the local N.E.S. Block. The road required to encroach upon a large area of individual territory held by the village of Khiroli. SM said that in order to help Bergram to work out this road, the people of Khiroli parted even with their own paddy land and it is strange that people of Bergram for whom the road was exclusively meant did not put forward the same gesture; but then they had gotten used to external manipulation. SM narrates another incident which throws greater light on the state of social consciousness of the people of Bergram where the mighty buildings of the *Palli Seva Niketan* are located (built with one hundred percent government grant). As per the rules of the West Bengal Government, a village where a school is to be located should offer free land for construction of the building. One was surprised to find that such donation from Bergram was forthcoming spontaneously when its leaders requested the land for building the school and a road in their village. SM alleges that this was done under a misleading stimuli falsely offered not only to the villagers of Bergram, but to others as well who had land in the village. "People are under an illusion," says SM, "that Bergram is aware and active about development and welfare work, now going on within and around their village, but a probing will unearth the clandestine current of mischievousness that flows through apparent and showy intelligence of the so-called leading people of Bergram. Then, and then only the cat will come out of the bag."

Khiroli and Rahamatpur are neighbors of Bergram. They displayed an unmistakable eagerness to the investigators that they are keen to take part in the activities which are going on around Bergram. Quite a few of them further felt that whatever one sees at Bergram, particularly the school, are all a result of the cooperation and active help that had once upon a time flowed from the neighboring villages; "but a firm conviction has grown in them today that they are being debarred from taking part in both deliberative as well as administrative aspects of the institution called *Bergram Palli Seva Niketan*, which has now become the close preserve of a small group." Two influential villagers of Rahamatpur, interviewed for this purpose said that "our boys and girls are on the rolls of Bergram schools; but we are not admitted to the Executive Committee of these teaching organizations." "Once in a while, in order to suit and serve their motives they took me," said one of them, "on the committee of the Junior Basic School, but they threw me out the moment they could pack up their own purpose."

Neighbors are certainly proverbial villains, and whether all that is said about *Palli Seva Niketan* is true or not, one finds the neighboring villages of Bergram at rivalry or conflict with one another and particularly hostile to the leaders of this institution. The conflicts first found expression over land donated for the school, and again the villages have turned their backs against each other on the issue of running the group of Basic Schools located at Bergram. SM of Khiroli says, "Bergram is on a proud footing today and this was possible because our people also helped them with all their might, and today they do not even care a fig for us. There is no one from our village on the Executive Committee of 'their' School, even though we send 'our' students 'there.' They not only ignore us but injure us too! On October 17, 1958, the Head Teacher of

PEOPLE AND THEIR INSTITUTIONS

Bergram Senior Basic School and the President of Adult
School then located at Khiroli (but its President was from
Bergram, that being a more influential area) came to tell
me with their red eyes "from now onwards it is a settled
fact that the Adult School will move over to Bergram which
has already become a center of education. You people have
not been able to collect students and hence the shifting has
to be carried out, come what may." This, I brought to the
notice of *Palli Samgathana Vibhaga, Sriniketan,* who were
pleased to bless me with their patronage by which we have
been able to retain the Adult school here."

Mr. X of Bergram represented this point in his own
way when he spoke in a complaining tone to our field investigator, that it was astonishing that Khiroli people
have come to feel that Bergram wants to go ahead 'in
spite of them.' He added that Khiroli was not 'behaving'
well and was refusing to listen to him. "They want to undo
all that Bergram wants to undertake, namely test relief
for roads, organization of schools, etc."

These instances show that the neighbors around have
developed an intensely negative attitude towards Bergram.
Their main grievance is that while Bergram is developing
by leaps and bounds, it is doing so at the cost of the neighboring villages, and by denying the latter their legitimate
dues. This becomes particularly evident from the attitude
of the people of the locality towards the Basic Schools. In
the guardians' meeting a serious question was raised about
functioning of the Basic schools at Bergram although their
existence was now an accomplished fact in these groups of
villages (the locality was provided with a big furnished
building, necessary equipments and other amenities). The
meeting played down complaints about roll strength and
lack of response on the part of the guardians in sending
their boys and girls in sufficient number. It is for this reason that the present investigator said in the beginning that
the heat did not generate enough light. The awareness
necessary to activize and stimulate the people for participation in the undertakings to which the organizers have
pledged their mite and material was probably also missing.

The *Palli Seva Niketan* sponsored meeting was scheduled
to be held at 3 o'clock but did not start before 6 or 6:30
P.M., and even then it was very poorly attended. The lack
of punctuality of the members and the level of their responsibility towards the institution indicated the interest

113

they took in the school programs. The subject was selected by the organizers and passed on to the group, not for its consideration, but for its acceptance. No real problems of guardians were discussed in the meeting, no sharing of needs with each other followed. No revelation of problems marked the discussion of the evening, and it is not surprising that no formulation of programs could have even been brought up. The meeting was a routine seminar, held in as mechanical a manner as are seminars that take place every day in so many urban institutions! The leaders of Bergram had obviously made an attempt to copy urban experiences and held a meeting for the sake of observance of a day! There were no indications that the guardians who assembled there for the first time since the inception of the school ever got an opportunity to express their needs, or to influence the programs of the schools, or to meet their unmet desires, if there were any, and of which they might have been aware. In sharp contrast to the A group of villages, where an inter-group integration was fast growing, rivalries and disintegrating influences were afoot here in B, even around the most important institution and its powerful leaders. The people of Khiroli—at least a representative section of them—doubted even the motivations of the leaders of Bergram!

Villagers of Khiroli and Rahamatpur felt that not only were they not invited to take part in the workings of the *Palli Seva Niketan* but that they were purposely kept away from it. From the experience described above, it seems obvious that the leadership which controls *Palli Seva Niketan* does not even seek to achieve any measure of group integration and popular participation in their work. Groupism blurs here the democratic process and reduces it almost to nothing. A few towering personalities—one or two in number—backed by external support and with motivations doubted by their neighbors are endeavoring to build here a program of work which does not recognize and grant any right of self-determination to the community for whom these services are being organized. The programs of *Palli Seva Niketan* thus, to a great extent, appear to be the handmaidens of its leaders; and even if one grants them the best of the motives, they cannot by any stretch of the imagination be fashioned as peoples' leaders, chosen in a democratic manner and functioning in a setup of mutual give and take. Neither were they found to be associating the beneficiaries and members of the community, or the guardians, with any of the decisions which could influence the destiny of these institutions. They are undoubtedly leaders, as Burt and Frances Strauss[1] describe, of the "dominator" type although the neighbors complaint was that they were "manipulators" too!

It is not the purpose of the author to observe that the institution called *Palli Seva Niketan* is not working efficiently; but it is certainly revealed by the facts of the matter that the leaders of this gigantic institution feel that they themselves should plan for the community, in view of the fact that the community had not yet reached a stage where the people were able to plan for themselves. The leaders, accordingly, did not feel the necessity of associating any individuals or groups from the community with the administration of this institution, much less that the community should have had any right to self-determination with regard to *Palli Seva Niketan*.

The leaders almost had, and moreover thought that they were perfectly justified in so having, a contempt for the community. They had not the slightest faith in the capacity of its members to govern themselves. Even by its very constitution, the *Palli Seva Niketan* was prepared to admit only such people to its council whom its original group of sponsors could trust and depend upon. Even at that, they agreed to admit these members initially for the period of one year on a trial basis! This attitude of fear and suspicion displayed towards new members may itself be regarded as the *sine qua non* of unstable leadership. The decision-making body of the institution thus remained like a lump of clay in the hands of a self-perpetuating and self-appointed body of rulers. The leadership denied the people of the community, by the very logic of the situation, their rightful role in determining their own needs and interests. The leaders did not think that the community had reached that level of growth where it could become aware of its own needs, nor that it was prepared to realize them through their own action. The leaders, therefore, preferred to act in isolation all by themselves; and what was of maximum significance was that the community seemed to accept the above contention with only a mild murmur of protest.

---

[1] Strauss, Bert and Frances, *New Ways to Better Meeting* (New York: Viking Press, 1952), p. 73.

SOCIAL WORK AND SOCIAL CHANGE

A Study of the Reaction of the People and Their Attitudes Towards Programming and Development Activities—SATTORE

Sattore is another important village which falls into the B group of our research universe. The village, big in size, seems economically somewhat better off than the other three. Hindus and Muslims form the two major communities of this area, although the Muslims account for 90 percent of total population. The situation is somewhat analogous to the village of Lohagarh of the A group.

Agriculture provides the main source of income here. There are however a few families whose occupations are shoemaking and leather work. The area of the village is divided into five distinctive regions, and people belonging to different religions and caste groups live in these different territories, thus dividing the village into five "paras," or zones, following the major communal grouping of the village.

The people of the area, as they generally remain busy in laboring for their bread, take hardly any effective interest in the affairs of the community in general, or in what could be described as "community projects" for the area. There is no common place in the village that could provide a meeting ground for people of different communities to assemble together at their leisure, to relax, gossip, or even to discuss their own problems. The people (caste groups mainly) who reside in the same zone or para, however, met infrequently, mostly in times of need. The best possible way of contacting the members of a given community and of being familiar with them, it seems, is to approach the residents of each para or zone separately, since it is the people of a zone or para who alone seem to possess any degree of homogeneity and integration. There is no one common leader for the whole of the village whose help could have been sought in establishing contact with the people of all the communities of the village, or for selling a particular idea or extension. A single individual, the richest man of the village, was probably an exception however, and seemed to wield considerable influence on others. When the workers of the research team sought to initiate some type of a community action in the village, it occurred to them that the zone-wise approach was the best possible way of establishing contact with the people of the village, and of suggesting to them the idea of an all-village action program.

The reaction of the people at the early stage of the action aspect of our research program (organized by the staff of the S.E.O.T.C.) was, however, confusing. The village community had hardly an integrated appearance at this time, since the Hindus, Muslims and the various other castes lay apart from each other. All of them at the initial stage, then, had to be separately approached in their own domestic areas. The Hindus, who were the first to be contacted, expressed a good deal of verbal sympathy to the overtures of the field team. They were very generous in welcoming the workers; but hardly enthusiastic about the purpose of the visit. They were, to say the least, passive and apathetic toward the program scheme, although a show of welcome was kept up. Repeated visits to this area, however, gradually melted this cool disregard and aroused their interest in the newcomers; and the community as a whole started becoming all the more conscious. Thereafter the programs were slowly introduced and gradually intensified by stages. The Muslims expressed in the course of time far greater desire for initiating and implementing the welfare programs suggested by the team, and the first effective overture came from them when they said that they would organize a Youth Club for the village! A suggestion was made at this stage to organize a celebration for the entire village, and this too came from the Muslim youth of the locality. Although they were hardly sure of the nature of the program to be introduced, and the details of its planning were yet to be drawn, they were keen to do something about it.

The field team requested them to work out the various details in connection with the program ranging from the items to be staged, area of operation, selection of formal leaders for the occasions, and so on. The response was very encouraging. Finding that some of the members of the village community were actively interested in the implementation of a program of youth welfare, the workers felt that the youth club was truly the need of the hour and should be set up on an organized and regular basis so that the club in its turn could involve the entire people of the locality in their action program. The ball started rolling without much delay, the whole village, the Muslim population in the main, showing great interest for the impending programs of action. It was suggested at this stage to a few early members of the youth club that they should meet in a common place and discuss the possibility of arranging a function, on the day of the opening of the proposed youth club. There was not much of either time or resources at the disposal of the people to pilot this project, yet the ready response was evident. There was the feeling of great movement in the air all around, and the people who became gradually interested were told that the function would be the forerunner for a series of projects to follow; they were assured that if they could build up their own strength and pool community resources to enable the members to realize their own responsibilities, a series of welfare programs could be brought in. These might be the reconstruction of the existing village roads, setting up of a night school for the adult illiterates, and so on. The integration and organization by itself could win supplies of amenities from the Government and solve many of the community's needs. After carefully weighing all these pros and cons, the field team and the youth leaders decided at this stage to organize a preparatory meeting in the village, where all sections of villagers could gather to discuss a total plan of action in all its implications and commitments. The members of the club were accordingly asked to take the initiative and convene a meeting to which all the villagers—adult men and women—were to be invited.

Following this decision, action, real and full blooded, seemed to have taken grip of the village. A whirlwind of activities suddenly stimulated the leaders of the youth; the meeting was called, and a program was prepared in detail. There were about a hundred people assembled in this first meeting. The oldest man of the village occupied the presidential chair, and one Haji Saheb, a religious leader of the Muslims of the area, was invited to attend. His opinion was sought in all these matters. The members belonging to Hindu and Santal communities also participated in the deliberations. The villagers prepared, after long discussions among themselves and with the help of the team of workers, a program of action, and it was decided that an opening function for the youth club should be held within a day or two. The exact date and timing of the various activities were drawn up by youth leaders with the active cooperation of the villagers assembled at the meeting, the local leaders playing a distinctive part in all matters of concern. Major enthusiasm and interest in this work were shown by the majority community of the village and a committee, consisting of some prominent members of the locality whose overwhelming numbers were Muslim, with fair representation of others as well, was set up to implement the program.

The day of celebration was observed with due pomp and solemnity; the various activities like construction of a road, inauguration of a night school and staging of a few cultural and recreational programs, preceded the general meeting. A high degree of enthusiasm shown by the people of the village was the chief feature of the day. People from the nearby villages like Khiroli, Rahmatpur, Jadavpur, Kondanga and Srichandrapur came to witness the function, and towards the end of the day the show was fully attended by a very large gathering of the people—nearly 600 in number. The most conspicuous aspect of the whole program was the active cooperation offered in the work of *Shramdan,* by the members of all communities, held earlier during the day.

The celebration, planned and deliberately hatched by the villagers, went off smoothly; but something happened in the meantime that introduced a new strain and changed the whole color of the situation. Some leading Hindus of the area who had felt neglected took initiative and invited on their own, and without consulting or informing the committee which was responsible for organizing the celebration, the B.D.O.[2] and a few government officers of the locality to attend the function. The latter were however not fully posted with facts; they knew precious little about the genesis and history of the event, and appeared almost unaware of the whole scheme as they arrived on the eve of celebration. When the idea of the celebration of the all-village event was originally sponsored, only a few Hindu leaders had displayed a sympathetic attitude towards the whole show; nor did they exhibit any positive interest or enthusiasm towards the future plan of work. But gradually as they became sure that the function was ultimately going to take place, and would be attended by the officers of the N.E.S. Block, they did a sudden about-face. Considering that more programs of amenities and welfare might now find their way into the village, and keen not to be left out from the situation of leadership any further,

[2] Block Development Officer.

they—the Hindu leaders—joined the celebration in numbers, and now demonstrated great and active concern for everything that was going on. With the sudden and undeclared arrival of the officers however, the entire picture underwent a rapid transformation. The main change on the occasion was that the common men of the area, who were quite active in the beginning, were pushed to the background, and the influential people, mostly those who were hitherto unconcerned and had played no part in earlier stages, surged forward to join and uphold the dignitaries. The entire leadership of the occasion immediately passed into the hands of a few of these influential leaders, who were previously absent but who now became suddenly active.

An objective, in-depth study of the dynamics of the situation will be interesting reading. This alone could reveal how and why the leadership of the celebration changed hands, and why the few Muslim youth who were the main sponsors of the program had suddenly to lapse back into inaction. The event took a new turn with the appearance of the bigwigs, and an informal and emotionally surcharged situation just degenerated into a formal and cold meeting. The common men of the village and those who had taken initiative earlier, being unknown to the influential leaders of the Block, fell back, and a new set of people who were nowhere in the picture earlier now came forward as vocal and enthusiastic members to monopolize the attention of the government. The majority of the young enthusiasts lost their way and felt that they were left out. The officers who arrived were hardly in a position to comprehend the whole situation, or to extend the much needed recognition due to the youth. The spirit of enthusiasm and spontaneous uprising of the area was checked in mid-course. It was previously decided in an earlier conference held in the village that the general meeting under review was to be presided over by one BA, who commanded the maximum respect in the village, and was actually in the Chair. But the idea was now given up and although Sri BA was right there at the ceremony, the new enthusiasts who had come forward and taken over proposed that the B.D.O. should be the president of the meeting. The minority who thus dominated the scene did not consider it necessary to get their decisions ratified by the majority of the people who had, they knew fully well, planned otherwise and had different programs in view. The villagers in an earlier meeting had not only unanimously selected their president, but also some others who were scheduled to address the gathering; but neither the people's chosen president nor their leaders were given any chance to fulfill any of their roles. All these were now replaced, and a small group of people came forward. The names of the selected speakers earlier commissioned to speak were dropped at the eleventh hour and some others, mostly outsiders who had accompanied the government officers, were called upon to address the gathering.

It is true that all these changes did not in any way affect the smooth running of the function, and that everything went on well. Yet it became clear to all present that the real villagers had ultimately lost face. They no longer had any say in the affair and remained there idle, watching a show which they had once planned with pride and were now made to witness as passive spectators. This position of inaction to which the villagers were reduced could be regarded as the ultimate defeat of the enthusiasts of the youth program. The villagers lost their much-needed opportunity to conduct their first community function on their own and thus the opportunity to experience, once at least, how it looks standing on one's own legs.

Given above is a report of one of the attempts of experimental action introduced by the field team, wherein efforts were made to bring a section of the villagers of the B group together and to give them some semblance of community organization for the purpose of observation and study. It is obvious that the village had no previous experience of initiating any specific social action which would permit the growth of community cohesiveness or integration. There were no recognized leaders or community apparatus in the village through which popular consensus could have been expressed. Consequently, the research workers felt the need for mobilizing village groups in order to initiate a typical case of action wherein the villagers could have an opportunity of working together and planning a program by dint of their own efforts; the people had therefore to be told that the function could be possible only if they could set it up on their own. The members of the club were asked to call a meeting for this very purpose, assessing their resources and measuring their strengths and potentialities. The external leaders (field team in this case) played their role, stimulating the community to action and stirring it into consciousness. When the community was thus organized, at least for the time being, and was prepared to put on a cultural function, and had set up a president and a committee of its own, quite suddenly the whole plan was marred by behind-the-scenes manipulators. The villagers then suddenly lapsed back into the role of passive witness to the new situation. The study also throws an equally interesting sidelight on the role of some of the C.D. workers. Primarily catalysts and enablers, they are seldom aware that when they change their hats and step into the role of village chiefs and doers, they throttle local initiative and enthusiasm! The incident depicted earlier provides ample evidence that a sudden and uncalculated visit, without sufficient data on the situation to be negotiated, may often upset the applecart of development.

The case study reproduced here provides an excellent example of a community which has immense potentialities of growth but which still lies unaware of its own strength. The members and leaders, interests and needs, all still remain to be integrated with each other. The village is yet to develop any degree of organizational awareness, which alone could enable the community to take charge of its own destiny. The potentialities of the community now lie shattered; its human and organizational resources must yet take concrete shape before responsible organizations and leaders who would hold their own could appear in the scene. Needs and consciousness of the people are yet dormant and the members of the community are unable to influence the flow of events. The community at Sattore is at a nascent stage of growth; it has yet to develop mature leadership, democratic apparatus, or the enlightened populace which alone could enable the community to realize its own needs by its own efforts and protect it as well from external invasions of undesirable events and actions.

ACTION-SITUATIONS IN A GROUP OF VILLAGES
Meeting of the Directors' Board of the *Ghani*

Cooperative Society held on Nov. 30, 1958: Benuria

The Secretary of the *Ghani* (oil-pressing) Cooperative happens to be one of the field investigators of the study and through his courtesy, it was possible for the recorder of this report (hereinafter known as the "worker") to attend a meeting of the Board of Directors.

PEOPLE AND THEIR INSTITUTIONS

CHARACTER AND COMPOSITION OF THE BOARD

There are nine members of the Board. Chairman: Block Development Officer (Ex-officio); Vice-Chairman: Village Level Worker (Ex-officio), a middle-aged man who carries general acceptability, as it appeared; Secretary (a young teacher attached to a school located in a village situated two miles away from the area of operation of the *Ghani* Cooperative; he is an important village worker; now a resident of the village, he is associated with organization of social services, cooperatives and all other organizational and developmental work of the area); Cashier: (he is the elder brother of the Secretary); and five other members (among whom there is a qualified physician who is the Medical Officer of the Health Cooperative of Benuria Group of villages, and mentioned in this report afterwards as "Doctor-member").

Unlike the Chairman and the Vice-Chairman, the seven other members all reside in the immediate vicinity of village and within the area of operation of the cooperative. Two-thirds (the one-third includes the B.D.O., the V.L.W. and the Doctor-member) of the Board including the Secretary and the cashier, have the background of hereditary avocation in oil-pressing, which is the sole business of the cooperative.

The Board meeting started at 3:00 P.M. Due to the absence of the Chairman, the Vice-Chairman presided. The worker checked up and found that the notice had been issued seven days before the date of the meeting through the village *chowkidar*.

The discussion started exactly at the notified hour when the following members were present:

The Vice-Chairman, the Secretary, the Cashier, four board members, two observers, (both were share-holders; one of them however was a honorary worker). Our field investigator for Benuria and the worker were guest-observers.

Three Board members came late by half an hour; the proceedings were reviewed once again, and their agreement achieved. As a matter of fact, all except the Chairman attended the meeting.

All the members of the Board who attended this meeting including the Vice-Chairman, whether they came in time or late, signed the log book while the meeting was on. This was just a part of formal procedure, as it was ascer-

123

tained by the worker that all the invitees were informed a week before about the meeting and the details of time, date, place and topics of discussion.

Among the members of the Board, all but one could read, write and understand well the objective of the society, as well as follow the deliberations of the Board meeting. Only one, who is conversant with the three R's no doubt, needed some help in reading and things were brought home to him on the spot by others sitting close to him.

The meeting started with the first item on the agenda and went on item by item as provided in the notice and announced in the meeting by the conducting Chairman, who was the Vice-Chairman of the cooperative.

OPENING ITEMS ON THE AGENDA

Confirmation of the proceedings of the last meeting came up first. The Secretary read out, word by word, the minutes of the previous meeting; after this was done, the conducting Chairman openly ascertained one by one the opinion of each and every member present and put the "unanimous decision" in the minutes of the cooperative, after making due changes wherever necessary. This took about half an hour; the time devoted to a simple item like this is an important indication that nothing is done by this group in haste, and that whatever is deliberated upon the group discusses thoroughly, with the express understanding of every eligible participant of the meeting. When this item was finished, two tardy Board members joined the meeting; the whole proceedings were gone through again and their express approval obtained and added to the proceedings.

APPROVAL OF ACCOUNTS

The second item was sanctioning of expenditures and checking of accounts to date. The work seemed to be of technical type. Here the Doctor-member played a very important part in assisting the secretary in writing the cash book, and checking and counter-checking every item of receipt and expenditure, with the supporting vouchers, against the balance in the bank book and the cash in hand. Barring one or two, all the rest of the members personally verified some of the book entries with the corresponding vouchers, before the accounts as of that date (i.e. up to November 30, 1958) were passed and adopted in toto.

PEOPLE AND THEIR INSTITUTIONS

TRAINING OF KEY PERSONNEL

It is necessary to mention here that, since the founder-secretary of the cooperative was away on deputation for his post-graduate education, the present secretary had to be persuaded to accept the obligation, and the "Doctor-member" is making every effort to train him up in the matter of accounts. It is needless to emphasize here that the present secretary is already showing signs of capability in all other spheres of the cooperative. Another worker, who acts as a messenger of the cooperative, carrying funds (deposits and withdrawals), and other materials like cement, iron rods, etc., is also getting training in maintenance of accounts and bookkeeping. He attends meetings and assists the secretary. This is mentioned here only to record that the Board is training up their essential workers in such a way that the normal functions of the cooperative do not suffer at any time from the absence of any one member, however important he may be; the worker ascertained that this training is an informal program having no fixed time, place, content or curriculum. This program has grown almost unnoticed, to meet day-to-day exigencies; but now that the program has come to the surface, the Board is increasingly becoming conscious of it and realizing its value. There are two Board members who had also had training in cooperative and *Ghani* work, at a Training Institute run by the Government of Bihar.

INDIVIDUAL LOANS

Next in the order came up the question of forwarding individual loan petitions to Khadi and Village Industries Commission at Bombay. The amount sought was 2,550 rupees to enable seventeen persons to start oil-pressing *Ghani* in their own houses. These individuals had already received an equivalent amount as grants-in-kind (the oil-pressing machine itself, one for each from the authority referred to), and the balance of 2,550 rupees mentioned above was awaited (it had already been approved); this was for the purchase of cows or bullocks.

It is necessary to mention here that the "cooperative" has planned a work center, where fifteen oil-pressing machines are to be set up; another seventeen *ghanis*—one for each of the seventeen houses who have joined the cooperative—will be at work around this center. The work center will thus be wholly a cooperative enterprise which will gear and guide the orbit of individual effort; and this enterprise will be restricted (for the time being) to those who had oil-pressing as their occupation.

THE LOAN—FIRST IN KIND, NOW IN CASH

The second part, i.e. the cash grant as already sanctioned by the Khadi and Village Industries Commission, Bombay, will be made available to the individual trader-member of the cooperative through the cooperative itself; the matter (which had already been discussed in one of the previous general meetings of the cooperative) came up again for review when the Secretary of the cooperative was requested to speed up the process and move the authorities at Bombay. The resolution was adopted unanimously.

EXIT OF THE OFFICIAL

The next item of business concerned the inspector of the *Ghani* oil cooperative (a government appointee). He had sent to the Board a letter of resignation from the construction sub-committee. The ground was that as a government employee, he could not be a member of the Board, could thus have no voice in the finances of the cooperative, and might thus find it difficult to work on the sub-committee.

ROLE OF OFFICIAL—QUESTIONED

One member wanted to know whether the matter of resignation could be favorably discussed when the Inspector was not present at the meeting. The Secretary disclosed at this stage that he had personally requested the Inspector to attend the meeting, so that all the Board members could ascertain his point of view directly from him. The Inspector was, however, absent. Expressing displeasure rather than vexation over the attitude of the Inspector, who sent in a resignation letter and did not attend the meeting in spite of a special request to do so, the same member observed, "here is an instance of non-cooperation in the name of cooperation."

Another member questioned the competence of the Board to discuss and decide the issue; the Chairman came in at this stage and ruled that since the sub-committee, from which the official tendered his resignation, was set up by the Board itself, the Board would be within their rights to dispose of the issue. After quite some discussion the resignation of the officer was accepted and the feeling of the members, as was evident, could be summed up as "no good forcing an unwilling hand to stay."

LAST BUT NOT THE LEAST

In the miscellaneous item, the "Doctor-member" introduced a very important resolution. The proposal came as a sequel to the acceptance of the resignation of the official, who was meant to be associated with the working of the cooperative.

The resolution urged upon the higher authorities to depute one of "understanding nature" instead of the present Inspector, "with the status and power of an Executive Officer," since there was a provision in the statute for such an appointment, for guiding the cooperative in its day-to-day work and helping it to grow further. The situation had cropped up in the first because of the unwillingness of the Inspector to help the society in fulfilling the objectives of cooperation. The purpose of this resolution, as discussed in the meeting, was to provide an official for help and guidance, who would lead as a co-worker of the villagers and not rule as a bureaucrat.

THE AFTERMATH

The post-meeting reactions mainly moved around the resignation issue. The members and the visitors all joined in criticism, mild and severe, of the resigning official. They said that they gave him their best available house in the village to live, entertained him with whatever food and eatables they could procure, but yet, they maintained, could not win his cordiality! They were sorry, but it was no fault of theirs that the Inspector could not adjust himself to their surroundings. He was occupying a house in the village with some of his belongings, but was actually staying at *Sriniketan* sharing a small room there with a peon. "He has stopped coming to us, see how unfortunate it is," said one.

When the meeting was formally over, the conducting Chairman of the cooperative, turning to the Secretary, said that "at the foot of every resolution there was an operative clause, like sending copy to so and so," ("Secretary authorized to speed up the matters to forward loan application," "sending copies of the procedings to appropriate authorities," etc.), and that these parts should be promptly taken care of if the normal functioning of the cooperative was not to be delayed.

Then all others present, joined by the conducting Chairman, entreated the Secretary to dispose of his obligations within 48 hours.

Some members inquired whether the work of transport could be performed with the services available within their own villages. This was brought up with the obvious intention of helping, if possible, their own men who had bullock carts and could let them on hire. At the moment, services for carrying bricks, cement, sand, etc., are chartered from neighboring villages outside the orbit of operation of their own organization, and transports were required to bring these to the site. It was found that outside services were cheaper than services available in the village, and that the capacity of the carts available outside the village was greater than those in the area.

The Secretary was seen explaining to an elderly person, who came to attend as an invited outsider and stayed on in the meeting as an observer, the need for cooperative enterprise. He asked, would he (the elderly one) now choose to become a member by subscribing shares of the cooperative, now that the ball has been set rolling by others—would he now care to cooperate and not stay away any longer?

DIVISION OF LABOR AND SPHERES OF SPECIALIZATION

The worker saw the different roles being performed by different members of the board. Some one is adept in office work, others in accounting and drafting of letters and resolutions, and still others in organization; some were expert in explaining the implications of a situation, and in helping the group to come to correct decisions. The importance of one as a coordinator, and of another as a voluntary worker, and so on, is duly recognized here. But no one is found indispensable, and in spite of everything, it seems, the caravan is on the move.

AN OPEN BOOK

It does not pass unnoticed that the working of the society is open not only to the members, but seemingly to the general villagers as well.

PEOPLE AND THEIR INSTITUTIONS

The Board, the other day, met under a tree and under the winter sky, on the sandy earth, with a carpet spread as a seat for the members and guests. Strangely enough even a passerby could drop in and join the meeting to see for himself how the affairs of the society were going on. The proceedings, including the minutest details about the accounts, were discussed in the presence of all, intimate or stranger.

It showed that the society had nothing secret about it— a very healthy climate for aiding cooperative endeavor to grow, and a pattern for others to follow.

A SECOND MEETING

As per an appointment with the Secretary of the cooperative society, the worker found it feasible to attend another Board meeting which followed the previous one forty-eight days later.

The meeting started exactly at the time, place and date specified in the notice. As before, some members of the Board signed the notice book only after the meeting had started. Since the society had no peon (information service) of its own, the notice book could not have been circulated among the members and what had reached them was merely hearsay. The Board therefore permitted its members to sign the notice book after the meeting had started.

OUT-OF-SHOP TALKS

The meeting started in the lobby of the house of the Secretary of the Society. The lobby was exposed to the heat of the afternoon winter sun so much so that soon after the seating began everyone had to quit his seat and all present got inside; the members and guests and some other village people who were also attending had to huddle themselves into whatever limited space that was available. Someone then remarked, "Don't we justify the requirement of a community hall for our group of villages where we are carrying on so many activities?" Turning to the worker one said, "We wish you bring this need of ours to the notice of some authority, why not of *Cheapkuthi?* (He thinks they meant S.E.O.T.C.) ; "they would not mind doing something for us without strings." The worker observed, "The authority is never and nowhere outside your orbit of reach. Don't you feel even by now that ultimately you all are the real authority, and that by this consciousness alone you can call any *'Kuthi'* or 'authority' at your doors."

A PLEASANT (?) COMEBACK

The Board soon set itself to the task for which it had assembled. But since a lot about the relation between the society and the *Ghani* Inspector had been mentioned in the last report, the worker feels inclined to mention that he was pleased to find that the Inspector was present this time, and participating in the proceedings of the meeting. Everyone seemed to take the come-back of the Inspector easily. "Easily" in the sense that nothing worth remembering had happened, and as if all along he was a non-entity to the society and none need take any notice of him, except by way of courtesy.

The Vice-Chairman again presided in the absence of the Chairman of the society, who seemed to be an "absentee landlord."

A BOLD AND MILD INDICTMENT

According to agenda, the proceedings started with the perusal and passing of the minutes of previous meeting held on November 30. The minutes contained comments and criticism on the non-cooperative attitude of the Inspector, who was now present. The Secretary read out the proceedings in a climate of unusual calmness (a stranger to the meeting might be tempted to term it as a "labored calmness" and not a usual one) and the whole proceedings were approved, also the accounts and cash-in-hand, as of date, after thorough scrutiny and counter-checking.

IN MIDSTREAM
(Financial deficit and non-availability of controlled commodities)

The conducting Chairman, on a point of inquiry, wanted to know how much money the society had already expended under the head of "Construction of *Ghani* sheds," and how much more the society would need in order to complete the estimated works taken at hand. The whole situation was then discussed threadbare by all. The discourses revealed that the society was in mid-course in respect to supply of money and materials, and because of this the work stood half-done. The prices of certain commodities (such as corrugated iron sheets for roofing) in the meantime had gone up considerably since the original estimates; and in making a revised estimate, which now became necessary, it was revealed that there would be a large deficit amounting to four figures, and this road-block stood in the way of successful execution of the project already taken up. It was accordingly decided to request the District Registrar of the Cooperative Societies to permit this *Ghani* Cooperative to meet the amount of deficit from the share money of the society for the time being, and to petition the Government and/or other sources for a grant in aid which could meet this deficit.

OBSTACLES AS OPPORTUNITIES FOR PEOPLES PARTICIPATION

A further clause was provided in the resolution that, before expending any amount from the share money (even if the sanction comes from the appropriate authority), the Board would refer the issue to the general body of the society and seek their unstinted understanding and approval in the matter. This would afford an opportunity to place all the cards on the table. All concerned could then know what was what.

The construction work was also held up for want of corrugated iron sheets, although the society had been permitted by the Government to buy from their stock.

The representatives of the society had knocked at the doors of the district authorities at Sewri.[3] They also had made requests to the State level authorities at Calcutta; and had then petitioned the Iron and Steel Controller, Government of India who had his office at Calcutta. "No stock," was the reply from everywhere. One put in hyperbolically "permit, permit everywhere, not a piece to buy."

A RESIGNATION REVOKED

The Secretary and the Cashier come from the same family; the former is the younger brother while the latter is the elder. In the miscellaneous item, the cashier's letter of resignation came in for consideration. Everybody including the conducting Chairman opined that the action of resignation was good in principle but not a timely one. The resigning Cashier was, therefore, persuaded to continue until the next annual general meeting, when a suitable

[3] NB. District town of Bhirbhum, the seat of the Government.

substitute would be found. The formative period of the society was deemed as a very inopportune moment for effecting any change among the officeholders, unless circumstances beyond control imperatively warranted such change. The resignation was then no longer pressed for, and it was taken as withdrawn.

AUDIT OBJECTION

The society's books of accounts were by now audited and certain objections, such as fixing of revenue stamps on the payment vouchers, proper entry of certain purchases etc. were mentioned in the audit report.

The Secretary wanted to know whether the Board would take up the audit report for consideration and action.

As the item was not provided for in the agenda, the conducting Chairman ruled that the consideration, as proposed, be left over to some other day and that the same be provided in the agenda while issuing notice of the meeting.

The conducting Chairman now left the meeting in order to talk to somebody outside, asking others to prepare the minutes in final form from the draft proceedings and then put them in the minute book of the society so that he could sign and go.

Before the conducting Chairman left the place it was also discussed and agreed to that a board committee consisting of the Vice-Chairman of the society, the storekeeper and the Doctor-member would next morning meet the Chairman of the society at his residence and explain to him the obstacles that arose over the question of deficit funds and non-availability of corrugated iron sheets, and seek his advice in order to overcome the hurdle. Besides the Doctor, some other members, if available, would also join the party drafted to inform the chairman of the present plight of the society.

A NEW FACE

There was at the meeting a middle-aged person, not a Board member, whom the worker met there for the first time. He was playing, it appeared, a useful role. In the matter of accounts, in preparing draft resolutions, in his comments about original estimates and remarks on the revised one, on working of details regarding carrying of remittances and modes of payments, in moving appropriate authorities to represent the cause of the cooperative as to the treatment of audit objections, how to proceed in the matter of procurement of government controlled commodities, and so forth, this gentleman had something to contribute. A new face is almost always an impressive one and arouses curiosity, especially in a close neighborhood. Inquiry now revealed that the new face was the storekeeper of the society (an employee appointed by and maintained by the Government) and had to his credit a good standing and experience in that line. The worker was sure that if the first impression was not deceptive, the storekeeper would prove to be an asset to the society. But this comment should not be taken too seriously as his role in the society's day-to-day working, for which this post had been primarily created, is yet to begin.

A GROUP OF VILLAGES

The proceedings of the above two meetings are revealing enough and provide to a very great extent an important clue to the understanding of the way of operation of a representative institution of the A group of villages. Case studies of these two meetings evidently reveal that the members had a sense of punctuality, an intimate knowledge of and respect for procedures, standards of behavior and formal decorum. They displayed a great interest in the responsibilities which their respective committees had assigned them. Matters here are not decided in a hurry or flutter. Neither are the decisions dictated by a few and followed dumbly by the rest. A good deal of discussion and initial give-and-take come before what is known as an "integrated decision" is arrived at. The members of this institution discuss things threadbare and so develop a thorough understanding of the situation before finally adopting a decision for action. All this probably indicates that a cooperative action which follows as a result of integrated thinking is the natural product of the group as a whole. The *Ghani* society's Secretary is scheduled to take all initiative for executive action. He acts on behalf of the society; yet there is no dearth of interest on the part of other members of the committee to offer and lend helping hands to the Secretary wherever and whenever such help is required. The members are not hesitant to assume greater responsibilities by themselves in undertaking specific work and initiating follow-up of actions.

It is the members of the committee who obviously decide all matters and take the ultimate decision for action; but whenever necessary and whenever it is so required by the constitution and/or by the consensus of the members, the matters are, without any hesitation, referred to the general body for their opinion. What is thus of great interest is the pleasant discovery that the members, although they form an official Board, do not ever hesitate to keep the general public informed of each and every step that has been taken by them. Even the Board meetings, as the worker reports, are an open book—held under the trees where any member of the public is welcome to join and see for himself how the affairs of the society is being run. All cards are thus laid bare before the beneficiaries for whom the institution is established. This state of affairs cannot and does not generally prevail where vested interests are scheming to eat up the vitals of an organization.

Beginning from the adoption of minutes, checking of accounts, formulation of the various proposals to be placed before the committee and follow-up of discussion, one can easily see that the democratic control of the members over the decision-making apparatus of the institution is firm. The programs and decisions here are thus not the works of a leader or two—official or unofficial; they are, rather, joint decisions, and this what is meant by the term "integrated decision" in the setup of group functioning. This integrated decision in its turn has been backed by majority decision, and functional and procedural correctness. The latter however may at once be an indication both of excessive love of ritualistic behavior as well as that of sound community organization practice. In either case it is however evident that the members have reached a degree of intra-group organization where procedures and systems could be upheld and maintained. The fact that this may one day lead to over-organization of the community, and a consequent de-emphasis on individuals, does not affect our previous contention. Democratic control over the institution as viewed in the above context is thus not only firmly established, but is being enhanced day after day by periodic appointment of various deputations and sub-committees which from time to time contact the Government officers at various levels and take charge of specific activities. It is obvious therefore that members of the institution, as well as its officers and executives, are prepared to share responsibilities of action whenever it is so required; and that a monolithic administration, where power is monopolized by only a few of the officials, is not allowed to grow.

Frequent references to general meetings, and the endeavor to acquaint the general public with its day to day work, further reveals the democratic character of the cooperative. The interest displayed by the members in the affairs of the cooperative can not be doubted. Every member who comes late, even due to perfectly valid reasons, signs the log book, and the whole business already covered is again re-opened and gone through. This shows, more than anything else, that there is great desire on everyone's part to take all the members into equal confidence as well as to maintain all regularities of formal behavior. Book entries are personally verified by the members, and every follow-up action such as procurement of brick, cement, sand, etc., are discussed in detail. Even after the meetings are over, members show their keen interest in follow-up work: we find them, for example, hastening to advise the Secretary regarding the need for initiating quick executive action. The capacity of the members to recognize their own needs is amply reflected in the interest they take in the affairs of the society; and it is this interested and vigilant membership, who discuss and decide about all matters, that go to form the greatest bulwark of democracy in the changing structure of the local rural society.

The proceedings of the above two meetings offer useful data for a comparative study of the working of the institutions in the two groups of villages, A and B. As already noted, an effective interest in work and sense of punctuality is altogether and strikingly absent at Bergram of B group. At Benuria, whoever might come late does so for a valid reason, and makes it up by the interest later shown in the running of the affairs of the institution. Here, meetings are held for more than the sake of holding a meeting, and every individual participant, by the vigilance and interest shown in the day-to-day affairs, makes it impossible for any "talented" or "official" leadership to dominate.

The Chairman of the Society could not attend either of the meetings. The members, all of whom belong to the village, show no sense of dependency on this outside government official. The Vice-Chairman who presides and is a representative of the state, is also not a dominator in any sense of the term. He is more of a "passive group coordinator." By no means can it thus be said from the proceedings of the above meeting that he is any more than just a Chairman. He is not even a "President" and no *de facto* ruler in any sense of the term. Neither he is the omnipotent bureaucrat. For he has to raise points of enquiry in order to gain from the local members information concerning the institution itself. It is thus the local people who genuinely rule and hold the reins. Here, there is every sharing of needs and interests between the various members of the cooperative; decisions are arrived at by vigorous discussion, and by piecing together the points of view of the various members in such a way that they are made acceptable to all. Although there are long and prolonged discussions (the proceedings themselves took about half an hour to be adopted), there was no voting and no throttling of the minority.

The way unwilling members or yet non-cooperative members are brought to the fold of the new institution stands in sharp contrast with the coercive tribal method followed at Khiroli. An unwilling member who had not still then joined the cooperative was thus invited to remain present at the meeting in order that, as an observer, he could himself realize the need for cooperative enterprise. It is significant to note how the Secretary initiated follow-up action with such a prospective recruit. After the meeting was over, the Secretary asked, "Would you now choose to become a member?" Quite a few others who had not yet joined the society were similarly invited as participant observers from time to time, so that their interests could be gradually aroused and brought in line with the interests of the others, and ultimately persuaded to join the society.

Three things which are of particular interest to social scientists, and which are evident from the study of the case records of the two cooperative society meetings, are important. These relate to (1) the continued emphasis which the organization placed on training of its members for new responsibilities, (2) use of experts and experienced members as consultants and guides, and (3) division of responsibilities and sharing of functions between members themselves. These techniques are necessary, obviously, in order to ensure that the right men are placed on the right jobs, and that the organization develops not one but a set of interchangeable leaders and workers.

The Doctor-member however plays an all-important role.

Being much advanced of the group in many respects, he probably has the capacities to do all the work by himself and could thus reduce, in the course of dominant action, all his colleagues into subsidiary allies, dependent assistants or sleeping partners. But this, as one watches the proceedings, was not allowed to happen. He was, on the other hand, merely used as a consultant by other members of the group. The Secretary, who is a village teacher and the real executive, is a local resident. The doctor, who is also a local resident, shows his readiness to train the former in undertaking secretarial responsibility. He teaches him to prepare cash books, to check receipts and expenditures, and to prepare supporting vouchers for the same.

Training of members in order that they might assume further responsibilities takes place as if by a natural process. This is done, however, in the wake of organizational action itself. The new members are thus assigned increasing responsibilities by stages, whereas the experienced and skilled senior members are required to offer specific coaching to the new hands; others, some of whom are also younger in age and experience have been deputed for institutional training in far-away places. The community in the A group thus realizes the need for training its leaders for future contingency, and is also ready to put up additional efforts for preparing the new members for greater responsibilities. This emphasis on training is of special importance in the context of an under-developed society. For the latter is often characterized by a set of traditional leaders who tend to hold the reins of power for good, in their own wrinkled jaws. This emphasis on training is therefore of special importance: training and preparation of new members is a step towards liquidation of their position of power and control. This effective co-sharing of responsibility both horizontal and perpendicular, i.e. between the colleagues of the same generation as well as between the leaders of the old and the new times is thus a special characteristic of this group of villages.

The Secretary here does not play the role of a dictator by "using" the doctor, except as his guide. Responsibilities are, on the other hand, equitably shared according to the acumen and capacity of the various participating members. Some members are thus placed in charge of office work and accounts, and of drafting of letters and resolutions; others are good at organizational work, and are found to be helping in the promotional side of the organization's endeavors. Some veteran members are at the same time busy in explaining the implications of the various situations to their less informed counterparts; some others are selected to serve on committees and deputations for contacting the government officials in order to meet the requirements of the organization.

The various procedures noted above concern training of leaders, assigning of specific responsibilities, formation of deputation parties and various other trends of democratic participation, cooperative group behavior and mutual give-and-take. These are rare features, which one seldom finds today in appreciable measure in institutions of the average run. Could these be considered the criteria of a good community organization? Would it be rash to conclude that these features could well be the results of scientific techniques of group work and inter-group process, in the context of a gradually awakening community? The use of experts and advanced members as consultants and guides, without surrendering to them as one surrenders to a dictator, as well as the fact that the members act in complete independence of government officers, indicate the level of development at which the community had arrived at the time of our study. These fulfill, it seems, some of the objectives which the Community Development Program had set before the advancing communities.

The Committee worked out details of future programs in advance. It planned for transport facilities as well as steps of financial administration for the construction of *Ghani* sheds. It ensured that the Secretary discharged his obligations within 48 hours of the meeting, and also finalized the names of those who would sit on deputation to the Chairman, without any loss of time. All this would show that the members were not only eager to decide things democratically, but also equally keen to get things done efficiently. A major weakness from which democratic institutions suffer in usual practice is that their members usually appear vocal only at the time of meetings and conferences and as soon as these are over they swing back and relapse into inertia. Situation in the A group seems to have however taken a different turn. Not only are the proceedings carried on in this organization in a democratic manner, but everybody here is willing to share and follow up by taking upon himself all such responsibilities which the organization chooses to assign to them. The Cooperative at Benuria, in framing its programs, had touched, it seems, some of the vital needs of its members; this and this alone guarantees the enthusiastic participation of every member of the group.

The Secretary of the cooperative society is both a follower and a leader. The members of the board guide and act, although they do not 'take over' by reducing the Secretary to a mere standard-bearer. Experienced elders also similarly guide and help. Each bolt, each nut in the social engine seems to act with harmony and carries forward the body of the community institution at a desirable speed. All these, together with the methods of program planning and the system of administration followed in the society, are the hallmarks of a self-propelling and self-satisfying social institution. The Cashier was the brother of the Secretary, and the way his resignation was submitted displayed a great sense of propriety, grace and professional integrity in terms of showing respect for the public cause. This grace on the part of the Secretary will strike even the lay observer as outstanding. The way the committee accepted the situation and persuaded the resigning Cashier to hold on till the next meeting displays the sense of etiquette, responsibility and strong elements of community cohesiveness, which the group evidently possessed.

On more than one occasion, thus, the group had shown extreme courtesy to the Secretary; but let there be no illusion that the existence of this courteous and harmonious relationship between the various members of the group even for a moment stood in the way of effecting proper scrutiny and check-up of the work of the Secretary. Accounts were personally verified by each member; every clause of the minutes was checked, and the Secretary was given clear mandates for action. The committee displayed in all these matters a great sense of respect for procedures. The signing of the register and checking of minutes; the acceptance of the resignation of the storekeeper; the removal of items of discussion from the table in view of the fact that they had not been previously included in the agenda—all these conclusively prove that the organization was not hurriedly dismissed by its members as a mere pastime, but that the members had a good deal of interest in realizing their responsibilities and owning these in a practical manner. Yet the group was probably not without its limitations. In a hurry to attain success for its work, the group was somewhat impatient, reckless and insolent at stages; and such behavior certainly provided some breaks in the smooth development of the group's integration into the larger democratic awareness of the community.

The group displayed impatience and restlessness at the speed at which things took place around them, and the way it delayed their effort. They had of course a set of real difficulties; yet even aside from that, the group was sometimes less than reasonable in its behavior. The Inspector of the *Ghani* appointed by the Government had resigned from the construction sub-committee on perfectly valid grounds, but his conduct was hotly debated and a resolution was moved to secure a more "cooperative" officer from the Government. Almost every member of the committee showed great interest in censuring the officer who was not even present at the meeting! The group ignored the absence of its Chairman, and the position of the Chairman in both the meetings was never more than that of a constitutional chief. The members of the group whose expectations from the Government officers and other outsiders were somehow very great, had consequently experienced a great deal of frustration and discontent from failure of the officialdom. The mounting suspicions were so tense that the group was possibly in a mood even to forget that it was these very non-cooperators—Government servants and outside leaders—who had helped it with loans, grants and state patronage, and had made it possible once upon a time to set up the cooperative. An analysis of the reasons for this aggressive behavior, which has been discussed in greater depth in a subsequent chapter, does not strictly fall within the scope of the case study here. It may however bear mention that the roots of this type of group response certainly lay in the inability to understand the other man's point of view, and especially when the point of view was that of those who, be they government officials or outside catalysts, were there to help them. Two distinct characteristics thus mark the behavior pattern of the leadership of the area. These are its "anti-officialdom" attitude, and a general dissatisfaction with the outsider catalysts as a whole. While the former is a quite natural phenomenon with almost all voluntary agencies in India (it may be a characteristic phenomenon of under-developed countries where the government is still identified to some extent as a hangover of the old imperialist machine, and where a dissatisfaction with it would be considered a "sophisticated form of social behavior"), the other shows that the group, however democratic it might have been within itself, was anxious to ensure that the outside world behaved properly and reacted to it in a manner in which the group would have liked it to do. Failure to find such positive responses from the latter naturally caused nervous impatience in the leadership.

All this became particularly evident as the members went on condemning almost unanimously the behavior of the Inspector. Nobody ever made an effort to understand that the Inspector might have had a feeling of embarrassment and/or other valid reasons to keep away from the meeting. This aggressive character of the group has been further revealed in the chapters to follow, where the results of an opinion study is embodied. The members' painstaking scrutiny of account books, repeated reminders to the Secretary to keep him aware of his responsibilities, the group's effort to dominate the official Chairman—all these probably indicate also that the group, zealous in guarding the community's own prerogative, was to some extent suspicious of its own office-holders as well!

The community in Group B also had a good deal of question and suspicion about its leaders. They were, however, to give expression to their discontent only after the meeting was over, and then only behind the back of its leaders. The A group on the other hand provided its members with regular institutional outlets for both positive and negative expressions. The aggression and suspicion thus ran into a constitutional shape in the A group and its outlet therefore did not affect the process of group integration.

Democracy cannot and does not claim to be able to wipe out all the frustrations of a human heart nor could it hope to do that in the case of a community; yet probably it endeavors to provide an effective institutional apparatus which might prevent negative, violent and too-radical expression of people's reactions taking place. Group A had such a democratic apparatus within its reach which B, it seemed, was still searching to acquire. The aggressive attitude of the people at A did not thus cause disorderly behavior, born out of emotional immaturity, towards the Inspector when he came back and sat at the meeting. He was received with good grace. The behavior of the members in setting him at ease made it possible for the Inspector to join the group as a regular member and function without any reserve. The atmosphere of the "labored calm" which was created when the proceedings (which included critical remarks about the attitude of the Inspector) was read out in the presence of the Inspector himself; and the toleration and expression of courteous compromise showed by the members was indicative of the level of emotional maturity of the group as a whole.

AN ECONOMIC CONFERENCE AT THE A GROUP OF VILLAGES

An economic conference was held in the A group of villages. Much initial spadework, in the shape of house-to-house contact, to sell the idea of such a meeting had preceded the event. The conference placed before the general public for discussion, ratification and adoption, a plan for total economic development of the area. The Department had for a long time been of the opinion that a good deal of community cohesiveness and mature leadership had come into its own in the A group of villages which would justify stimulation of plans for total economic development. The Department therefore decided to prepare a plan for the development of the area, and informally discussed the matter with the leading villagers of the A group.

The following decisions were then arrived at:

  i) A tentative plan will have to be first prepared by the villagers in collaboration with the department.

 ii) The plan would then be discussed in a conference of a few selected workers.

iii) The department took initiative in approaching the Doctor-member referred to earlier to collect village data with the help of the youth of the area, and to prepare a tentative plan to be considered in an economic conference especially convened for this purpose, which would be attended by representatives of all the four villages of the area. A few young men especially selected for this purpose, and those who were previously active in the now defunct youth clubs, came forward to assist the doctor by collecting required information from the villagers. The doctor requested the Department to prepare a guideline and a questionnaire which would provide the basis for collection of data. The data was then collected, not by the workers but by the youth of the village. In order to prepare these young men in the correct manner of approach for securing the information from the villagers, a four-day orientation training was later arranged by the Department officials in the village of Benuria itself. A report of the proceedings of the economic conference, which lasted for two hours and fifteen minutes, as reported by our workers, is given below:

The Economic Conference at Benuria:

Subject: The economic problems of the village and their remedies.

Place: Benuria mango grove in front of the Basic School.

Number of people attended: 30.

The Economic Seminar was held at Benuria, where the villagers had the benefit of having a series of four talks delivered by Shri Dhirananda Roy, the "Doctor-Member" (Benuria), Sri Binod Paul, and Sri Sailaja Nanda Mitra.

A good many of the villagers participated in the seminar. Since the conference was held at the same place where the Social Education Organizers under training were holding a village camp, the latter gave a warm welcome to all who came to witness or participate in the conference. The simple manner of decoration of the site accomplished by the Social Education Organizers endowed the meeting place with due grace, and at once attracted the notice of the children, men and women of different villages who were passing by.

The Director of the *Palli Samgathan Vibhaga* opened the Seminar at 2:30 P.M. with a lucid speech. He pointed out that the area must have a well-defined plan and a set of goals before itself. This was, he said, a necessary prerequisite before one could undertake a new program or hope to solve any of the vital problems of a community.

The next speaker in the course of his talk, said that the plan or the scheme must come out of the minds of the villagers and not only from outside. The problem, its cause and effects, should be realized by the villagers and then they should try to find out the ways of solution; in this task all the speakers, including the outsiders, assured the villagers the combined assistance of the Social Education Organizers' Training Center, the *Palli Samgathan Vibhaga* and the National Extension Service Block.

After the introductory speech, the Doctor-member read a long paper full of economic data and figures regarding the villages of the A group. He suggested that attempts might be made to introduce selected cottage industries on cooperative basis, which could increase real income and promote the economic stability of the adjoining villages. He especially pointed out the seasonal unemployment of the villagers. In order to employ such seasonally unemployed, he said, we should introduce schemes of small-scale industries and cottage industries as much as possible. Further, he added, the village had potentialities to float such scheduled schemes of economic improvement as poultry, soap manufacturing, knitting cooperatives, etc., in order to help the unemployed of the villages to settle down. He next presented before the villagers the staggering problem of the per capita income of the villagers of the area: this was only 13.80 rupees per month. The villagers of this area were mainly agricultural people and their only source of income was in the land. The average holding of the area was only three *bighas* per head. The area was well in the grip of the law of diminishing returns. In his concluding sentence the doctor observed that the villagers were then standing just on the verge of an impending crash. Now, he emphasized, was the time for action, and it was for them to ponder whether they would allow the village to fall from its past glories, or agree to put up efforts to stimulate the latent energies and help its survival.

The data presented by the doctor revealed that a large number of villagers were landless and under-employed, whereas another equally large number of people were unemployed. Some of the elderly and accredited leaders of the village—belonging to upper income group—were suddenly shaken by this revelation, and they challenged the validity of the data presented. The discussion centered around this topic for some time and when the staff of the Department, as well as the youth group which had collected the data, succeeded in establishing its validity, discussion took a different turn.

The Director referred to earlier appreciated suggestions put forward by the doctor which dealt with the three aspects of a development plan, namely those of (i) individual development of the villages, (ii) group development of a few villages, and (iii) the regional development of the area.

Sri —— of Lohagar said "we must undoubtedly have a well-knit plan, sufficient resources, advice from the experts and experienced members, as well as the services of efficient and sincere organizers to solve the problems of the area." "Secondly," he emphasized, "we must develop a cooperative attitude and have mutual give and take amongst us; otherwise, all plans, however good they may be, are bound to fall flat." Mr. G said that the position of the health society was no better than that of a skeleton ship on a wide ocean, having not much of cooperation and monetary aid from the community.

The Director, in reply to Mr. G, said that in order to make the health society the very center of community life, one should prepare a three year or a four year plan, and within this period ensure that one hundred percent of the inhabitants of the community have been enrolled as the members of the society.

The question regarding average yield of crops broached by the doctor next came up for discussion. The villagers from Lohagarh said that "we must apply scientific methods in our cultivation to increase the agricultural out-put" and quoted the example of Kirnahar (a neighboring sub-division) where the villagers had increased returns and yield by applying scientific methods for cultivation.

Sri Binod Paul of Islampur raised the traditional problem of irrigation; though the main canal runs through neighboring fields of Benuria, he said, we need some sub-canals. The Director referred to a sub-canal five miles in length which was recently dug by the people of Jadavpur area for purposes of their own irrigation. He paid a very high tribute to the people of Jadavpur for their growing awareness of common problems, as well as for their ability to solve one such problem by sacrifice of their leisure. So, observed the director, "Can we expect that we may follow the above example and make some little sacrifices for a big common interest?"

Some of the villagers observed that it was not possible to take up such work in their villages since there were so many conflicting groups and interests in their area, and no one was willing to part with his own personal land, which would be necessary for bringing out a sub-canal. Sri Binod Paul and Mr. X intervened at this stage and observed that unless we were prepared to make sacrifices, and that too to our fullest capacity, there was no alternative but of facing utter decay and collapse.

Some more discussions followed in which almost all the villagers took part. The plan presented by the doctor was then taken up for discussion and amended clause by clause.

The conference was over at about 5:45 P.M. with a vote of thanks to the chair.

The conference and its preparation provide an excellent study of the relationship of the workers of the Department and the villagers of the area. The Department stimulated the initial action; some prominent leaders of the village took up the idea from there, offered the village youth the questionnaires and schedules meant for survey work, and trained them to collect the information required for the conference. The actual work of collection was, however, done by the villagers themselves. The plan was prepared by a leader of the village and checked up and amended in a meeting.

The plan reflects the needs of the villagers and shows the degree of understanding which the leaders themselves had regarding their common problems. It is difficult to believe that such a plan could have been chalked out without any external assistance. But this was possible in the A group of villages. The villagers of this area, after being in touch with the Department for a long time, had themselves become plan-minded, and the final plan which was thus evolved reflected to a very great extent the exact needs of the villagers of the area.

In the short reviews given earlier of the two meetings of the Board of Directors of the Cooperative Ghani Society and the Economic Conference held at Benuria, one can note the stage of development where the communities of the A group of villages were resting at the time of our study. The preparations for the conference, the nature of discussions that followed, the way the data was collected, the manner in which village experts and departmental officers were utilized by the community—all go to show that the individuals and groups of the area play no mean role in controlling their own destiny, rather than leaving the task solely to outside initiators. Personality cults of leaders, it seems, have failed to dominate the rank and file here; discussions are not imposed in meetings; neither are the outsider-leaders, nor even the advanced sections of their own people, allowed to "impose" any program, or to "establish" any line of action independent of the villagers' decision-making units. The villagers develop plans of action slowly and cooperatively. They talk together, discuss together and gradually a consensus, created in the process, makes it evident that the time for limited action is ripe at hand.

The economic conference threw special light on the ability of the community to reflect its needs and to formulate specific schemes of action. The ability of its leaders to integrate the interests of the people and to secure their consent—a step which required considerable sacrifice on the part of the leading members of the community—shows a good deal of emotional maturity, not only of its leaders but of the conscious sections of the people as well. This level of emotional maturity, social consciousness and integration of interests which have thus been achieved as a result of continuous interaction of the departmental workers with the people of the area, is clearly revealed in the case studies of action-situations noted in this chapter. Detailed earlier (in Chapter III) were certain recent incidents, which had initially moved the community out of its stage of inertia and molded it into a powerful agency for social action. The state of functioning of the village institutions related here, their merits or otherwise, are however in no small way due to the plans of social development which had started the initial interaction and created a new element of leadership.

CHAPTER VIII

EDUCATION AND RECREATION IN THE TWO COMMUNITIES

EDUCATION—A STUDY OF ASPIRATIONS AND ACHIEVEMENTS

A number of references have been made earlier regarding the educational and recreational aspirations of the two groups of villages. It is evident from the position stated therein that both groups of villages are very eager to send their children to schools so that the future generations are not denied adequate opportunities for schooling and self-preparation. The two groups of villages do not, however, stand on an identical footing as far as actual accomplishments are concerned. The percentage of school-going children in the A group of villages is larger. The following table, reproduced from Chapter II, for ready reference, will make this evident.

A group of villages	Percentage "A"	"B"	B group of villages
Percentage of children going to school	75.5%	60%	Percentage of children going to school
Number of literate adults	65 %	35%	Number of literate adults

A larger percentage of adults have been declared literate in the A group as compared to B. The questionnaire for opinion-study referred to earlier had however evoked the same type of response from both the groups, almost all the villagers interviewed having expressed themselves in favor of sending their children to school. The replies to the questionnaire have thus established that villagers of both the groups would, if facilities are available, utilize educational institutions to full capacity. But as the facts of the situation establish, only a limited number of parents of both the groups had sent their children to schools. A fundamental analysis of the dimensions of expressed desire and of actual capacities of a community for supporting that desire with required sacrifice and efforts would thus reveal interesting data and provide a more correct estimate of the total situation. Social workers, in their effort to measure clients' attitude towards stimulation and service, need therefore to recognize the gap which may often exist between "needs" and "felt needs," and between desire and demand. The needs have to be supported by adequate willingness on the part of a people (who conceive these needs and desires) to make necessary sacrifices for their satisfaction, so that "needs" may assume the character of "felt needs" and the desires become demands.

An effort was, therefore, made to collect necessary evidence from the every-day life of the two communities to find whether adequate follow-up action, in terms of organized efforts, were initiated by either. The A group of villages, a number of interesting incidents revealed, made extraordinary effort to secure not only more facilities for schooling, both for children and adults, but also made simultaneous efforts to utilize the same. The need for sending children to the school in the A group of villages had, it seems, become a felt need of the community, inasmuch as the village leaders of the area had followed up their desire with adequate social action. Instances have not been lacking. In the A group of villages where some of the selected representatives, either of the attendance committee or of the youth group, had gone in the beginning of each session from house to house to motivate the reluctant parents to send their children to school. A healthy competition among the social education organizer trainees (see Chapter III) themselves, to stimulate participation in adult literacy classes, had also created a special impetus in this direction. Not infrequently the literacy centers organized by the trainee-apprentices (there were ten such centers existing during the period under review in the four villages of the A group) would appear as the centers of educational activity, and the hubs of community gathering. A number of special devices were introduced and initiated by the trainees to secure parents' participation for sending their children to the schools, as well as to encourage people to attend the literacy classes. This had changed the whole situation, and a time came when the prestige symbol of the village was no longer the number of schools it built, or the roll strength, maintained for the sake of routine administrative satisfaction. The quantum and quality of actual participation of the community in the school curriculum was perceived on the other hand as the major target to be reached.

The SEO trainees organized mass drills and recreational groups before and after school hours. Visits to the homes of unwilling parents, who were initially not at all bothered about the future of their wards, together with organization of craft classes for winning subsidiary income for the housewives, aided the process. For these stimulated participation, both of the housewife in the women's class, and that of the child (whose expenses could now be done away with) in the school. The adult classes increased their attendance as indigenous recreational programs, organized with very great care, became attractive; specific schemes of incentive for adult literacy were also drawn up and initiated. An unwilling adult member narrated the process of his own conversion to the adult literacy program in a public gathering especially convened to evaluate the work of the trainees. He said: "I returned home in the evening after the day's work and found that my children had gone to the recreation center, my wife to the craft class and my mother to the "Ramayana" study circle. The house was empty. What could I have done, you think, besides rushing to the adult study circle, which gave me, I discovered to my delight, not only instruction in letters but also the company of other adults, music, recreation and fun."

The total program of educational development, it seems, had worked; and what lent effective means of sustenance to the entire program of educational development was certainly the multi-dimensional approach, and the efforts made to enlist people's participation for each of these activities. It proved that the solution lay not by acting in isolation, but in associating the leading and enthusiastic youth leaders of the area with all its activities. The new devices, which brought success to the educational drives of the area, thus gradually became, from being imported techniques to begin with, a part of the technique of community action owned by the village itself. The villagers could not only now redefine their aspirations but were able also to realize them by their own efforts. The goals and ideals of a community are not established in a vacuum. They have to be built with sustained efforts over a period of time, and the members of a community can only accept these goals and ideals when they themselves provide the necessary wherewithal in terms of both resources and techniques.

EDUCATION AND RECREATION

Adults of the rural areas, especially in India, are proverbially realistic, and unnecessary kite-flying in terms of upholding unrealistic aspirations are not in their vein. The level of expectation of a community can only go up when the ideas are well within the reach of the community's resources and potentials. In the A group of villages, the aspirations of the people in terms of educational attainments were now no longer simply to have schools in greater number, but also to ensure that every member of the community join these schools irrespective of their age, sex or status. This changed definition of the situation led to a changed environment as well, and new standards of accomplishment became gradually visible, leading the way for a further rise in levels of aspirations and expectations.

The leadership of the area, now acquainted with new techniques of working with people, found the new aims realizable and within their terms of reference. Pitching of targets at a higher level was now possible, and the leaders took effective steps to evolve new targets and to work for their realization. They moved to change the location of the school, which was at Bahadurpur, a village approachable only to the children of the immediate locality, to a more central place, the barren "danga" of Benuria, which was equally accessible to all the villagers of the zone, and belonged to a no man's land. A new building was accordingly constructed. A section of the people of Bahadurpur who could not reconcile themselves to this loss of an institution from their own village, had to be appeased; and although the main school shifted to Benuria, a small subsection which could be attended by the children of Bahadurpur continued to hold classes in the old building. The new school of concrete construction and with many more resources, was shifted to a central place, so that children from all the four villages could have easy access to it. The Bahadurpur school still stands today on the Benuria danga as the symbol of the great unison of four little communities which sought to develop into a greater community by inter-group integration. The new community school also gave its sponsors the satisfaction of much increased attendance of students, rather than the mere physical "feel" of owning a school.

In the B group of villages, the scale was turned upside down. The desire for sending children to school, as revealed in answer to our queries, existed here, too, in a wide-spread manner. But no follow-up action was initiated by the elite of these villages which could have crystallized its aspirations into concrete realities and facts.

If we recall the case studies of action-situations detailed in Chapter VII, it will be evident that although there were in Bergram two schools with massive structures, the attendance in both these institutions was poor. This was so, as is obvious from the recorded consensus of the people of adjoining villages, mainly for two reasons. First, the other villages were not allowed to sit on the managing committee of these schools; and secondly, the people of these adjoining villages could, for this reason, never be reconciled with the status which Bergram wished to acquire for itself by owning for itself several prestigious physical structures. This led the people of the adjoining villages to virtually boycott the services of these schools. The leadership and the ruling groups of B group were apparently more interested in physical achievements, and had consequently ignored the wishes of the community and continued to act in isolation.

The concept and state of educational needs in both the groups of villages thus manifested themselves in different shape and form. In one of the groups the need for education seemed to exist in an academic manner and could not have been given practical shape by the members of the community, for want of appropriate agencies and desire for action.

More adults have thus been made literate in the A group than in B. The two groups of villages were very near, we have seen earlier, to each other as far as their social and political consciousness were concerned; but they occupied very different positions on the question of formal literacy and schooling of its younger members.

The results achieved in A have been just enumerated. There were several well-defined adult literacy centers set up by the Department in A. The members of the A group attendance committees which were composed of local villagers, took a positive interest in increasing the number of participants in the adult literacy classes. All adult literacy centers everywhere in this district have their attendance committees, which almost as a rule, function more or less as advisory bodies, more to satisfy the requirements of rules of law than to fulfill the felt needs of a community. In the case of the A group of villages, however, it was found that these formal committees had not been existing only for name's sake, but that its members had taken live interest and had converted these committees into effective instruments of village development.

The percentage of adult literacy in the B group of villages would have, in our opinion, been even less if the data had been collected at the very beginning of our study. As has been observed earlier, the very fact of the presence of our research workers had initiated a process of development in the villages of the B group, and had stimulated its commoner members (as distinguished from the leaders of the established agencies) to take upon themselves greater responsibilities of welfare work. A few adult literacy centers were accordingly opened in this group, as the people of the area made direct approaches to the Department soon after the data collection work was started in the year 1957. A few interested villagers from the neighboring villages of Bergram also became very much interested in adult literacy during that period, and displayed positive interest in securing community participation in adult education programs; percentages of literacy in the B group accordingly shot up. Adult education centers by themselves are no guarantee of community education, unless they are backed by sufficient community action initiated by the leaders of the community and of its various institutions.

The A group of villages had obtained a greater measure of success, not only in this direction but also in securing community integration, only because community efforts were not lacking here and a positive interest in the realization of the community's educational needs was visible.

The B group of villages, on the other hand, had lingered behind. This was so because there in B, the need for educational programs was still to become a real need. When the leaders of B had started realizing this need on more than an academic level however, they succeeded in initiating appropriate follow-up action and in achieving more tangible results within a short period of time.

RECREATION AND DEVELOPMENT—
A STUDY OF THE TWO AREAS

A further inquiry, in order to find out what recreational facilities and programs actually existed in both the groups of villages, forms an important chapter of this study. Members and a number of non-members (selected as per

our sample referred to in Chapter II) belonging to the Defense Party (Khiroli), *Palli Seva Niketan* (Bergram),
and a number of other organizations, were interviewed so
that data regarding types of varieties of recreational programs prevalent in the two areas of study could be acquired. Questions were directed to similarly ascertain
whether these recreational facilities existed in an organized
manner and had specific purposes in view, or were merely
of sporadic nature. The position of the villagers, and their
urge for more outside help for stimulating organization of
new recreational programs, was likewise ascertained. The
data which was thus made available and presented below
is, it seems, very revealing from the point of view of our
study.

In the village of Khiroli it seemed that readings from the
Koran, the Sacred book of Islam, was a regular feature.
Games like *Hadu-du*, volleyball, *Dhapas*, and cards were
occasionally played in the village by interested groups here
and there. Groups of children similarly got together in the
B group of villages on their own and ran about and played
from time to time; there was also a radio in the village of
Khiroli which was listened to by groups of people especially
interested in it; yet there were no organized attempts in
the villages of Khiroli and Sattore to conduct recreational
programs, whether for the grown-up adults or the young
children, in a systematic manner.

Out of the total number interviewed, 88 percent of the
villagers of the B group observed that they would welcome
help for the setting up of recreational organizations which
would stage religious dramas and *Kavigans*, and show religious films. The people of the village of Sattore were,
however, not prepared to set up any recreational agency
which would organize programs for the mere sake of it,
as this would go, they maintained, against the sacred tenets
of Islam.

In the village of Bergram the interviews revealed that
the children of the school played *Hadu-du* in their off hours,
staged dramas and had volleyball equipment at their disposal, but that there were no specific organizations in the
village earmarked for the purpose of sponsoring recreational programs for them. The reaction of the total number of clientele interviewed in this connection revealed that
they would require help to set up recreational organizations
to meet their growing needs. In the village of Rahamatpur

the *Kirtan* and *Manasa Mangal* party referred to earlier held their sway; there were no other recreational organizations in this village either.

In the A group of villages, on the other hand, recreational programs existed in abundance and efforts were made, through well-formed secular organizations especially devoted to this purpose, to develop them in an organized manner. *Badhugan, Kavigan, Harinam-Samkirttan* and recitations from the *Ramayana,* and the *Mahabharata,* were among the traditional and religious recreations still available in the village. There were also *Kirtan* parties and regular arrangements for *Raibeshe* dance in the villages of Islampur and Lohagarh, two of the four villages of A group. Modern recreational programs had simultaneously been patronized by the villagers of this area. Sports, football, *Dhapas,* variety entertainments, dramas and cultural shows, had become a regular feature here, and a part of its life. During the traditional religious celebration of *Saraswati Puja* the villagers of this area combine with the worship a number of "variety entertainment" shows, which provides opportunities to the talented young children and adults to contribute programs of dances, songs and recitation.

The two groups of villages thus differ widely in number, type and methods of organization of recreational functions. The attitude of the people towards the existing programs of recreation and their future development also vary. In the B group of villages recreational programs exist in a sporadic and disorganized manner. The traditional religious celebrations which are the main study here are conducted only by a limited number of institutions. Their paucity as well as their sporadic and unplanned nature show that they are, if not decadent, then certainly not in the way of revival. Yet the people of the area, aware as they are of their recreational needs, admit that they would welcome help for setting up organizations which could develop specific recreational functions; there are many however, who would only welcome religious and traditional recreational forms and their celebrations.

The situation in A group is different. What is of special significance here is that the recreational facilities in this group of villages exist in an organized manner and reach wider sections of the society. The youth clubs (a number of them are in functioning order) organize sports and recreation programs, football and indoor card games for its members. They also stage dramas and cultural shows for the benefit of the wider sections of the community almost at regular intervals. *Mahila samitis,* ten of which exist in the area, organize programs of a religious and secular nature exclusively for women, as well as make special efforts to ensure that their members also attend selected village festivals along with others. The children's organizations have their special function, and stage specific items in all-village shows. There have been several occasions when the children's club and *Bratibalakadals* have organized exclusive functions of their own through their own efforts. Apart from celebrations of the traditional festivals, worship and other caste functions, they organize, follow-the pattern set up by *Santiniketan Ashram,* some of the special festivals initiated by the latter. These include *Silpa Utsav* (the industrial ceremony) and *Vriksha Ropana* (tree planting), which present both traditional and new items of recreation for which they raise their funds, select their own programs and site, elect a president from among them and conduct the proceedings by themselves—adults being invited to attend as guests. One such function organized by the children on a children's day was carefully studied. The records reveal that every detail of the various programs thus introduced was drawn up on the basis of a previous plan, and the show was carried on in a neat and disciplined manner, which made a great impression on all those who attended. A careful analysis of the program revealed that all the children were allotted specific duties and regular assignments, and each one in charge of an assignment was not only held responsible for the discharge of those specific duties but performed them conscientiously and well.

The villagers of this area and their recreational and cultural organizations had introduced a series of new types of cultural functions which I choose to call "secular." Some of these have been enumerated earlier; others include organization of public exhibitions, baby shows, tree-planting ceremonies and Independence Day Celebration. These ceremonies combine in their presentation selected items of traditional recreation, such as *Kirtans, Bhajans,* and so on, as well as those which are of a non-traditional nature, composed of drills, sports, chorus songs, etc., which are open to people of all castes and communities. Regular prior announcement for each function and systematic notification of the same coupled with simple yet tasteful decoration of village sites, and the "not too long duration" of each function are some of the improved practices introduced as a result of the impact of new trends of organization. These celebrations were, of course, introduced at the initial stages by the extension workers of the area but some of these have now become a part of the cultural pattern of the community.

The recreational programs which thus exist in the A group of villages in an organized manner are many in number and varied in type. The people here take pleasure not only in participating in the traditional social functions which they continue to support, patronize and thereby nourish, but also in attending modern sports and recreational ventures of multifarious variety.

Bahadurpur and Islampur *Kirtan* parties, the study revealed, introduced the practice of appointing regular teachers to train new recruits and young participants. The youth who joined as new recruits, some of them as members of the youth clubs, continued to stage modern drama (with historical and social themes) and organized variety entertainment shows, literary symposiums and economic conferences by themselves. An attempt is thus made in the A group of villages to harmonize and balance traditional programs with the new types of modern variety and to realize the proper place of both in their day to day life. As the younger generation takes to traditional programs and as older people come to witness the secular and modern shows staged by the youth, a new process of synthesis in the recreational and cultural field is automatically initiated. The people in the A group of villages observed, in answer to research queries, that they did not require any outside help for organizing recreational programs of the new type, although they admitted that there was considerable need of toning up the existing organizations which sponsored recreational programs in the area. They maintained, however, that they would welcome outside help to build a high school, for which enough resources from the community were now forthcoming. At the same time, it was their feeling that they could mobilize their own resources to improve the existing recreational program as well as to set up new ones by their own efforts.

Recreation is a part of the culture of any community. It

contains in itself the mechanisms of social adjustments and defense. A community which does not know how to recreate, sing, play and laugh hardly possesses the potentialities and dynamism which are required to initiate larger programs of reform and action. Ability to draw upon the existing recreational facilities of a village and especially from the traditional recreational programs, after these have been reorganized by elimination of their irrational and vulgar traits, were as far as Sriniketan was concerned indicative of a higher measure of community consciousness and have been looked upon by the founder of Sriniketan as an important criteria of success in extension work. Is it too much to say from what has been described herein that the A group of villages, judged from this point of view, have gone a long way in realizing one of the fundamental aims of development?

In the variety entertainment shows staged in the A group of villages, we observed *Kirtans* staged side by side with modern songs and Raibeshe dance presented with modern sports. The traditional recreational performances were previously held, as is the practice everywhere, for a long stretch of hours, usually starting from about midnight. The situation has changed today as one finds in the A group that most of the shows and functions are held in the evenings and present a variety of different programs lasting for a period of two to three hours on an average. People willingly donate funds for such recreational evenings and seem to enjoy these short duration programs. I am, however, not attempting here a detailed review of the pattern of changes which have taken place in the recreational programs of the A group of villages since this could be the subject-matter of a separate study in itself. Yet it is necessary to emphasize that while the leadership of the B group of villages is mainly concerned with setting up of schools, construction of roads and organization of defense parties, all of which fulfill essential needs of a community, those of A group have learned to understand the essential values of apparently non-essential programs as well! The A group, it thus seems, treats recreation on a par with other development schemes and has sponsored both with care and eagerness. As a result, in every function held in the A group, one finds that recreation programs are staged as its indispensable accompaniment. Little pieces of decoration used to beautify the sites of village ceremonies and meeting places similarly endow the same with aesthetic appearance and sober color. Social and recreational functions have thus become a part of regular community life in the A group of villages. The new types of recreational programs, as well as the old and traditional ones harmonized in a new form, have become an integral part of the culture of the community.

The recreational program in the A group of villages go hand-in-hand with its development programs inasmuch as they sustain the children's organizations, strengthen the ties of the youth and frequently bring adults on common platforms. In the early stages of the development of youth clubs, as we have noted before, the leaders were merely concerned with recreational programs, but gradually these very programs brought them together and welded them into a socially integrated community, functioning as interested and powerful bodies for the purpose of development administration. Recreation in the A group of villages thus plays a totally different role from what it does in B. In the B group, it is a mere religious activity, and that too without having any effective bearing on the religious life of its people. In the A group, the function of recreation is very much distinguishable. For apart from providing pleasure and enjoyment to its participants, recreational programs in A have led and still lead to an integration of community life, and serve as springboards of social action. A few interesting incidents reproduced below will make it evident how in the A group recreation groups started shifting their areas of interest to more concrete social functions of development and catalyzed the whole community in action.

The youth groups of Bahadurpur and Benuria had only recently tried to organize popular opinion for the removal of a toddy shop (tavern) existing in the second village for a long time. The boys suddenly considered it the duty of the youth, now organized and coming into their own, to remove this social vice. They further realized after quite a campaign that, as it was not possible for them to remove the toddy shop from the village altogether, they had to content themselves with prevailing upon the shop-owner to move it to the backside of the village where he was to be given compensatory land. The youth considered it a step toward the ultimate removal of the shop, at which time the keeper, they recognized, would need to be rehabilitated. Some others, a group of adults who met every evening to play cards decided after a few days to take advantage of their togetherness and raised contributions from each other to pay for a teacher who promised to make them literate. Social consciousness and adult education in both these cases have been linked to recreation. These and many other examples like these could be quoted from the A group, which would suggest that recreation functions in the A group of villages not as a mere program of enjoyment, but as a tool and aid to developmental organization as well.

The clientele of the B group of villages needed recreation more often for religious purposes than for its own sake. They found themselves inadequate to meet these needs by their own efforts. The leaders of the group, as yet unaware of the values of recreation, took no cognizance either of these special areas of need, and concentrated merely on more direct schemes of development. In the A group of villages the need for recreation existed in a varied type and manner. Recreation was required here for the very sake of it, although its value in religious ceremonies has not been minimized. Organized groups of individuals have found in recreational programs of the A group a useful medium for their own expression, as well as an effective tool for community development and social integration of existing relationships. Does not this special meaning of recreation give a special significance to the community itself? Recreation, no more an idle phenomenon, has been here the very spice of life and an important component of its culture. That enhances, probably, the value of the cultural bonds of the community itself, and endows it with the added virtues of vigor and life.

CHAPTER IX

PEOPLE AND THEIR OPINIONS—
AN OPINION STUDY

Ideas travel, it seems, quicker than activities. That is the finding of this chapter. Enclosed in the pages to follow are the results of an opinion and attitude survey. The purpose of this particular study was to find out the opinions, perceptions and images prevailing in the two areas regarding a variety of social issues and facts which are of vital importance from the point of view of social development and growth. Information in this direction was collected from 190 valid forms filled in by the clientele of the A group of villages and from 120 of the B. All the people thus interviewed were associated with either of the institutions whose detailed functioning have been examined in the preceding chapters. Most, if not all, of the respondents were also the members of the administrative or policy-making bodies of one organization or another.

Forty-six different questions were framed for this purpose. Replies to these, it was thought, would provide an indication of the attitude of both groups of people regarding a variety of issues. These include attitude towards development work initiated by: (i) the Government; (ii) the Department of Rural Reconstruction; (iii) other agencies—as well as the general attitude towards (iv) Vishvabharati[1] and (v) a few selected social and religious problems of the day. The questionnaire also included a set of queries for a comparative measurement of the level of general knowledge prevailing in the two groups of villages; (vi) of their perception and awareness pattern vis-a-vis the local self-government institutions functioning in their respective areas; and (vii) their attitude towards the various political agencies functioning at the state and national levels, such as the West Bengal Legislative Assembly and

[1] The Institutions founded by Rabindranath Tagore of which the Department of Rural Reconstruction is a part.

the Indian Parliament. Since the people of the two areas were called upon, from time to time, to elect the representatives of the various tiers of administration, the questionnaire also sought to ascertain the state of people's awareness and understanding regarding the role and place of these political bodies in their life and society.

The study likewise sought to measure (viii) people's attitude towards the educational programs of their villages, (ix) their own social and religious opinions, and (x) awareness regarding a group of leaders of national fame.

This opinion study, which comes at the end of the book, does not however provide a summing-up view of the situations obtaining in the two group of villages. Neither does the author believe that whatever answers were given by the people have invariably reflected their correct positions regarding the many vital issues on which their opinions were sought. For, more often than not, what people generally express on an oral level, regarding their contemplated behavior pattern in imagined socio-religious situations, and consequently, what their opinions are regarding the various burning social and moral issues of the day, may be quite different than what they may actually do when they have to deal with these issues in reality situations. In actual practice, when the occasion for action comes, one may find that the same person whose opinion has been recorded, is behaving in a manner which will be very dissimilar to his expressed estimate of the situation. One may, for example, say that he believes in inter-caste marriage at a time when there is no possibility of any inter-caste marriage taking place in his family. But when the eventuality actually arises in his own personal context, the same person may be found unable to accept the proposition. It is for this reason, therefore, that the present author believes that emphasis should be laid, in any study of applied social sciences, on the collection of data from observation of human beings under actual situations of action—as well as on study of social relationships during processes of interactions—rather than on mere opinion study. People's opinions regarding social and intra-community relations may be very different from the actual practices they follow. What the people think they would do may thus seldom agree with what they may actually be doing in situations of reality.

The emphasis during the course of this study therefore,

has all along been on finding data from action-situations rather than on mechanical collection of "opinions" of the *vox populi*. In a place like Bolpur police station it is but in the fitness of things that all the villages including these which belong to the B group have been, in some measure or the other, influenced by the impact of Rabindranath Tagore and the radiating influences of his university. This becomes evident from the replies that the villagers of both groups have given to our queries. Both the groups have thus evinced a high degree of social and political consciousness, and the difference between the two as revealed by the comparative study is also not very striking. This chapter, therefore, presents some significant data on the intellectual awareness of the two groups of villagers, and of their life. The data collected from actual observation of action-situations presented earlier forms, it is needless to mention, a complementary part of this study. A comparative perusal of the gap, if any, that exists between the practices and professions of the two groups—as may be evident from such a cross-reference study—is also of significance.

Out of the total number of people interviewed in both groups of villages, almost all of them had a very positive awareness of the need for education. All adults should become literate, they said, and all children should be sent to schools. They were unanimous in their opinion that children should go to schools for the purpose of acquiring knowledge as well as for getting a job—either in the city or, if there were opportunities to earn enough to help their families, back in the village. Only a limited number of people, i.e. 15 percent from group B and 14 percent in group A, felt that their children, after they grow up should and must stay in their own villages and not migrate away.

SOCIAL RELATIONS

The attitudes towards social stratification and social relations were equally encouraging. Sixty-three percent of people in the A group of villagers stated that they were willing to drink water in the houses of Harijans and about 53 percent of the people belonging to the lower caste of the same group said that they would be prepared to offer water to the people of higher castes. Similarly 57 percent and 48 percent from B group of villages stated that they would be willing to drink water from the lower caste and offer water to the higher castes. Fifty-three percent of the people were prepared, in the A group of villages, to dine with Harijans, but would do so only in general assemblies. They had no objection to this even where cooked (pucca) food would be served. Another 53 percent agreed to dine under similar circumstances with people of higher caste. Forty-eight percent of people from B group of villages agreed to dine with Harijans if it became necessary to do so (out of this about 27 percent will dine willingly and the others with some reservation). An equal number of people from the B group of villages were prepared to dine with the higher caste willingly. The people who are prepared to drink water and dine with Harijans are also agreeable to visit their houses. The rest of the people from both the group of villages feel that it is not possible for them either to dine with Harijans, or with any higher caste.

Fifty-three percent of people from A group are prepared to marry their children to the families of lower caste and another 45 percent will accept inter-caste marriages only when they are forced into it; but 60 percent of people interviewed from A group of villages are prepared to offer their daughters to higher castes.

All people from both groups of villages are prepared to send their children to the same school where Harijans, too, send their wards.

The data presented above makes interesting reading and there does not seem to exist much gap between the position of two groups of villages. Diffusion of ideas thus takes place quicker than changes in social behavior. The people of A group of villages, however, are somewhat more liberal in their social relationships with people of the other castes; they have scored heavily in the matter of inter-caste marriage. On other matters, a detailed discussion of which follows later, the differences in the attitudes of people of Group A is not strikingly at variance with those of B. The people who say that they are freer in social relationships obviously feel that they are a socially emancipated community and therefore take pride in fraternizing with the "lower" castes. It is thus not strange that while a larger number of people are prepared to take water offered by the people of lower castes, a lesser number of people are willing to offer water to the higher castes. Caste thus acts as a two-way process and our study reveals that not only do the higher castes refuse to enter into certain prohibited social relationships with the lower castes but the lower castes have their inhibitions as well. The socially emancipated people referred to earlier are prepared to take possible risks of contravening religious mandates by themselves such as taking water from people of lower castes. Yet they are not prepared to take a greater risk and break away from religious sanctions by offering water to the people of the higher strata.

This has probably two implications. Development, at least on a level of ideas and aspirations, travels downward in the hierarchy structure rather than upward, and the people of the two areas have taken to new attitudes more from charitable disposition towards "the lower" than out of deliberate effort to break caste laws. The contention however does not hold good as far as other sectors of social intercourse are concerned. People who are ready to recognize inter-caste marriage are more willing to offer their daughters to higher castes than to entertain brides from the lower castes. The evidence on this score should also be examined from the point of view of the terms and reference of community development and social growth. Whereas a higher caste in these days of liberalizing traditions finds infraternization with the underdog a measure of development, this is not so from the point of view of the lower. To them, however, a marriage in the higher caste is to be treated as a process of definite progress and may be following Srinivas' argument, a major leap towards 'Sanskritization' of the family. Most of the people from both groups of villages were, however, reluctant to answer questions pertaining to inter-communal marriages as they possibly recognized that they were unable to offer socially desirable answers in this matter. A few (20 percent) who replied, however, felt that such marriages were not desirable, 63 percent of people of A group and 42 percent from B were, willing, however, to "accept" inter-communal marriages if they were "forced" into it. The data provided in this sector of our study also needs careful shifting for a deeper analysis. The sweep of development, liberalization or Sanskritization, whatever the case may be, it is evident, has been strictly kept confidential within the respectable bounds of the Hindu society itself. The methods of the social work process for village development, like the limited traditions of social reform in this field, have hardly ever employed a program or climate of inter-communal assimilation. If development makes inter-caste social amalgamation a fashion, and if the time-honored movement for breaking caste barriers has made good strides over the historical scene, no efforts even in the area of village work at Sriniketan have ever been made to secure social assimilation of the two communities. The dimensions of the whole tragedy however becomes somewhat thinner when we find that the lapse of efforts on this score is probably a universal phenomenon in the country at large.

People of both groups of villages were, however, very liberal in allowing *Harijans* to visit the places of worship. Ninety-five percent from the A group and 85 percent from B were prepared to allow them to enter the places of worship exclusively meant for the higher castes (temples). Harijans themselves were also likewise prepared to participate in functions of higher castes, if they were so invited as observers. Almost 100 percent from A group are also similarly prepared to participate in social functions (like marriage) of other communities and 85 percent from B are also ready to allow the people of other religious groups to practice their own rituals just as they liked. One hundred percent people from A group were similarly agreeable to allowing freedom of religion to all villagers, irrespective of their caste or religion. The A group of villagers thus displayed a high degree of social awakening, though it is not that the B lagged behind.

As we stated at the very beginning, our attempt in this chapter has been to collect opinions of people on a variety of issues and to provide on the basis of these a measure of social consciousness of the area. It was not possible to initiate appropriate action-situations to actually test how the two communities would have functioned if and when they were to face reality situations and facts of life. A few experimental situations organized in A and B groups of villages, however, had provided some limited opportunity to measure comparatively the reactions of the villagers in selected action studies.

The S.E.O. trainees had once organized a three-day camp in the A group of villages and a subsequent one in the B. People of all castes and religious groups were invited on the second day of the camp thus organized, to dine together along with the campers. It was a pleasant surprise to find that the villagers as a whole responded to the program very favorably. They all sat together and about one hundred people from various castes and communities partook of meals cooked with "water and salt." A similar attempt was later made in the B group to plan such a joint camp and inter-dining. It was observed, however, that the people of the locality were not too enthusiastic about the idea. The plan had accordingly to be given up and the effort to organize an inter-community and inter-caste dinner was abandoned.

Similarly the *Domes* (a lower caste) of Lohagarh (a village of the 'A' group) had once expressed a desire to organize *Swaraswati Puja*[2], a festival usually celebrated by high caste Hindus. The plan, however, was certain to upset. For the *Puja* required the services of a Brahmin priest, and no Brahmin was prepared to come forward to perform the rituals or to participate in the ceremony. However, a trainee of the S.E.T.O. Center (himself a Bengali Brahmin) volunteered to deputize for the village priest and took the toll upon himself. The *Puja* was ultimately celebrated and attended by the trainees and members of Sriniketan, both of which groups belonged to all castes and description. It is interesting to note that people of the village, those of the higher castes, had thereafter joined the puja as participants, and that this particular trainee had no difficulty in retaining his position of informal friendship with the high castes of the area, either then or thereafter. Although every effort was made to organize a similar situation in the B group and to find the reaction of the inter-acting community to such a situation, the leaders in B remained very cold, and both the "lower" and the "higher" castes of the area were found to be in no mood to get involved in an experiment like that, or to provide data for study of the after-effect, if any. The role of the S.E.O. trainee, the apprentice social worker in this connection, seems to be open to question. As an outside catalyst engaged in a program of social interaction and integration, he might have possibly done better, according to the principles of worker-client relationship, to wait and to help motivate the higher castes to release their own priest for the work, rather than to step himself into the saddle of a "doer," and force the pace of events. But rarely has a professional social worker in India functioned in a situation like this, often handled either by a social reformer or by a social revolutionary.

---

[2] A caste Hindu worship.

Here, a change of role on the part of the social worker—from more conventional overtures—seems to have been well warranted in view of its effect on the total community. A two-fold conclusion emerges from the situation: The problems of social relations in underdeveloped societies must be dealt with by new tools; the role of the social worker must be flexible enough both to affirm the old patterns and maintain accepted social behavior, while indicating new directions in situations of crisis. If the goal of social work is the expansion of the sealed areas of human understanding, this latter point cannot be overly stressed, and the tools must function not only for a group's established ways of dealing with reality but also serve as a catalyst for integrating the unknown. If "action" and "doing" help to create the necessary impetus to self-criticism in a given situation, social work methods should not hesitate to incorporate such approaches into their own structure.

ATTITUDE TO MEDICAL AID AND FAMILY PLANNING

Ninety-five percent of people from A group of villages have no prejudices against modern medicine. They believe that diseases are chiefly due to unsanitary living conditions and malnutrition, and that medical treatment should be by qualified and trained doctors. In matter of family planning, they further believe that children are born due to our 'own acts' rather than as an act of providence, and that childbirth should therefore be and is capable of being spaced and planned. The people of A group were accordingly further prepared to call for birth control measures and practice the same in their own life. "Child marriages should be avoided," they say, adding that "early marriages are equally undesirable." About 84 percent of people in B group share the same opinions as those of A regarding medical treatment, family planning and marriage. Almost all the people in both these groups were prepared, by their own admission, to change their old traditions for new ones if something better was really ready at hand.

ELECTIONS AND PROMINENT PERSONALITIES

The schedule for opinion study also contained a few basic questions aimed at a comparative assessment of the general level of political and social consciousness of the people of the two groups of villages under study. The data obtained in this area provides equally interesting material.

AN OPINION STUDY

Ninety-eight percent of people interviewed in the A group of villages were "enrolled" voters and a great majority of them took part in the last general elections. All people interviewed from the B group villages were also voters. All the people of the two areas had voted in the union board elections, whereas only 98 percent from the A group took part in the "general" suffrage, and a similar number from B had also so done. One hundred percent of people in the B group of villages were aware of the age qualifications required for a person to enroll as a voter whereas only 75 percent of the A group were acquainted with those qualifications. All the people in both the groups of villages had known of at least one candidate for office, and his name. (Incidentally, the person known to all was the one who had contested for the assembly seat in the last general elections—and won), whereas only 72 percent of people from the A group of villages and about 65 percent from B group knew the names of every one of the three candidates who had contested from this area. Almost 100 percent people from both groups of villages were aware that the Congress Party was ruling the State and leading the Government at the center.

AN OPINION POLL

A comparative statement provided below incorporates the results of an opinion poll on a few prominent political, social and spiritual leaders of the country:

TABLE I

Name of leader	Village Group A Recognition Percentage	Village Group B
Mahatma Gandhi	100%	100%
Ramkrishna Paramhansa	74%	60%
Swami Vivekananda	70%	65%
C. R. Das	30%	40%
Raja Ram Mohan Roy	32%	56%
Netaji Subhash Chandra Bose	96%	93%
Shyma Prasad Mukherjee	41%	65%

TABLE II

Name of leader	Village Group A Recognition Percentage	Village Group B
Jyoti Basu	20%	21%
U. N. Dhebar	9%	21%
C. R. Rajagopal- achari	9%	23%
Jayaprakash Narayan	9%	18%
Pundit Iswar Ch. Vidyasagar	93%	93%
Ashutosh Mukherjee	69%	23%
John Cheap	38%	25%

SOCIAL WORK AND SOCIAL CHANGE

The poll had aimed to ascertain a few political facts such as whether and how many people knew the *names* of the various leaders and the knowledge and communication pattern of the area vis-a-vis the names mentioned in the tables. Negatively, the poll did not aim to ascertain the political popularity of the incumbents on the list since the latter had a number of leaders on the roll who were no longer alive.

It seems evident from the above that the leaders of the B group of villages had greater political consciousness, or at least more information regarding the developments taking place in the political scene. More people from B group had known, among the dead, of the late C.R. Das and Shyamaprasad Mukherjee; and among the living, of Rajagopalachari, Jayaprakash Narayn and U.N. Dhebar. All people knew of Gandhi and 100 percent and 96 percent and 93 percent of people from A and B respectively knew Subhash Bose.

In the social and cultural sphere, 93 per cent of the people from both the groups had known of Pandit Iswar Chandra Vidyasagar, a leading educationist *cum* social reformer of the mid-nineteenth century. Ramakrishnadeva was known to 74 percent of the people from the A group, and to 60 percent of the B. Seventy percent from the A group and 65 percent from the B knew of Swami Vivekananda. Raja Ram Mohan Roy's name was known to 56 percent of the B group and to only 32 percent of the A. This big gap in perception structure of A and B regarding Raja Ram Mohan Roy was due to the fact that the period of study had coincided with certain celebrations which were going on in the B group of villages for commemorating the memory of the Raja at that time.

From the data given above it is equally evident that far more people of the B group were interested in elections and took part in them. More of them had known of C.R. Das, Subhash Chandra Bose, Shyama prasad Mukherjee, U.N. Dhebar, Jyoti Basu, C. Rajagopalachari and Jayaprakash Narayan, than of the A group.

It is difficult to explain the significance of this political poll.

The B group, it seems, however had experienced a greater impact or free play of political winds. More information and knowledge about the political scene and its action-potential had freely entered its area of thought and action.

170

This is certainly in sharp contrast with the situation obtaining in the A group where such free play was possibly retarded by the "personality" impact of the leaders, and of the catalyst institution of 'A,' namely the Department of Rural Reconstruction. A further analysis of the situation provided below will make the picture clear.

The leaders of the A group had been village leaders par excellence. They had little or no ambition toward or connection with the outside political world. By motivation, leadership, aspiration and impact the elite of the A group were concerned only with the facts and events of their villages in particular. Caught in the whirlwind of socialization, the community in A was also likewise immersed deep in its own internal process of village action and had little or no time at its disposal to look beyond its own frontiers. The A group has thus by its very upbringing been more interested in the local and community affairs than in the world at large. More people of the A group than of the B had therefore known of Mr. John Cheap, a local historical figure who lived in the area 150 years ago. The ruins of his fort still remained at an elevated spot situated four miles away from both groups of villages, and provide a sight of historical importance where the S.E.O.T. Center is now established.

The A group of villages had developed under the shadow of *Vishvabharati Sriniketan,* an institution which had by its philosophy and mandate kept away from party politics and active political association. Its interest in the villages of the area was thus merely academic, and its contacts with the villages were for the sake of welfare work only. However, this complete dissociation from political interests had not, it seems, brought an unmixed blessing to all its clientele and all the inhabitants of its field of operation. It had on the other hand cast a somewhat negative influence in the area of its work, and made people of these villages politically immature. Less conscious and even unaware of certain basic political facts of the world which every socially educated individual and a growing community, even if they be interested only in their own affairs, must learn caused the A group to remain in backwaters. The Department of Rural Reconstruction as an institution of social service had been chiefly responsible for initiating social welfare activities in the area. The Department had cast the net of its influence far and wide, deep down in the feelings of human mind, leading to a modification of values and personality structures of the people of the A group of villages. The institution with its protective influence and powerful paraphernalia of communication and contact had reduced the people of the area, although socially and culturally advanced, to considerable political incapacity. Somewhat apolitical in its feelings, aspirations and political overtures, the people of the A group were much less advanced from those of the 'B' in this particular area of development. The B group had thus stolen a remarkable lead on the political front. Its leadership had demonstrated visible interest in the current affairs of the world. This achievement without the help of any well-defined democratic agency administering regular adult education programs in this area is no mean achievement.

The impact of the Department, and the limitations of an institution wedded exclusively to scientific welfare work, are equally well brought out by the material served in this chapter. A community which gets bogged down in too many details of the welfare movement, and has little time to do any serious thinking beyond this dimension, may not be able to develop all its important faculties although such development is certainly the key objective of social work activity. Social workers of a developing society should be fully aware that severe limitations accompany the complete divorce of social work from the fields of political action and awareness, and so avoid the purist approach.

CHAPTER X

ATTITUDE TOWARDS DEVELOPMENT WORK— AN INDICATION OF GENERAL KNOWLEDGE OF THE PEOPLE

The National Extension Service Block of the contiguous areas was started in the year 1955 by the government of West Bengal in order to cover the group of villages where *Sriniketan* had been operating for the last thirty years. The Block was not integrated with the administrative machinery of the Department of Rural Reconstruction, but functioned as an independent agency of the State government. The area previously serviced by *Sriniketan* was included in the field of operation of the Block; however, the full coverage of the block included 185 villages, and was a much bigger area. A specific questionnaire designed to measure the attitude of the people of both groups towards the N.E.S. Block and the Department of Rural Reconstruction, as well as towards developmental work in general, was accordingly framed and administered.

It seems that ninety-five people out of one hundred from the B group of villages had heard of the N.E.S. Block and known that their own villages came under the area of its operation. They were also aware of the name of the local Block Development Officer. In answer to a pointed question whether the advices of the Block had been of any help to them, a general feeling was expressed that the advices offered by the block administration had been helpful to the people of the area. Eighty-five percent of the people interviewed felt that the establishment of better communications, i.e. building of roads, etc., have been moderately satisfactory, whereas about 81 percent of the people expressed that the supply of manures and establishment of night schools have been accomplished in a "moderately satisfactory" manner. Thirty-six percent of people felt that the supply of improved seeds, establishment of health facilities, the work of controlling of malaria, the development of health and improvement of cattle (i.e. in the field of animal husbandry), have been only just useful, i.e. "moderately satisfactory."

An overwhelming number of people ranging from 95 percent to 70 percent expressed, however, that not much progress had yet been made in the matter of establishment of social education centers, night schools, hospitals, cooperative health societies, irrigation facilities, demonstration pumps and marketing facilities.

As we turn to the A group, we find that 100 percent people from A group of villages had been aware that their villages came under this N.E.S. Block and had known the name of the Block Development officer. About 95 percent of them felt that the help rendered by the block has been generally useful but while questioned about specific improvements, which might have taken place under the leadership of the Block, 84 percent of people felt that the supply of improved seeds has been "moderately satisfactory," and about 50 percent felt that supply of manures had similarly been a somewhat successful endeavor. Almost all the people of the area seemed to be of the opinion that the help rendered by the Block in other spheres such as the supply of fertilizers, provision for marketing, organization of kitchen gardens, control of epidemics, provision of irrigation facilities and establishment of better communications, schools, social education centers, night schools, hospitals and dispensaries, have been ineffective. Forty-one percent however admitted that help rendered by the block for organizing village industries had been somewhat satisfactory.

Eighty-five percent people from B group of villages felt that they wanted the Government to bring measures of improvements to their villages, and are prepared to contribute their mite (i.e. 'as much as they can') ; 67 percent of people feel that they are prepared to contribute only to some extent to the development work; 83 percent of the people are prepared to donate their manual labor, if asked for; and another 2 percent are prepared to offer their carts and equipment on loan.

Ninety-eight percent of people of the A group of villages wished that the Government would bring improvements to their villages and are willing to cooperate with the Government in this task. Ninety-eight percent of people feel that they are prepared to donate their manual labor, while others are prepared to offer their carts and the use of their influence. Nobody in group A is prepared to help by giving money to the Government. Ninety-five percent of people of the A group of villages have, they admit, been from time to time approached with offer of help by N.E.S. Block authorities, the Department of Rural Reconstruction and the Social Education Organizers' Training Center.

Fifty percent of people in the B group of villages revealed that they have been approached by outside agencies with offer for help from time to time. Out of this, 41.5 percent of the people said that the N.E.S. Block and the Department of Rural Reconstruction had approached them for help. Nobody from group B named the Social Education Organizers' Training Center as having approached them with offer of help, but observed that political parties and independent village leaders had approached them with aid and support. It is interesting to note that neither any political party, nor any independent leader had approached the A group of villages with such offers; the only approach to them came from well-defined and well-recognized social service agencies and institutions. Our findings reveal, as has been noted earlier, that the independent leaders and political parties referred to had played a prominent role in the B group of villages and wielded a good deal of influence in shaping and determining the pattern of social services in this group.

Excepting one solitary individual, from the B group of villages, all villagers of this area had heard of *Santiniketan* and *Sriniketan* and had visited the institutions located therein. Excepting him, everyone could give the correct name of the founder of Vishvabharati but only 45 percent of the people interviewed could give names of six other persons connected with the university. Thirty percent of people could detail a few of the purposes for which Santiniketan had stood, 25 percent of people of the area knew of some of the objectives of the local Union Board and the name of its President, and 86 percent of people knew the name of the representatives of their respective villages to the Union Board. Eighty-six percent of people had voted at the last Union Board elections, and 90 percent knew the functions of the Union Board and could point to at least one of the most important sources from where its revenue was drawn.

All the persons of A group of villages had heard about *Santiniketan* and *Sriniketan,* knew what they stood for, and who was their founder. Almost 100 percent of people knew the names of six other persons connected with *Vishvabharati* and 20 percent could explain the meaning of the word *"Vishvabharati."* One hundred percent of the people were acquainted with some of the purposes for which the Union Board was established, and with the names of their respective representatives to the Union Board. Nearly 100 percent of the people could name some of the functions of the Union Board and 85 percent could name at least one of the important sources from where the revenue for the Union Board was drawn.

Out of the total number interviewed in the B group of villages only 30 percent felt that *Sriniketan* had rendered them appreciable service. But questioned further about it, 57 percent stated that they were not aware of the help rendered by *Sriniketan* whereas 25 percent of the people were of the opinion that *Sriniketan* had rendered them yeoman's service. In the A group of villages, 100 percent of the people observed that *Sriniketan* had approached them with offer of help. But 40 percent of people were of the opinion that *Sriniketan* had ultimately not been able to be very helpful. A good percentage of people, about 30 percent almost, said that they were not aware of any concrete help given by *Sriniketan* to their villages.

The usage of the word *'Sriniketan'* in this context, however, needs some elaboration. From some time in the past, the people of the area failed to draw a clear line of demarcation between the Department and the local N.E.S. Block, as the two organizations worked with a good deal of understanding and cooperation, although they never failed to maintain respectable distance from each other in areas where their policies were likely to clash. The villagers were confused by the similarity between the two organizations, and especially so in view of the fact that a number of former workers of *Sriniketan* were functioning under the N.E.S. Block on loan service. It should be recorded here that the role of the N.E.S. Block itself was still not very clear to the villagers of the area. The image of an effective block administration, almost invariably meant to them its ability to offer material aid and to act as the agent of the supply line. As we have noted earlier, since the two agencies, the N.E.S. Blocks and the Department, were being identified with each other, the effectiveness of the Department was also judged from the point of view of its ability to offer material benefits. The role of a stimulative educator and community organizer, which was *Sriniketan's* main sphere of activity seemed to have lost somewhat of its significance in the light of these new developments.[1]

In the B group of villages, although the acquaintance of the villagers with *Sriniketan* had been very meager—and by the admission of the Department itself, these were the villages where they had not been working at all—even then, 25 percent of the people felt that *Sriniketan* had rendered them yeoman's service. This reaction, one surmises, was mainly due to three reasons. First, with the entry into these villages of rural workers from *Sriniketan* for the purpose of research work, the villagers of the area were hopeful that a stage of collaboration would now begin where much could be expected from such a powerful institution. The tribute paid to *Sriniketan* was therefore both a show of courtesy and an early wooing for a hopeful alliance. It is also true that *Sriniketan*, although it did not take any direct interest in the B group of villages, always gave all the help to the leaders of this area which it could offer from a distance. Since the achievements of the community of B group, in terms of its own social awakening and awareness of its goals and ambitions for social and welfare services, were not very high, whatever aid came from an unexpected source—a source on which the villagers of the B group of villages had no right to fall back upon—was gratefully received and widely cheered.

Expectations in the A group of villages had on the other hand risen high. They had achieved a great deal, stimulated a lot of their individual interests for common causes, and had pitched their targets high up. The urge for development was visible, and the requisite organization and leadership to step up development were not wanting. With more and more needs being satisfied by their own efforts, new needs were being gradually discovered and new goals had therefore to be established. In this setup, where expectations were rising rapidly, if the supply line of the N.E.S. Block of the locality (whose total administrative and economic resources were suited only to serve an aver-

---

[1] A former employee of *Sriniketan*, who was then working as a Village Level Worker in the Block, commented on this change of image, when he said; "Formerly under Sriniketan people came to us for advice, help and guidance, today they come to me for loans, seeds, and fertilizers.'

age N.E.S. Block area, where people lie steeped in lethargy and inertia) fails to keep pace with the rising tempo of enthusiasm, as it seemed to in this case, the inevitable corollary of such a state of affairs is bound to be grim. The expectations of a community from a development agency working in its area has thus a direct relationship with the stage of development where the community is resting at the moment. Its attitude towards development is therefore a product of the relative growth of its consciousness, which in turn is a result of the developments already achieved in the community. The attitude of the community under such circumstances is often an indicator of its rate of growth as well.

The relationship of these villages with *Sriniketan* was, of course, very intimate. They came to develop, along with a sense of dependency, an awareness of their right to call for help, the more so since they were prepared to mobilize their own resources. Since the relationship had assumed a very closely knit structure, Sriniketan's (which was a purely educational and welfare organization) inability to offer direct material aid was considered disappointing, and the feelings of frustration had started mounting. It is only at a certain stage of development that urges for further progress in a community becomes stronger; and with the willingness of a people to make more and more sacrifices, these cravings and desires become all the more irresistible. If a community, thus firmly pledged to reach certain goals, fails to satisfy its needs and finds that the goals they had set up are receding into the background, (chiefly for want of resources), frustration develops at a cumulative rate and soon takes the shape of aggression and hostility. At all such times when urges have been created and mobilization of resources in a given community have taken place, the only way to prevent frustration is to offer all such material aid which could supplement the efforts of the people and help them to reach their goal. Supply line must keep its pace with the steps of a developing community and failure to do that will lead, more often than not, to renewed frustration and anguish. "Satisfactions," says Mr. T.R. Batten, "are linked to wants and wants manifest themselves as tensions—feelings of discomfort or restlessness, which continue until the wants are satisfied or abandoned." [2]

---

[2] Batten, T. R., *Communities and Their Development* (London: Oxford University Press, 1960), p. 218.

ATTITUDE TOWARDS WORK

The Department of Rural Reconstruction at Sriniketan has been acting as the stimulator-catalyst of the A group of villages. It could raise resources from among the people, but could not undertake to act as the agent of the supply line. It does not speak well for a community to mistake the role of the educator-stimulator with that of a supply agent. The A group of villages, which long lay within the area of the Department's orbit of work, seemed to be unable to appreciate and understand the role of the agency, and its confused estimate of its role made the leadership of these villages somewhat intolerant of, and aggressive towards, its sponsoring agency. This by itself could be interpreted as an interesting sidelight on the community's varied dimensions of development. The inability of the Department to extricate its role from that of the Block, or to keep up its image of catalyst, is also a serious factor which may well be the result of the state of confusion existing among the image-builders themselves.

The expectations of the people toward the N.E.S. Block were, however, pitched rather high; even at a stage when a cooperative *Ghani* society was being backed up by the N.E.S. block with all its resources, only 41 percent of villagers interviewed thought that improvements in the sector of village industries in this area had been moderately successful. It is interesting to find that, although all the people of A group of villages had agreed that the N.E.S. Block had approached them for help at some stage or the other and admitted that adequate efforts were made to reach the villages, only a few had felt that adequate services had been rendered to them, either by the authorities of the Block or of the Department. A group of villages, where substantial work had already been done by the N.E.S. Block, seemed to feel dissatisfied with the rate of achievement, whereas in B group, where systematic efforts of the N.E.S. Block are hardly yet visible, satisfaction in abundant measure has been noted.

Two conclusions emerge from this anomalous situation: namely, that the people of the B group of villages were of an easily satiable type, whereas the A group, which was well along on its journey of development, was becoming increasingly impatient for greater results. The pace of movement of A group was becoming more and more irresistible, and the inadequate speed of the supply line (a speed which had satisfied the B group), failed miserably to come up to the mark in the A group of villages. The frustrations and aggression displayed by the A group were thus of a community which, armed to the teeth and mobilized to its last man, is unable to move forward for lack of fuel. Such a development by itself may not necessarily constitute a negative attitude towards development but a significant potentiality for self-engineered growth seems evident in a community like this. Yet, here is a situation where A group of villages, not hostile to but anxious for development, accelerates its pace of growth only to find its catalyst-agent crumpled up in its decisions and speed of progress. What will happen to the future of such a community, is difficult to predict; one thing however seems certain: that the community would either, on its own, mobilize its resources to move forward and outstrip the agency in achievement and growth, abandoning the latter altogether in its onward march, or get submerged, together with the catalyst itself, in waves of demoralization and self-annihilating inertia. To this characteristic of ambivalence of the A group of villages, we shall have occasion to return again in the chapter to follow.

CHAPTER XI

TOWARD FULLY INTEGRATED COMMUNITIES

The other objective of community organization is to create a sense of self-reliance and reciprocal relationship among the various members of a developing community. In India, where the differences of income are so great, one of the ways in which members of a particular locality engaged in development work could be given a feeling of togetherness is by ensuring, in an equitable manner, a certain degree of community participation in some of the vital matters of the area. There could thus be a common participation, despite the differences of income, in the decision-making process of the village. But the making of a decision is, by itself, not good enough. What is more important is the implementation of the decisions, as well as administration of the welfare programs of a villege. Both these require finances. In a poor country where state resources for welfare and development are far short of the requirements, the question of raising at least some part of the cost from the client community becomes important. The members of a village where development work is going on should, therefore, be encouraged to make a substantial contribution in this regard.

This is required for more reasons than one. First of all, the economic resources raised in this way, however meager the amount, is bound to be of great assistance to the community itself; secondly, no community can preserve its self-respect unless it raises some part of the cost by its own efforts. The question of equitable co-sharing in this matter is also of vital importance. If it is granted that some of the necessary funds are to be raised by the community, then contributions should be forthcoming from all sections of the population, irrespective of their economic status. It is absolutely necessary to emphasize that the resources so raised should not be a gift merely from the affluent sections of a village, but the common contribution of all members.

There is a natural tendency in economically handicapped societies, and especially where the State has already started developing social security before welfare programs have been stabilized, for the local voluntary organizations to become entirely dependent on outside grants, or on the charity of its richer citizens. But excessive dependence on outside aid and/or outright grants have a tendency to cripple local initiative. Excessive dependence on the wealthy elite would similarly ensure the rise of a domineering leadership whose only claim to the hierarchical position is that they can secure grants from the outside world, or pay it from their own pockets.[1]

A community which does not raise its resources from within itself suffers, then, on two counts. Firstly, it becomes over-dependent on outsiders and secondly, its own leaders become domineering and dictatorial, looking to the outside world or only to themselves for their support, and can safely ignore the village community of whom they are the leaders. A democratic organization becomes almost impossible in such a situation. Since there is no reciprocal relationship of give-and-take between the leaders and their rank and file, the integrative aspects of community life are naturally threatened. An important objective of community organization, in India is, therefore, to ensure that the client community becomes economically self-reliant and raises at least some part of the total cost of welfare or development from among its own members.

It is, however, not the author's contention that the development services in a village should be entirely self-sufficient, or that they should be able to raise all the resources required for the purpose. No single village, not even a group of them, could in fact finance an optimum level of social services from its own coffers. Nevertheless the budget of an institution should not in any case consist of one hundred percent outside grant. Any democratic welfare plan must have, a share—an effective one—of community finance. An important aim of community organization in India—and a principle that applies universally— is therefore to enable the members of a community to raise a part of the total cost of development by their own contributions, and to ensure that the local institutions do not depend entirely on outside grant, thus becoming parasitic appendages of an external body.

---

[1] For example, the position of catalyst leaders in 'B'. The institutions there had no community contribution and were run by the grants secured by the leaders.

INTEGRATED COMMUNITIES

EQUITABLE SHARING OF ECONOMIC COSTS

It has been mentioned that there should be a democratic base of collective contribution, and that all strata of population should be involved in the process. The fact that a community's concept of self-reliance and respect depends on the economic contributions forthcoming from the community itself, makes it imperative that the contribution must come in an equitable measure from all stratum of society—rich and poor alike. It is equally important that all should pay at least a part of their contribution through a common mode of payment that is within the ability of all.

This mode could obviously be payment in one's own labor. For that is the only resource which all sections of people own in common. If the poorest have to participate in the fund-raising campaign of a village, it should certainly have to be open to them to contribute in labor or kind. In order to create a sense of co-sharing it would be necessary therefore to see that even the most affluent section of the population offers some part of their contribution in labor. That would open the way for emotional integration, and help those various sections whose economic status is obviously uneven to come closer.

Community organization in rural areas needs therefore to recognize this new objective, i.e., the raising of community contributions, if not matching grants to what is received from outside, from among the members of the community. A part of this contribution should come in the form of community labor voluntarily donated by all, the affluent and the under-privileged alike;[2] this would go a long way toward making the process of co-sharing a democratic one.

The question of donations in labor or kind becomes all the more important in a country like India. A majority of people, for whose welfare the programs are tailored, cannot make any effective contribution in cash. The logic that those who have the capacity to pay in money need not therefore participate in community labor raises the question of equity and status. Unless all members of a community agree in a limited way to take part in some common activities together, some sections of people would suffer from a sense of inferiority, and the matter of community cohesion would become a doubtful one.

What we aim to achieve in the economic field, however,

---

[2] Labor donation is popularly known in India as *Shramdan*.

is not self-sufficiency but *self-reliance*. No community can at the present stage of national and international collaboration remain in isolation. For one thing, all villages would require large measures of outside help, both financial and technical; furthermore the fact of isolation is not a healthy phenomenon. Self-sufficiency however has two facets: one emphasizes isolation; the other is concerned with self-help, and self-dependency.

SOCIAL SELF-SUFFICIENCY

Since it is neither possible, nor at this stage desirable, to think of economic self-sufficiency, the village communities should develop a feeling of self-sufficiency as far as their other resources are concerned, such as in the introduction and execution of programs and leadership, for example. A given geographical area may not be economically viable; but the society there must at least be a viable unit of planning and growth. A psychologically self-sufficient community, to express our meaning in concrete terms, should have an adequate number of competent leaders and institutions. Side by side with this, the community should also be able to give some attention to the type of relationship that would exist between the leaders and their followers, so that the two could act as a team and look to each other for psychological support and help. In fact, they should be in a position together to use all their own wealth, as well as being able to call for outside help and resources on their own terms. Far from becoming dependent on outside help, as was the parasitic plight of the villagers of the B group, the client community should then be able to stand on its own legs and lean heavily on leaders, institutions and consultants (as in A) whom they can call their own. This state of psychological self-sufficiency is, however, not only a theoretical proposition. Villages which were so organized under their own leadership and institutions would be in a better position to raise some of their economic resources from the world outside. Economic self-reliance and psychological self-sufficiency are two of the most important milestones in the ongoing journey of a developing community. When they are realized, the targets of social development will be seen to be nearer hand, as they will help to fulfill a community's essential aims in the context of its own peculiar needs.

INTEGRATED COMMUNITIES

INTER-VILLAGE INSTITUTIONS

It has been stated earlier that no single village could finance, on its own, all the services it requires. No village, be it a revenue area or a Panchayat, could likewise be considered as an economically viable unit. What is required, therefore, is the formation of inter-village institutions which will cater to the needs of bigger regions, and attend to the needs a number of individual villages at the same time. The health society of A, or the new credit cooperative born out of a merger of two others, provide excellent examples of this. An aim of community organization should therefore be to develop inter-community or inter-village bodies.

There should be no theoretical objection, however, to the one-village, one-institution approach. One may, in fact, plan for development of village units of regional institutions, or even for independent institutions in the village itself, in areas where the villages are big enough to sustain them. There is a great need to demarcate the areas of functioning of these two types of institutions, and to discover which ones should function at the village level and which others would federate on inter-village basis. Most of the Indian villages for example could easily maintain on their own a primary school, a youth club, a women's league (*Mahila Mandal*) and an adult literacy center. Outside this limited area of services, it would be futile to expect that the villages of the present shape and size would be able to support other institutions and facilities. The new emphasis of the community organization process is therefore, on inter-village bodies, which may have sub-units functioning at village levels. These would help the villages to open up, through new contacts; they would be able to rise above the parochialism or regionalism which lead to disintegration, and perhaps even to discover more resources within themselves. The inter-village institutions would also give the area a wider range of choice in the selection of leaders. Helping to promote inter-regional integration and development, they would help the villages to take a more rational view of the many pressing problems which face them every day.

UNIPURPOSE COMMUNITY INSTITUTES

The other important aim of community organization should be to offer unipurpose rather than multifarious services through the inter-village institutions, that is, they should specialize in offering a *single* type of service, such as health, credit, oil, or agricultural equipment.

The Community Development program in India had wanted to set up multi-purpose village institutions, for the combined administration of agricultural development, social service and economic welfare. There is a widespread belief that these institutions have failed. Whether this failure is due to the multipurpose nature of these organizations is a separate question; but the conclusions of this study have specifically pointed out the merits of single-purpose institutions. (One may well plead in this context that they should now be given a trial. The needs of the Indian villages have become complex enough to require expert diagnosis by specialized institutions and help of specialized services.)

It may be that extremely specialized bodies will never have any place in rural areas, but the time has come when we should give up rigid adherence to the old belief that a few institutions set up in a few villages would be able to attend to most of the vital needs of an area. Let us not forget that the mortality rates of the multipurpose institutions in India have, in the past ten years, been alarmingly high, and that administration of more than one service may often retard the growth of optimum capacity of a single trade. Unipurpose institutions may develop the required efficiency in administration. Its inter-village structure may also bring in the necessary viability.

The need for inter-village institutions would not, however, undermine the role of single village agencies. What has been suggested earlier is, in fact, a demarcation of the two roles. It is necessary to discover which institution could operate on a single-village basis and which others must have a wider area of functioning. A number of institutions could thus operate in the village itself, while there are others which would not be able to stand all by themselves and require a larger operational basis. More social work research is thus the need of the hour. A scientific probe to find out which type of institutions could best be supported at the village level, and which others should develop inter-community contacts, may help in this matter. There is no doubt, however, that most of the vital services required for development and growth of an area will have to be administered on an inter-village basis. Thus, the important objectives of community organization in creating a small, pluralistic society should be the adoption of inter-village bodies, with areas of specialization for each, and the assurance of smooth teamwork between the larger units, their village counterparts and independent village institutions.

The concept of inter-village institutions would not in any way interfere with the more vital question of village self-reliance. Growth of development potentials of a single village or of the small community would not be retarded by this concept. The larger cooperation will, on the other hand, be a matter of the alliance of mature village leaders. They would unfold the latent potentialities of dormant resources over a wider horizon, and lead to the growth of an inter-village pattern as the basis of rural development.

SECULARIZATION

The other aim of community organization is secularization. Secularization of the objectives of village institutions and creation of a broad-based leadership drawing from the ranks of various castes and religious groups would go a long way to strengthen the process of planned social change in the grassroots community. This could not only create a vertical integration of ideals and needs with the aims of a secular state, but may also facilitate horizontal amalgamation of various interests and groups.

The indigenous welfare institutions in India have a rather doubtful tradition in this regard. Quite a few of them, even those in the towns and those functioning on an all-India basis, cater to the needs of members of particular castes, sects or religious groups. The village institutions which are now being set up as a result of rural development should eschew this path and uphold a broader objective.

Secularization is the ideal and should be aimed at not only for the realization of a mere moralistic goal, but for strengthening the very base of rural development. Villages in India are small units, and permit little enough developmental work to take place in an efficient manner; the caste and religious divisions fragment this work even further. Sometimes the division is also cross-territorial. This infinitesimal factionalism is not exactly a source of strength. Thus it becomes absolutely necessary that one of the objectives of community organization should be to develop secular outlooks in all institutions. Such a process would obviously help the opening up of closed units. It is easy to see that secularization would also lead to the best mobilization of available resources, and bring within the reach of an institution much larger human and material assets than what could be found in limited groups and communities. Positive antagonism of forlorn groups could also, in this way, be won over. This would foster emotional integration and act as the most powerful single agent for modernization of the rural community.

The institutions of both A and B groups, our study reveals, had thrown open their gates to all religions and castes. The inter-village institutions of A group had a Muslim village as one of its members, and brought within their fold the so-called scheduled castes as well. The process of secularization in A group had indeed gone a step further and included among its constituents representatives of tribal hamlets, too.

Development in India, following the ideology of the State, accepts secularization as an accredited policy. A persistent drive, pursued at the level of the village community, may well help to realize its full implications. The lesson of the Sriniketan experiment is that the process of secularization is not a difficult one; a uniform policy of community organization would hold good for all sections of population— Hindus, Muslims, tribals and the scheduled castes included. Contrary to popular belief, what is required for the various racial, religious or caste groups is not a series of separate approaches or processes, but a varied program of social welfare suited to the common needs of the different groups and communities.[3] An important aim of community organization should therefore be the conscious promotion of this process of secularization. The trends of development permit this overture, and all that it requires is a determined push by a cadre of trained communtiy organizers.

DIRECT PARTICIPATION IN AN OPEN SOCIETY

The village community often appears to be a loose federation of a number of competitive and unequal groups. One way of promoting integration is systematic exercise in community participation. What is required is the widest possible participation of all groups and individuals in the various decision-making apparatuses of the community. Such participation should, however, be homogeneous and

---

[3] No separate tribal policy, for example, is required.

equitable. All of the various sections of population, and not only the so-called leaders or elected ones, will have to take part at all stages of decision-making, planning and execution. This means that the agencies of development should not have indirect constitutions. Neither should the decision-making bodies be, once they are elected by the populace, left entirely to the care of the selected few. The institutions in rural areas may, on the other hand, be direct democracies and give all their members enough opportunity for intensive participation. Planning and execution of programs should be made in open sessions, so that all adult members can associate on their free will with the various processes of execution. A sense of community identity and integration cannot grow when the general members of an institution vote only once a year to elect their few representatives, and then leave the elected chiefs to take care of the remaining business. It may seem somewhat strange that formation of inter-village institutions and direct participation are being advocated at the same time. Would that not mean too unwieldly and cumbersome an affair? While it is true that an inter-village base would increase the number of participants, the fact that the inter-village bodies would be single-purpose in nature would obviate this difficulty. Regional institutions with multifarious programs would simply not be able to serve the purpose.

An aim of community organization should be to dismantle closed circles wherever they are, and encourage development of direct democratic behavior in an open political atmosphere. That would help to provide increasing opportunities of socialization to all members. Continuous participation and co-sharing will reduce social distances, draw out the latent resources of the last man of the group, and provide its members with an intense feeling of community belonging.

Methods of Obtaining Community Decisions

In the direct democracy that is now envisaged [4] the method of decision-making cannot be left to majority vote. The aim of community organization is to ensure development of mutual tolerance, respect for each other's point of view, willingness to sacrifice one's own immediate satisfaction for the benefit of the community. Community decisions

---

[4] Found in existence in some of the institutions (*vide* the case records of Ghani oil cooperative societies).

should, therefore, be the "integrated decisions" of the group as a whole, and not only of its dominant section. The purpose of community action is group cohesion. Imposition of the views of a section of population over the rest who might lose in a voting, would leave the latter dissatisfied and may tear apart the community. Arriving at an integrated decision, in which all members of the group find their points of view reflected, is the other name for "consensus." Intermittent discussions, frequent consultations and mutual understanding should lead to the integration of interest and development of a consensus. Majority vote or the traditional method of social coercion (as in the conflict situation in B) in an unhomogenous and stratified society may well threaten the integrity of community life. Development of the machinery and traditions of mutual consultation and constant sharing of interests could, on the other hand, replace the practice of majority rule. To provide this integrative base to the rural community should be another one of the aims of community organization.

Voluntary Basis of Community Organization

Community organization is a democratic process. In the Indian context of community development, where the role of the Government is increasingly becoming all-pervading, the aim of democratic development should not only be to ensure direct participation in institutional functioning, but also to promote voluntary processes in every facet of rural development work. A democratic community must necessarily have a built-in process of voluntary action. Its institutions should be non-governmental in nature, run preferably by voluntary organizations or local bodies.

As in the case of secularization, so also for the development of a voluntary infra-structure: the ethos of social development easily permits its planned encouragement. The government-sponsored program of Community Development had in fact once been keen to promote non-official associations and organizations under the immediate aegis of the Government. The effort, self-defeating in many ways, had met only with limited success. For there are many preconditions for development of voluntary bodies, and a government, however genuine its interest, may often fail to take note of them. The first condition in this regard is that the village institutions be as far as possible economically self-reliant. The other is that outside voluntary welfare organizations, rather than the government, should be gradually encouraged to take interest in community welfare work.

SOCIALIZATION OF THE IMAGE OF RURAL ELITE

Development in a growing society is often reduced to mere realization of a series of physical targets. Of the many purposes that the latter serve, one is that they become the prestige symbols of the village elite. Big buildings, concrete structures and long winding roads add to the feathers of the leaders, and cast their spell on the general body of people. These external achievements often help to win over the government leaders who are anxious to spend money, and also to develop a monopolistic control of village affairs. Items of development in such cases often do nothing but fulfill the leaders' needs for recognition. They also build the titantic images of these leaders, and frighten away the lesser men. A great stumbling-block to rural development is the projection of these images and the monopolistic control of village leaders (compare the widely discussed "cult of personality").

They provide a perennial source of resistance to development. The leaders who earn great prestige with the State quickly move into the upper echeleon of the affluent sector and eat up most of the benefits themselves. The villagers, consequently, have to lie low in poverty and despair, deprived of their due. The higher the rate of upward mobility of the small group of leaders, the larger is the area of stagnation of the weak and the poor. One must break through this resistance by socializing the image of the "big brother." It is equally necessary to ensure a vertical mobility in the leadership structure. Whereas the leaders must understand that the aim of social development is not only to help those who are already overprotected, but to achieve for all sections of the population the satisfaction of their basic social and economic needs, the clientele of development must treat their leaders as mere guides and aids. The former should always be in a position to grant leave to their leaders as soon as there are others to take over or when the control they manifest becomes oppressive. An important aim of community organization is to emphasize this earthy character of the leaders of community institutions. In a country where hero-worship and idolatory go hand-in-hand, the basis of democratic development can never be safe unless and until this "image breaking" becomes a professional responsibility of the community organizer. There is no doubt that such an assignment would require courage on the part of the social worker, and also inflict quite some pain into the otherwise peaceful life of the community. But the aim of community organization is not the establishment of a cowardly peace of adjustment and surrender, but to create the fire of development in many a stagnant soul.

CHAPTER XII

CONCLUSIONS AND THEORIES

CONCLUSIONS

The balance-sheet ends in the preceding chapter. A comparative account of social work and social change—the type of developments which took place in A & B groups of villages, as a result of the different methods of approach—have been described at length. One wonders whether it is not time now to pull together the threads of these discussions and sum up the major conclusions of our study. This may also bring out a few important lessons.

On the basis of case studies, opinion and attitude surveys of leaders, institutions, programs, methods, and their impact, a comparative assessment of the qualitative growth that had taken place in the two groups of villages has been provided. Social changes in A and B were related to the two methods of work, one analogous to the social work method of community organization, and the other a different approach followed by the catalysts of the B group of villages. The methods helped to develop in the individuals and groups who live in the A and B clusters of villages the power to identify their own needs in some form or other, and enabled them to meet them as well, each in their own way. The extent to which the individual and groups in either of the areas have been able to control the institutions and make them their own agencies for the satisfaction of indigenous needs have, in my view, signified the measure of growth arrived at.

The roles of the institutions, the leaders and the pedestrian clientele—the men-in-the-street, who form the communities of the two groups of villages—these three together represented (to my mind) the ingredients of what one may well call a "system" of social development. The primary purpose of the study was to find the relationship of the people to the total apparatus of development which was to help solve the needs of the area. The fact that this

search and a cause-and-effect study of the social work process led to the discovery that a specific system of social
development could be found, and that there was some variance between the system's operational features in two different areas, may be considered as an important lesson of
this comparative account. The other aim—namely, that of
finding the gap, if there was any, between the two types of
developments that had taken place in A and B groups—led
to the discovery that differential emphasis did exist in the
operational appearances of the system in the two groups of
villages. The focus of our study has thus been on determining the correlation between the methods used by the catalyst bodies of A and B, and the types of social changes
which took place. The divergences in the operational features of the two systems represent the difference that the
impact of the two methods produced. While the structure
of the system is described later, it may be worthwhile to
sum up in brief the major differences which existed in the
development of the two groups of villages.

The pattern of development in A group followed the
reciprocal lines of mutual feedback. It was the people who
controlled the institutions. The institutions provided the
layout for the design of development; but the fact that they
—the institutions—themselves were amenable not only to
the influence of the members of their formal committees
or boards of control, but also to the general rank and file,
was of the highest importance. The design for development
was determined by the local institutions, the institutions
were controlled by their formal committees and the latter
remained responsive to the influences of all its members,
the general bodies of the local communities. If this represented the web of developmental relationship in A group,
the help that was available from the State government was
to be secured by the village elite in the manner in which
the committees and general bodies of their institutions required them to do. The aid that came often took the shape
of (matching grants) and the relationship which held the
elements together, i.e. State, local institutions, village elite
and the general body, were more or less democratic, based
on reciprocal relationship and mutual feed-back. The job
of the catalyst agency in A, that is, the Department of Rural
Reconstruction was merely to activize the group of village
leaders. They in turn, depended on the people of the base

line for their support, and to the catalyst-agents for guidance.

In B group, the catalysts remained estranged. They were a number of outsiders who functioned through the instrumentality of a few indigenous village leaders. The latter controlled the institutions and laid down, in their name, designs of development. The State supplied finances; and while the catalyst agency, the State, the village elites, institutions and the general body, were all closely linked to each other, the process that held them was not an interdependent democratic one. This absence of the democratic process was, (to my mind) due to the fact that the method followed in B group was not analogous to the method of social work.

The ingredients of the two developmental systems or models were generally the same and provided a uniform structure. Composed of six major elements, the system in fact was common to both, and may well be described as indispensable to a growing society. Those elements were: (i) external catalyst body (an institution in A group and a group of political leaders in B), (ii) the State, (iii) community organizations or local institutions, (iv) the general members who compose the community for whom all development is required, (v) the village elite and members of the governing bodies of (iii), and (vi) the process or method of work. The ingredients of the developmental system thus appeared to be the same in both cases, but since the process or method which make the system what it is was different in the two areas, the operational shape took divergent forms. The social changes which occurred in the two groups could hardly, therefore, have been considered of equal significance. For the type of social changes which take place in an area depend on the type of relationship which exists among the various elements of the developmental system, and in turn determine its operational feature.

In B group, the external catalysts and the indigenous elite, (i) and (v), stood at the apex; whereas the indigenous elite and the general members, (v) and (iv), occupied this position in A. But what characterized most of the differential phases of the two systems, however, was the "vertical mobility" of both the general members and the indigenous elite in one, and its absence in the other. This possibility was evident in A, and did not exist at all in the status-quo-oriented society of B. If we have been looking for a gap in the developments or changes that had taken place in the two groups of villages, it lies here in the inter-actional process of the six elements—a process which represents and follows the method of work utilized by each group of catalysts.

The types of social change that took place in A, then, were different from those which were evident in B. The changes in A were brought about by a democratic process of self-help and self-determination. It was people-centric and self-propelling. Decisions here were a result of pro-longed deliberations of the members of the decision-making apparatus and the final decision-making body, meaning thereby the leaders who were on the committees or boards of the institutions. Due to the factor of vertical mobility, the power blocks in A had no fixed points for themselves. The opening chapter of the study makes this clear.[1] It shows how the leadership in A was transferred to the younger generation; and there also we saw that the onus for "integrated" decision lay not on one single individual but on the group as a whole. The systematic division of roles and defined assignment of functions among the de-cision-makers in A were evident. The vigor with which these were adhered to and furthered had likewise left the impression that the group had almost an ethical commit-ment to democracy. If ours has thus been primarily a study of perceived needs, as viewed from the standpoint of social work, it is evident that the villagers in A, the lead-ers as well as rank and file, were well able to fend for themselves. They could verbalize and define their needs, enumerate them in formal committees and gatherings, and make a democratic effort to meet them as well. This did not happen in B. The reins here were in the hands of outside leaders. It was they who surveyed and defined needs, not of their own but of the people of the B group of villages. The changes which took place in A were accord-ingly of a very different character. Based on a conscious appraisal of their own needs, what was achieved here was at least a reflection of the aspirations of the people.

Leadership in A was therefore widely diffused. A part of it was technocratic and professional such as the leader-ship of Mr. X and Mr. P, whereas real decision-making

---

[1] Chapter 3.

was entrusted to less-equipped but democratically-elected representatives. The institutions in the A group of villages were also the centers of development. Planning was institutionally perceived and institutionally implemented, although sometimes it proceeded at its own pace, at the cost of rapid physical development. What was thus emphasized in the wake of this democratic growth was the responsibility of each institution to work its own sphere, and also the great value of institutional democracy. This pattern of democratic development received further impetus in A. This was due to the willingness of the people to make substantial contributions for financing their own welfare services. Self-helpful to some extent even in finances, the institutions in A were thus not so very grant-minded as they were in B. Neither was the spirit of self-help and development confined to the formal administration of social service institutions. It spread its roots far and wide, and grew with the development of a variety of programs—recreation and education included.

The changes that were brought about in the A group of villages were concerned not so much with the achievement of physical targets, or institutional growth merely for the sake of it. The focus, on the other hand, was on development of the individuals and on personal change. Growth of dormant potentialities of the members of a community to the point where they could identify their own needs and resources, and thereafter prepare a program of change by their own efforts, was the objective. The efforts toward the preparation of new members of the Ghani Oil Cooperative for higher responsibilities, through division of labor and through committee meetings, bear ample testimony to this. The pattern of development was not to be laid down by the hierarchy of these institutions. The individuals who manned them, rather, were at the center of all development. Recognition of their role in the process of decision-making and implementation thus helped the task of actualization and self-development. The various persons who composed the rural community were therefore at the vanguard of the decision-making process. Their interests were at the center. Quite often this commitment to democratic processes was almost irksome and looked like stale ritual; yet it showed the way and indicated what the values of the community were. The changes that had taken place in the goals of its present day leaders, as distinguished from the goals of their older counterparts whom the process of social development had replaced, had also become clear.

The institutional developments in the A group of villages had made the area a psychologically self-sufficient unit of development. This was due to the fact that the community institutions in this group well served the needs of the area. The people of A functioned in an integrated manner, and exercised complete control over these bodies through a well-developed leadership that was responsive to the needs of the community. All these led to a feeling of psychological self-sufficiency, a feeling that the villagers could stand on their own legs and did not need external support of outside leaders. The situation might not have, and in fact did not, lead to a self-sufficient economy; but it certainly developed a feeling of social self-sufficiency and self-reliance. The community now considered that its technical and organizational resources were good enough to provide a plan on the basis of which they could call for such outside economic assistance and aid as might have carried their vehicle of development forward.

An important aspect of change that took place in A was that the programs which were introduced became gradually stabilized. They spread their roots in the minds of the clientele and did not hang loose as an external imposition. In my opinion, it was due to the methodological support the programs received from their catalysts that this process of integration was achieved. In A these were introduced through the institutions and the village leaders, who were chosen in turn by the people themselves. In B these were pushed in by a group of self-appointed benevolents, and therefore did not become a part of the indigenous setup.

The aim of social work is not only to offer help to a vulnerable group at a certain point of time. The purpose is rather to strengthen the clients' own hands. A certain degree of financial self-reliance, organizational development, and growth of indigenous leadership is therefore imperative for determining the basis of change in a social-work-directed client group. The infrastructure of indigenous resources is therefore to be considered a basic minimum requirement. *What is required for this purpose is not only institutionalization of the process of social change but its socialization as well.* The latter should not be imposed from the top, and even when so imposed, should in the shortest possible time become the choice of the humblest of its members. This is precisely what had happened in A. Realization of the fact that a "community" is made of innumerable cells of individuals, and that development means the growth of attitudinal changes and individual potentialities in as many members of the community as possible, is the other aim of social work. The developments which took place in A did, in my view, attend to these needs of social work, and certain essential features of a society which social workers strive to bring in could have easily been found there.

In a country like India, the social work process should further develop the concept of regional development, as opposed to communal or centrifugal tendencies which create unworkable units; unworkable not only because they become uneconomic for providing an optimum quantity of welfare services, but also because the leaders and institutions of the area cannot find enough psychological satisfaction in such a limited milieu. Their efforts consequently get dispersed and the leaders turn for their satisfaction elsewhere, sometimes even in socially undesirable channels. Secularization of the decision-making apparatus is likewise equally necessary, and particularly so in a developing country. To sum up, what we look for in social work is all-around changes in some key elements of the society. Changes in individuals and their personalities, changes which would lead to the growth of corporate personalities in any field of development, are the aim. The area where the system is to operate should therefore be large enough to ensure that the decision-making is not confined to a few or guided by sub-regional and communal considerations. The broadening of vision, the expansion of the territorial base, personal change, vertical mobility, and democratic give-and-take, are some of the vital features of the type of change that social work endeavors to bring in.

If these factors were achieved in the A group of villages, it needs to be pointed out that it was also for this very reason that the process of development took slow strides in the area; neither did it always yield what could be considered as positive results. The physical targets, for example, were, as compared to B, far less impressive. The rate at which tangible targets, e.g., construction of schools, buildings, and roads, were fulfilled, was slower than that of the intangibles. The changes evident in the area led on the other hand to the development of psychological self-sufficiency, organizational growth, democratic leadership and correct procedures of work. The all-absorbing democratic process, however, had also made the community self-engrossed and self-centered, concerned merely with its own problems and worries. The people of the area had consequently become apolitical, and apathetic to the needs and interests of the outside world. Psychological self-sufficiency had led to comparative isolation from the rest of the country. An extreme concern for self-development, the natural corollary of excessive welfarism, added fuel to this process. The fact that the leaders and the institutions had to function within a democratic setup accentuated the cumulative impact of all the negative results, and often led to conflicting circumstances.

Since the leaders in A group had to depend mainly on the support of their rank and file, the natural tendency was to wait and secure everyone's concurrence, and postpone any precipate development. The absence of a sense of immediacy and vigor were its results. The continuous democratic exercise of give-and-take had also led to a spectacular development in the aspirations of the rank and file, and their ability to make sacrifices was enhanced. The latter led to a rise in expectations, and hunger for more and more services. The democratic framework had thus held back the paces of rapid physical growth; it created at the same time far-reaching community expectations. The inevitable result of this was some amount of irreducible frustration, which, as we have seen earlier, had steadily mounted and eaten into the vitals of growth.

The leaders and the followers in A had reached quite a level of democratic practice and institutional development. They had also mastered the art of planning and coordination. They knew how to hold meetings, keep proceedings, prepare records, maintain decorum, and also, through well-recognized division of functions, roles and jobs, to mobilize the community as a whole. The leaders in A were thus successful not only in associating the general public with the process of decision-making but also in obtaining substantial financial and material support from them. Respect for democratic values and recognition of the merit of individual contributors had invoked a wholesome response in the larger community, and made the latter responsive to the developmental processes initiated by the catalysts.

The process of conversion of indifferent members were

indicative of this response, and of the level of growth obtained in A. The unwilling citizens who were not prepared to fall in line were won over with patience, respect and educative endeavors. This commitment to democracy gave a sense of direction to the community in A, a sense that B lacked in substantial measure. If all these were to the credit of A, the debit side of the balance-sheet was not altogether encouraging. The fact that the leaders of A found themselves unable to move forward at a faster pace often frustrated the planners. Since the process of decision-making was democratic, the sense of frustration quickly traveled downwards to the various members of the community, the rank and file included. This led to widespread dissatisfaction, and often had a cumulative effect on the community as a whole. The latter developed as a result of this an aggressive temperament and displayed obvious signs of imbalance, which in the course of time became as if a part of the developmental system. In spite of the many hallmarks of qualitative development, it was interesting to find that the community in A—its leaders as well as the rank and file wore the aspect of frustrated and persistent combatants, although their targets of attack were not always evident even to them.

The situation in A sometimes led to doubtful reactions. As the people in general became dissatisfied with their own rate of physical achievement, quite often it led to a frantic search for a scapegoat, one on whom they could squarely put all their blames. The officers of the Department naturally came in handy for this purpose. This tendency to find a scapegoat was further aggravated, as the present leaders of A remembered that the catalysts of the Department were in the past responsible for perpetuation of the older group of leaders and the vested interests they represented. The fact that, even now, quite a few of the Department's officials were, in remembrance of the past relationship, prepared to support the older generation, created a sense of near-hostility. It was interesting to note that the weight of democracy and the process of socialization had thus led to uneven results. Not only were the physical targets low, but the built-in impatience created a vicious circle of mutual persecution, the wrath against the outsider being ultimately turned to one's own company.

The B group of villages had secured, on the other hand, impressive physical targets of development. Here the determined group of indigenous elite, backed by a number of powerful political leaders, introduced quick developing programs of welfare and amenities. The fact that decision-making was the prerogative of a small group of people did not prevent its leaders from going ahead. That the amenities so created by the exclusive efforts of the benevolent leaders lay almost unused and untapped by the vast number of villagers, and had touched only a few, also did not matter to them. Quite often the group that really forged ahead—the limited group of decision-makers—bore, as a result, the burden of massive institutions on their own shoulders, almost all by themselves.

This separated the leaders from the rest of the community, and created a sense of isolation. The programs and amenities introduced in B, therefore did not become stabilized or integrated with the culture of the community. Nor did they become a part of its resources or potentialities of development.

The process of work in B was leader-centric. It did not stimulate a great many people, much less provide them with democratic opportunities for self-determination. The needs of individual villagers were not at the center of the focus here. What the group of political leaders who lived at Belpur or Calcutta wanted to be done in B was more important to the local leaders than the wishes and desires of the village community. The process of work could not, therefore, relate the programs of development to the needs of the community. The institutions were on the other hand, used to translate into action the needs of the elite. What the outside catalysts and the local leaders conceived to be the needs of the village, the institutions promptly took note of. The latter did not therefore fulfill the villagers' needs, nor were they amenable to the control of the general community. The individual members of the village community, accordingly, did not develop the requisite quantum of community integration, such as that which might have led to the growth of a welfare community.

Not that the extent of aggression or frustration prevailing in B was any less. In A, the community stood together to share the frustrations stemming from the inadequate paces of development and the incapacity of the community. The victim of agression in A was the outsider catalyst, i.e., the Department itself. Frustration in B originated from the discontent of the rank and file and led to polarization of forces, estranging the leaders from the community and the community from the institutions. The only cohesive impact it had was to bring the outside catalyst and the local leaders together. Quite often it also led to the surrender of the villagers to the small group of self-appointed headmen, who in their turn were eager to function as tools in the hands of the well-intentioned political leaders.

The system we have spoken of was common to both A and B; only the operational features were different. Out of the six elements mentioned earlier, three were most active in B—the State, the outside catalyst and the local leaders. The community in B lay passive, and the process that held the elements together was not democratic. In A the responsibility and onus of action were with the local leaders and the community. The process was democratic. The former led to substantial physical development, and the latter to inner development of the rural community. It is difficult for a developing nation to choose from among these two techniques and types of development, and say which one it is opting for. There is in fact a national ambivalence in this regard and it has often led to strange conclusions. In their professions, the leaders of the developing societies have always been clear, that the type of development the A group signifies is just what they are looking for; whereas, in their practice, the same leaders and the catalyst bodies have often leaned toward B. Anxious to get results, they have preferred to move forward with physical accomplishments and often ignored the cause of "inner" social development and sustained democratic growth.

My main purpose here is not to recommend either of the types but merely to state that the outlines of a developmental system have now become evident as a result of our study. The changes which take place in a specific group of clientele is, however, determined by the respective roles of its various components. If the social work process is followed, the sixth element would lead to a strengthening of the community itself whereas a mere amenity deal would lead to a consolidation of the position of a few and follow a pattern of development where physical accomplishments may be impressive. If one succeeds in the short run the feeling is that the other would produce long term results of more enduring value.

We have stated before that the process of change had

been stabilized in the A group of villages, and that far-reaching results were visible there. This might indicate that I am convinced of the durability of these developments, and feel that they are of greater permanence as compared to what had happened in B. Again, it may also seem that the rate of *physical* development in B was higher than that of A, and that the speed at which motivational and institutional processes of social and personal development had made their headway in A was of a comparatively much higher calibre. Social workers will, of course, find in the type of changes introduced in the A group of villages the desired impact of their methods. Yet it must be made clear that the two positions stated above regarding A and B cannot be treated as final conclusions of this study. How permanent or durable these changes will be in A will only be ascertainable after a lapse of time, when, as has been mentioned before, a repeat study is conducted on the basis of some schedules and questionnaires.

If there is a clear danger that the physical development of B could crumble in course of time, there is an equal danger, if I may say so, of a similar collapse taking place in A as well. The setback in B may come easily, when the present leadership, fostered from outside, either gets estranged from its catalyst advisers or is led to complete isolation from their hostile clientele. The collapse in A may, on the other hand, be due to the nervous tension to which it has voluntarily subjected itself. This tension may increase, as frustration mounts. The gap that exists between aspirations and capacities, the will to work and capacity to mobilize, may well create a tragic psychosis in A. The community in withdrawing into itself, and shutting its doors to the "unreasonable" outsiders to whom they have already raised wrathful eyes, may pave the path of self-destruction. But that would be, it is my contention, a failure of the future process of work; and even a total collapse like the one feared will not in any way reduce the value of the changes which social work methods had once brought to a given society at a particular point of time.

Even if the methods used by the Department of Rural Reconstruction may not be regarded as those of scientific social work, their impact, nevertheless, did produce different results in A than what was achieved in B group of villages. A group had, as it were, become a different society. Differing in norms, institutional equipment, social ethics, motives and perspectives, it had opted for a totally different ethos of development— an ethos which is greatly in harmony with the ethos of social work. The type of changes —process-centered, individual-based and democratic—which characterized the developments in A cannot but therefore represent the very dimensions of social change which social work introduces in the context of a developing society.

THEORIES

A review of the growing relations of social work and social change is bound to remain incomplete without an analysis of their theoretical implications. What follows in the ensuing pages, therefore, is an examination of a few basic principles of social work, as they have emerged in the context of Indian culture. As social work sets the pace of social change, the latter too brings its impact on the structure and functions of social work methods. The modifications, worth taking note of, in the theory of social work in India, are discussed here.

American contributions to theories of social work still remain the most outstanding. Historically, the early beginnings of the profession can be traced in the labor settlements of the United Kingdom, the methods of social work[2] were carefully developed in the United States. What is true of practice is also true of theory and at least of the theory of social work. For both of these, developing hand in hand, had their most wide-spread trial in the American society and have now attained a great deal of sophistication.

The development is particularly due to the systematic use of "skills" or "methods" in specific groups and communities. The twofold problem faced by "the new world" —the need for providing a democratic infrastructure to the small community, and the integration of a heterogeneous group of immigrants who belonged to diverse racial, cultural and linguistic origins—had, indeed, called for an extensive use of social work skills. The fact that this integration had to take place in the orbits of small communities made application of social work skills all the more important.

The behavioral norms of the respective units of habitat where these groups lived, be it the town or the country, had

---

[2] All three methods: case work, group work and community organization.

also to be democratic; for that led to social cohesion and cooperative functioning. These factors, as well as the urge toward stimulation of the leadership and organizational know-how available in small groups and communities, led to further sharpening of social work tools. Development of interest groups and functional communities, once composed of heterogenous elements, and the tendency toward self-help and self-reliance, had likewise established the need for social work. If these accounted for widespread use of consistent methods and led to a refinement of those methods, theoretical sophistication developed as a logical corollary and further helped to round out the body of practical knowledge.

Social work knowledge is practice-based, and although it draws extensively from other social sciences, the core of the practical know-how or the 'theories' of practice stem from the field itself. It is small wonder, therefore, that production of social work literature, growth of schools of social work, as well as the development of the body of knowledge, have all been most phenomenal in the United States; for the practice itself has been the most widespread there. Barring a few books,[3] published in Great Britain and fewer still elsewhere, theoretical contributions to social work outside the U.S.A. are almost negligible. In India, the writings have been peripheral. The bulk of it is in the area of philosophy. Although a few sociological, psychological and historical contributions are now forthcoming, writings in the area of methods have been very meager. Even Peter Kunstler's studies on group work and community organization,[4] which merely deal with structural description of the two practices, have no counterparts in India. The result of this limited interest has, it is obvious, severely retarded the growth of the profession.

UNIVERSAL AND SPECIFICS OF THEORY

If social work knowledge derives from practice, the theories of profession can only grow when the theory-builders, themselves practitioners, are free to draw upon their own recorded experiences or to study field work practices conducted by others. The inability to learn anything beyond what is available from the recorded experiences of the

---

[3] The list is hardly a dozen in U.K. and even fewer in India.

[4] See Peter Kunstler's *Community Organisation in Great Britain* (London: Faber and Faber Ltd.), pp. 15-24.

limited use of social work skills in one particular cultural setting, however rich may be that experience, has in a way deprived the profession of much of its vitality. Although social work, like any other social science, deals with basic theories that are of generic value and could be universally applied, the fact that the knowledge from which the profession could draw its methods stemmed only from a limited social situation must have adversely affected its position. As social work develops, acquiring new insights and perspectives, the more diversified is the base from where its knowledge flows, and the more varied and purposeful will be its growth. For one must remember that although generic postulates are of universal value, specific sub-cultures have their own peculiar needs too. Universalized theories, when tested in the particular conditions of specific milieus, may therefore often require modification.

It is not my contention that different theories of social work are necessary for different countries of the world. What is important, in recognizing the universal value of social work, is that its various theories and methods have to undergo necessary modifications in different conditions of life. The theories so modified in a variety of cultures could then emerge empirically richer, and acquire greater universal validity. It is for this reason that we regret the lack of Indian contribution to social work theories. The fact that the contribution is particularly poor in the area of methods has indeed led many to believe that their value yet remains to be established in India.

The universal base of social work cannot, however, be disputed. Viewed from the perspectives of fundamentals, the components of social work practices are three in number. First of all, there are the basic postulates, which are as valid in India as anywhere else; these are of generic significance. The other two are called for the specifics in the particular context of the needs of an indigenous culture, and those born of the peculiar demands of our philosophy of social work. The philosophy of social work in modern India has, however, been greatly influenced by the liberalism of the West and its sciences. To the extent that the core of the Indian philosophy, shaped by its leaders like Raja Rammohan Roy, Ranade, Gokhale, Tagore and Gandhi, has drawn from the impact of the great revolutions of the

West,[5] its fundamentals cannot be very different from the philosophy that had mothered the profession there. If out of the three components, the scale weighs heavily on the side of the universals, it will not in any case undermine the value of the specifics. For the latter are of particular significance in making the universals applicable to a definite area, as well as in reshaping its structure and functions. The need for Indian contribution to the theory of social work, and particularly in the area of methods, cannot therefore be over-emphasized. Its importance lies, if I may say so, not only in discovering how these theories could be made more applicable to India, but also in making the social work skills more applicable to different human situations and in giving them a *global* validity.

COMMUNITY ORGANIZATION—NEW ACCENTS IN THEORY AND PRACTICE

The second half of this chapter is, therefore, devoted to an examination of some of the important theories of social work, or at least of one of its methods, that of community organization, or inter-group work.[6] On the basis of the empirical data presented in the book, my effort is to bring out certain specific principles of community organization which are of special relevance to the developing society in India. While most of the theories of social work as found in the West[7] are applicable to our conditions as well, there are certain principles and objectives which are of special importance to us. These, I claim, have become obvious as a result of this study, and if properly understood and practiced would make social work in India more purposive and meaningful. While a few variations and developments of community organization, its objectives and principles, have come to our knowledge from this study of "methods," and are of specific value to us, there is every reason to believe that a grafting of these would make the general theory of community organization itself of greater relevance to the field of social work at large. This chapter records some of

---

[5] Industrial Revolution, French Revolution, American War of Independence, Bolshevik Revolution, Growth of science and technology etc., etc.

[6] (a) Community organization definition is:

   (b) Group work definition is:

[7] Theories enunciated by Murray G. Ross, Sanderson and Polson, etc.

CONCLUSIONS AND THEORIES

these theoretical conclusions and underlines a few specific trends.

It has been noted earlier that the methods introduced by the Department of Rural Reconstruction were not completely identifiable with those described in social work literature. However, the discrepancy, obviously stems from the demands of cultural reality; a practice that is recognized as correct may, in different circumstances, emphasize different sets of principles and objectives. The structure of community organization, undergoing a basic transformation in a different sub-culture, may look very different from its traditional image. The changes that take place need not therefore be considered as deviations from any basic norm, but as adaptations required to suit the needs of a growing society. Some of the principles and objectives which have become evident in the course of this study may give a new meaning to theories and methods, not only as they apply to this country, but also in the development of the theoretical content of the teaching and practice of social work itself. It may be that the specifics we talk of were already there, latently embodied in the structure of methods, and have only become more obvious in the context of Indian rural development. There could, however, be no doubt that even this limited recognition will go a long way toward realizing the role of community organization in India, and make its theory relevant to the context of her rural society.

A FEW TRENDS

It has been my endeavor to show in the previous chapters that the two methods followed by the two types of catalysts in A and B had led to different results. In the diversified developments that occurred in the A group was reflected the type of changes social work seeks to bring in, and this was owing to the fact that the method used in A was akin to "community organization"—the sixth element in the "developmental system" referred to earlier. This empirical review has brought to the fore certain characteristics of special import. Some of these important trends of community organization found in the context of our culture and society are described below.

It would be evident that community organization is the most important element in the developmental system, the chief agent of social change in village India today. Rural community organizations must also, if they are to be of value to our specific background, be socially self-reliant and psychologically self-sufficient units of development. Inter-village in scope and democratic in structure, they should permit vertical mobility of the leader-follower relationship; for that alone can enable the agencies to remain responsive to the needs of its clientele. Community organizations in a developing society should also be secular in nature. The institutions built as a result of the workings of the community organization process should be the products of *participatory democracy*—socialization rather than coercion or majority vote being the method of obtaining agreement and consensus.

COMMUNITY ORGANIZATION AND THE DEVELOPMENTAL SYSTEM

The question of determining the exact role played by the sixth element of our developmental system (the process or method of work) in developing communities is inextricably linked with the understanding of the functions of the developmental system. A new emphasis in the developing society is on this model. The various features of the community organization process could so orient the parent system that its directions became one with those of scientific social work. A matter of major significance is thus the working of this system, and the role of the process of community organization in it. Community organization is in fact a major adjunct to it as well as its chief pace-setter. The system with its six parts is a common feature in rural India, wherever developments are taking place in a serious and planned manner. If this system thus provides the main basis of social growth, the type of change which it ultimately produces depends on the process itself: the process guides the interaction of the other five elements, and therein lies its importance. For while the *system* is common to all developmental situations, the results it produces will vary, according as the *process* of community organization utilized to secure the desired type of development varies.

The developmental system was common to both A and B groups of villages. If the model is tested on a wider basis, it will be evident that all programs of development concerning the small rural community operate through the same system. Definitionally the system has a static as well as a dynamic role, a pure as well as an operational structure. While the identity of the system is more readily evident in its pure form and static state, it is the operational structure and its dynamics that leads to interaction among the various elements and sets in motion the process of change.

The aim of all development is undoubtedly the good of the individual, his increasing welfare and happiness. The value of a developmental project is therefore determined by the type of impact it produces on the people at large. Individuals, who form groups and communities (and give meaning to all institutions), are its clientele. While a proper relationship between the six elements determines the character of the end product, the relationship between the various elements depends on the dynamics of the system itself. The dynamics in turn depend on the method or the process, i.e., the sixth element. The process or the method therefore provides the key. It determines the quality and character of changes that take place in the client community, and influences the dynamics of relationship in the system itself. Similarly, whether development would lead to the benefit of only a chosen few, or ensure that its fruits reach the general members of a community, "the last man first," would depend very much on the way the system operates. Quite often it may lead to aggrandizement of the catalyst body, helping the latter to fulfill its vested interests and establish its own suzerainty. The system may likewise lead, in a different situation, to purely sectarian development of a few select groups of rural elites, or help the state to fulfill some of its own preconceived targets, such as those which may secure its political stability. In certain circumstances, I then, the client of development may be left high and dry. The winds of welfare may blow well over the heads of the clientele, for whom the programs are ostensibly tailored, and enrich only a few vested interests.

An understanding of the role that the developmental system and its various elements play in securing planned social change of the small communities is therefore very vital to the understanding of the theories of development in an underdeveloped area. Caste, economic condition, geographical situations and technological aids, all have some role or other to play in this process of development. Any one of these may either block or stimulate the pace of development, depending on the form they take in any area of development. An understanding of the functions of the system and its structural inter-relationships cannot therefore be complete without a clear appreciation of the role that factors like caste, kinship, and other groups play in the life of the rural society. These factors by themselves are not sufficient to undercut the basic values of the system, or undermine its influence on the process of social growth and change; the role that caste, kinship groups, geography, economic condition, or any other factor plays cannot be effective unless it influences the dynamics of the system. For example, a particular caste or other group might conceivably block the way of development, try to enhance its own status by developing the "elites" of the small community at the cost of its general members or of the institutions. Kinship groups might likewise strengthen an elite that was susceptible to its influence, by estranging the state from the community, or the catalysts from the people. Similarly, economic variables might hold back the process of social recovery, and consolidate gains in the hands of a few; this can happen when the role that the third element (organizations and institutions) should have played is usurped by the fifth (rural elite). But a durable, democratic and self-propelling process of social development, such as that which produces a change-prone and growth-oriented society, is possible when all the six parts work in harmony and concentrate their real gains in the third element of the system.

Two conclusions emerge from the foregoing analysis. These relate to the structure of the developmental system and its role. A significant result of planning for social change in India has been that a definite system can now be discovered in areas of development. The process of social control let loose by the six-part system has today the most far-reaching impact on the life of the village community. It is the chief agent of social change. In which of the many probable ways its impact will be most felt depends very much on the sixth part, the method, and the orientation that it gives to the system as a whole. The method sets the direction, visualizes the objectives, and enables the system itself to cast its eyes on a single indivisible goal.

CONCLUSIONS AND THEORIES

What is also evident at the same time from this analysis is that an understanding of the process of planned social change in a specific community cannot be complete unless one realizes the exact role and dynamics of the developmental system of the area. Whether the fruits of development reach a few or the masses, whether the process is 'catalyst-body' centric or 'people' centric, depends on the operational structure of the system. It is on the system, again, that the pattern of development of an area would eventually depend. The changes that take place in a given community as a result of planning and purposive development may thus be of varied type. Whatever may be the result of development, however, the system is a reality in India today, and cannot be overlooked.

The developmental system is a basic feature and integral part of a growing society. The position of the social worker in such a system can be of several descriptions; he may be employed by the State, by the village institution, or he may be a free-lance, honorary social worker. Whatever his actual position, his potential role cannot be conceivably any other than that of a catalyst. This role is obviously a difficult one and can be fulfilled only when the worker has, by means of training and equipment, acquired a firm grasp of the broad spectrum of village development and sympathetic methods of working with people. In line with the goals of the developmental system, he must give a sense of reality and direction to the totality of design and change in the small community.

The needs of a developing society warrant that the new directions of social work be indicated by leading concepts. It should also be evident from the foregoing discussion that social work techniques, viewed in the sense of static categories applicable to all cultural configurations, will remain useless to an area unless they are able to modify their structure to fit the specific needs of that area. Throughout this study it has become increasingly apparent that integrated communities are comprehensible systems of logical and functional relationships, each with their own very special complexes for ordering the impact of reality.

In viewing underdeveloped communities as "functional wholes," it is clear that any alteration in one segment of culture will necessarily affect the whole social configuration. The implication for social work is that, in introducing new ideas, practices and institutions, the process must involve more than a mere addition or subtraction of elements. Failure in development programs has more often been due to the superimposition of material culture, thrust on a community from without, rather than a lack of resources or technological aid. Instead, the first step must be the discovery of a multi-dimensional method of *transformation;* only then will social work create an internalization process by which new and unfamiliar elements will be incorporated with a minimum of conflict into the living fabric of the community.

GLOSSARY

Bhajans	—Devotional songs.
Bighas	—0.33 acres.
Cheapkuti	—The site once owned by Mr. John Cheap, an indigo planter, and now occupied by the SEOTC.
Chowkidar	—Village watchman and police agent.
Compounder	—Doctor's helper, executing his prescriptions (colonial English).
Dhapas	—A folk song of Bengal.
Domes	—A lower caste.
Ghani Society	—Cooperative of oil-presses.
Hadu-du	—A rural sport.
Kavi-gans	—Competitive on-the-spot poetic composition.
Khadi	—Homespun cloth (the main platform in the Gandhian program for rural renewal).
Kirtans	—Devotional songs in chorus.
Mahila samiti	—Women's club—an activity under the Indian Community Development Program.
Palli Seva Niketan	—Village service center.
Panchayat	—Village council.
Raibeshe	—A widely prevalent folk dance of Bengal; originally of Santal tribes.
SEOTC	—Social Education Organisers' Training Center.
Shramdan	—Voluntary labor for community projects.
Silpa utsav	—Industrial ceremony.
Sradha	—Death anniversary.
UGC	—University Grants Commission.
Vriksha Ropana	—Tree planting.
Vaishnavism	—A secularized sect among the Hindus.

METHODOLOGICAL NOTES
IN COMMUNITY DEVELOPMENT

BY PHILLIP BOSSERMAN

This volume gives concrete case studies of community development processes. The central thesis is that community development must ultimately come from within. The method of *Sriniketan* depends on the "social worker's ability to create an environment in which a community could be motivated to perceive its own needs, and be prepared to organize its resources to achieve their fulfillment." Or put another way, "What is required, . . . is a determined effort to create, in the community itself, its power to resolve its own needs."

We cannot get into a discussion about the origin of enablers or catalysts or outside workers. Where development is needed there is a parallel need for the right kind of leadership. Probably in the beginning the community must depend upon outside personnel. However, the ultimate goal should be the training of indigenous leaders. Presently, I am involved with a very effective program of leadership training among the communities on the off-shore islands of South Carolina. Penn Community Services, Inc. has received a sizable Ford Foundation grant to develop and execute such a program. Their efforts are pioneering.[1] Consequently, our methodological notes will be for an external worker who seeks to "create the power of self-development which would enable a community to determine its own welfare . . . To give the community through its individuals and groups of youth, adolescents and children, the wish, the impetus and the method of making use of their own aptitude and dormant potentialities for the solution of many of their problems." The social worker is there not to impose or establish anything but to ensure that "any action taken is the action of the community itself."

> Talking together and planning together (is) to develop silently into "acting" together; and perpetuation of this togetherness into institutional shapes and forms is . . . the greatest guarantee

---

[1] The address of Penn is St. Helena Island, Frogmore, South Carolina. Mr. Courtney Siceloff is director of the project.

for meeting the needs of the community, by the efforts of its own members, on a permanent basis.

These goals summarized by Dasgupta may be profitably compared with the excellent discussions by William and Loureide Biddle in their volume *The Community Development Process*[2] and the fine materials produced by several members of the staff at the University of Missouri.[3]

As an enabler or catalyst or worker there are perhaps four major factors in an adequate methodology:

1) Appraisal of the situation.
2) Energizing the planning of a solution to the problem.
3) Implementation of the plan.
4) Critical estimation of the results.

Keep in mind we are attempting to work at these four procedures within the spirit and context of the goals previously stated.

"Entry" into the community becomes an over-riding concern as a first step in the appraisal of the situation. The manner of initial contact is crucial. This means, among other things, the worker must have a comprehensive understanding of the community as a functioning whole. Hence, the development of an accurate antenna system which is sensitive to both feelings and roles becomes his first obligation. The techniques of cultural anthropology tempered with a profound appreciation of the culture and its values serve well here. When I speak of sensitivity and appreciation I do so in the same way James Agee does in his remarkable book *Let Us Now Praise Famous Men:*

> No one is at home, in all this house, in all this land. It is a long while before their return. I shall move as they would trust me not to, and as I could not, were they here. I shall touch nothing but as I would touch the most delicate wounds, the most dedicated objects.
>
> The silence of the brightness of this middle morning is increased upon me moment by moment and upon this house, and upon this house the whole of heaven is drawn into one lens; and this house itself, in each of its objects, it, too, is one lens.[4]

---

[2] New York: Holt, Rinehart and Winston, Inc., 1965.

[3] Department of Community Development, University of Missouri, Columbia, Missouri. Cf. Dunham, Arthur, *Currents in Community Development.*

[4] Boston: Houghton Mifflin Company, 1941.

Not only is there sensitivity, profound respect for those tangible and intangible expressions of another culture but Agee suggests the "optic" for comprehending the situation. One must learn to *see* what is there in the material and nonmaterial aspects of the culture. This means going below the surface of things, digging deeply into the varied strata of the culture, the community. Depending upon where one is and the so-called sophistication of the community, a most concrete way to begin is to map the community. This tells us where people live, it helps us identify the households, and then enables us to begin to see relationships among families, within families, ecological factors, location of stores, markets, bus lines, and town hall. A technique used by Professor Jack Donaghue of Michigan State University is to have his students or trainees go to a supermarket and follow a customer or several customers through the shopping process. One can develop a "flow chart" of these movements and from what one observes make some low level generalizations about the individual or individuals. We are interested in developing sensitivity, making it possible to draw into one lens the various aspects of the community.

After mapping and beginning to piece together the patterns of relationships among people, the next step might be to ask who makes the decisions in the community, and what is the "pecking order."

How do they make a living? What is their religious practice? What myths are important? What traditions or historical events influence? An over-arching question we are seeking to answer is simply this, "What do you need to know in order to act like a member of the community in which you find yourself working?" Obviously language is indispensable for learning about the meaning of behavior. It is the most powerful carrier of a culture. It is the entrée into a culture which cannot be neglected. If you are in a foreign speaking community, then your first task is to learn the language.

Allen Hoben of the University of Rochester suggests we look at the social life of a community as a drama. Hence, "your task is to identify the characters in the community and find out how they are supposed to act out their parts with respect to one another in various settings. It is only after you have done this that you can interpret how well or how badly and with what intent a particular 'actor' is playing his part." [5]

He puts it another way:

> I think it is crucial to emphasize . . . three aspects of any society: its repertoire of social identities; the permitted combinations, or "grammar" or possible interaction between these identities, and the modes of behavior appropriate to this interaction. [6]

Entry into and assessment of a community are particularly difficult if there is a real cultural difference, i.e., the differences that exist between a middle class white American and a member of a Negro ghetto. Fitting into this very different culture is difficult because "the recognized social identities, the grammar of possible interaction between these identities, and the roles, the modes of behavior appropriate to interaction, differ from one society to another. These differences provide abundant opportunity for intersocial confusion and misinterpretation." [7]

Thus, the antennae must be sharpened, lengthened, directed, and sensitized to see what is below the obvious, and to interpret the social situations as they are and then act appropriately within them. This takes practice and training and criticism. It must be a conscious effort on the part of the CD worker.

Second, once entry has been accomplished and a comprehension of the situation developed, the enabler, the worker begins the processes of community action which are based on collective identification of the problems which the community sees itself facing and the subsequent plan of action which it employs as a total unit. Here the foundation of "friendship and affection" upon which *Sriniketan* operates must be coupled with certain broad principles: [8]

> Free and open participation by any and all interested persons in episodes which have under consideration public policy or action affecting the welfare of the people of a given area. [9]

[5] *Community Study Guide.* Unpublished mimeographed paper distributed by the Peace Corps, Wash. D.C., 1966, p. 6.

[6] *Ibid.*, pp. 6-7.

[7] *Ibid.*, p. 8

[8] *Ibid.*, p. 8.

[9] Schler, Dan, "Some Generalizations Regarding Community Development." Mimeographed, University of Missouri, Columbia, Mo., 1964.

METHODOLOGICAL NOTES

How does one accomplish such open participation? There are no set rules or formulae. Rather the tone of your approach is the crucial factor. Once you understand the decision making processes, identify leaders, put the various groupings in their context, you next seek to meld these persons and groups into a collective unit in which free and open participation obtains. The "how" comes from that antenna system once again. Each situation calls for its own method. Patience is the essential ingredient. Moreover, the existing group processes provide a foundation upon which to build. The emphasis here is upon *seeking* wherein the community may find its *own* culturally relevant methods. The beginnings start, as the Biddles point out, in a small nucleus of concerned citizens who have a particular interest in seeing something develop.[10] It is from this small group that initiative, vision, the "what is possible" emerge. The enabler starts by bringing such a group together. Again, assessment of existing leadership and types of leaders is important in this initial organization. Understanding of the community patterns and expectations is a prerequisite in order that the sources of eventual influence and power are not alienated.

Next, the small group selects a project which is visible, possible, and certain of success. This becomes the initial experience which influences others to participate once they are aware what collective action can accomplish. It is also the beginning of the development of that infrastructure which makes the handling of other problems possible.

The group then works out the plans, makes assignments, and designates the calendar of action. It is implemented.

The final step is evaluation. How was entry accomplished? Was assessment of the situation adequate both by the enabler and the action group? Was the project a good one? Did it meet the criteria? How well did people participate in the planning and the implementation? Were the desired results realized? How did the project square with the community sources of power?

The process we have described compares favorably with the "Outline for the Flow of Process" developed by the Biddles. Their major stages for the formation and work of a nucleus group started by a community developer are 1) *exploratory:* initial discussions with certain key concerned

---

[10] *Ibid.*, pp. 88 ff.

persons; 2) *organizational:* identification of a problem of interest to local citizens; 3) *discussional:* definitions of the problem plus looking at possible solutions and final decision on a proposed action; 4) *action:* carrying out the project of action, reporting the work done, analysis of what happens and happened and final evaluation; 5) *new projects:* discussion and action on new or redefined problems with wider involvements resulting in increasing controversy and conflict which might call for pressure action and leading subsequently to a coalition of power elements; 6) *continuation:* a permanent nucleus now operates; the community developer can withdraw; problems of increasing complexity are undertaken which in turn calls for increasing responsibility.[11]

As Professor Dasgupta so clearly and effectively illustrates, the emphasis for lasting and beneficial change comes from creating an atmosphere and a structure in which all people, and groups are represented, feel included, may be heard in open discussion; reciprocity of perspectives and positions becomes the foundation. In Dan Schler's words "programs of action and change (consequently) are built from the bottom up, rather than from the top down." [12]

To conclude we shall indicate certain publications which illustrate the methodological principles we have discussed. Happily the volume of materials is increasing. I will only touch on a few items which hopefully will whet the reader's appetite. Much of this is in the form of case studies which help the practitioner in community development assess his methods and refine his approach.

General Works:

William W. Biddle and Loureide J. Biddle, THE COMMUNITY DEVELOPMENT PROCESS, New York: Holt, Rinehart and Winston, Inc., 1965. This previously mentioned work contains an excellent bibliography. The first part of the volume deals with two case studies in which the Biddles were involved. The second section discusses principles and processes on the basis of these two experiences. The emphasis is on the United States but much of what the book contains would apply throughout the developing world.

---

[11] *Ibid.,* pp. 90-91.
[12] *Op. cit.,* p. 4.

METHODOLOGICAL NOTES

Conrad M. Arensberg and Arthur H. Niehoff, INTRO-
DUCING SOCIAL CHANGE, Chicago: Aldine Publishing
Co., 1964. The authors attempt "to assemble the basic cultural factors which should be understood for the successful
introduction of new ideas or techniques." They do this with
great success. They especially help the community developer
from the perspective of the social sciences and what they
have learned about cultural change.

Arthur H. Niehoff, A CASEBOOK OF SOCIAL
CHANGE, Chicago: Aldine Publishing Co., 1966. This is a
companion work to the volume on Introducing Social
Change. These cases illustrate what worked and didn't.
They are world-wide in range and cover a number of problems from public health to agricultural extension. The cases
are very helpful for purposes of analysis and critical assessment of one's own efforts.

Arthur Dunham and Ernest B. Harper, COMMUNITY
ORGANIZATION IN ACTION, New York: Association
Press, 1959. A basic introduction and discussion of CD.

Bennis, Benne, Chin, THE PLANNING OF CHANGE.
READINGS IN THE APPLIED BEHAVIORIAL SCI-
ENCES, Holt, Rinehart and Winston, 1962.

Pamphlets:

Donald L. Beran, COMMUNITY DEVELOPMENT, AN
INTRODUCTION TO CD FOR VILLAGE WORKERS, Re-
printed from AID Training Material Series A, Vol. L, April,
1965. An excellent manual, concrete, specific, essential.

Arthur Dunham and William Biddle, CURRENTS IN
COMMUNITY DEVELOPMENT, Department of Community Development, University of Missouri, Columbia,
Missouri, 1964. This is a thoughtful assessment of the current scene. Other materials are available at the Department
of Regional and Community Affairs, University of Missouri,
303 Professional Building, 909 University Ave., Columbia,
Missouri 65201. The University of Missouri has one of the
best programs in the United States. They offer a very fine
correspondence course which deals with the theory and
principles of community development.

The Peace Corps has been working in the field of community development from the beginning of their programs.
They have developed some excellent training and "how to"

materials. Unfortunately these have not been collated. However, if you would write to the Latin American Regional Office, Peace Corps, Washington, D. C. 20525, they will be happy to share what is readily available. J. D. Mezirow of the University of California, Berkeley, put together a bibliographic guide for the Peace Corps entitled THE LITERATURE OF COMMUNITY DEVELOPMENT, 1963, which is extremely comprehensive up to 1963. It needs to be brought up to date. However, the materials described are indispensable.

Cornell University, MEASUREMENT OF PEACE CORPS PROGRAM IMPACT IN THE PERUVIAN ANDES, 1965. This study was conducted for the Peace Corps and constitutes a fascinating look at the effectiveness of volunteers in certain villages contrasted with villages which had no external aid and those which had other types of external aid. The results are favorable to the Peace Corps and the practice of community development principles we have outlined in our notes and illustrated by Professor Dasgupta in this work. Moreover, the method of measuring impact is highly suggestive and gets at one of the most difficult problems we face in CD. Just how does one judge whether a certain type of change has taken place as direct result of certain strategic programs?

Finally, I would mention the very helpful periodical published in England entitled THE COMMUNITY DEVELOPMENT JOURNAL, 22 Kingston Road, Didsbury, Manchester 20, England. This publication is world wide in its scope and very practical in its orientation. It is highly readable and useful.

Across the channel, Le Conseil International de Recherches Coopératives, 7 av. Franco-Russe, Paris 7, France, is beginning to publish widely in this field. I would particularly mention the very fine work of Henri Desroche, Directeur du Centre de Recherches Coopératives, Ecole Pratique des Hautes Etudes, VIᵉ Section, University of Paris, Paris. His institute is doing some excellent work in training researchers and developers coming from the developing world itself.

University of South Florida
Tampa, Florida

PHILLIP BOSSERMAN
December, 1967

INDEX